The Stages of Age

The Stages of Age

Performing Age in Contemporary
American Culture

Anne Davis Basting

Ann Arbor

THE UNIVERSITY OF MICHIGAN PRESS

✴ to the generations of my family

Alice Davis Cantwell

Dr. Arthur Cantwell

Alice Koehn Basting

Abe Basting

Sally Cantwell Basting

Tom Basting

Brad Lichtenstein

Copyright © by the University of Michigan 1998
All rights reserved
Published in the United States of America by
The University of Michigan Press
Manufactured in the United States of America
⊗ Printed on acid-free paper
2001   2000   1999   1998   4   3   2   1

A CIP catalog record for this book is available from the British Library.

Library of Congress Cataloging-in-Publication Data
Basting, Anne Davis, 1965–
    The stages of age : performing age in contemporary American
culture / Anne Davis Basting.
        p.   cm.
    Includes bibliographical references and index.
    ISBN 0-472-10939-1 (cloth : acid-free paper)
    1. Aged—United States.   2. Theater and the aged—United States.
3. Arts and the aged—United States.   4. Intergenerational
relations—United States.   I. Title.
HQ1064.U5   B287   1998
305.26—ddc21   98-9015
                                                                CIP

Acknowledgments

The support network that encouraged and guided me through this research and writing process was an elaborate tapestry. My debt of gratitude to Kathleen Woodward rivals the national debt of 1995. She recognized and kindled these raw ideas when they were just a well-meaning first chapter of a dissertation. Her courageous steps into this largely uncharted field of Age Studies made it possible for me to even imagine this project. Her generosity as a scholar and her skills in orchestrating and nurturing conversations continue to build interest and support research in this growing field.

The Rockefeller Foundation Grant in Age Studies brought me to Woodward's Center for Twentieth Century Studies at the University of Wisconsin–Milwaukee, where I could develop this material while looking out over the Milwaukee skyline and beautiful, turbulent ice sprays of Lake Michigan. Believe me, the Mediterranean's got nothing over Milwaukee. I thank my fellow fellows, the staff, and students at the center for challenging and opening my work on aging and performance to new directions—particularly Elinor Fuchs, Sharon Keigher, Hillary Harris, Dale Jaffe, Patricia Mellencamp, Cecelia Condit, Robin Pickering-Iazzi, and Nigel Rothfels.

Thanks go to my editor, LeAnn Fields, for her plain-spokenness, her patience, and her support of a project that could have so easily fallen between disciplinary boundaries.

This research began during my doctorate program in Theatre Arts at the University of Minnesota, where the tenacious support of friends and mentors got me through the hoops and over the bumps. Particular thanks go to Michal Kobialka, who fed me salmon and taught me to fight, and to Jaqueline Zita, Helen Kivnick, Pascale Bos, Melissa Burchard, Jane Olmstead, and Mary Petrie, who provided undying intellectual pep talks and keen constructive criticism. A grant from the University of Minnesota's All University Council on Aging supported part of the early research for this book.

Many colleagues helped read various versions of this material in its many incarnations as conference papers for the Association for Theatre in Higher Education (ATHE) and the American Society for Theatre Research (ASTR) and as articles in theater journals. A consolidation of chapters 2 and 3 appeared in *TDR* (fall 1995) and the *Journal of Dramatic Theory and Criticism* published a version of chapter 5 (winter 1996). Along the way Kent Neely, Alice Rayner, Philip Auslander, Stephen Katz, Carrie Sandahl, Lisa Bernd, and Stacy Wolf shared their invaluable reactions to my ideas, both spoken and written.

Thanks go to directors of the senior performing groups, particularly Susan Perlstein, Peggy Pettitt, Ann McDonough, Bob Dryden, Dennis Lamberson, Joy Reilly, and Kirsten Bonner, for supplying an infectious passion for the magic of theater and its transformative potential. Arthur Strimling's ability to flip my worldview with a simple, unassuming story remains a constant source of amazement.

The men and women of Roots & Branches, Elders Share the Arts, the Artreach Players, and the Geritol Frolics gave me the gift of their stories, stories that made the word "research" fall away. I thank them all and give posthumous thanks to Barbara Myerhoff, whose writing helped make me unafraid to experience and describe the mutual sense of transformation entailed in the exchange of stories.

The final thread of the tapestry is one of family. Thanks are due Tom, Sally, Tom Jr., Susan, Ellen, and Art, for teasing me endlessly and believing in me completely, even, and especially, when my own belief wavers. Without knowing, Alice Davis Cantwell, Alice Koehn Basting, and Rose James sparked unending questions, ideas, and stories. And to Brad, for his presence in my life, for his fire, and for his flair for knowing what counts.

Contents

1   Acting Your Age: Performance and Performativity
    in an Aging Society   *1*

2   Feeling and Being Young: The Geritol Frolics   *24*

3   Radicalizing Oral History: The Grandparents
    Living Theatre   *56*

4   Generations of Change: Roots & Branches and
    Elders Share the Arts   *83*

5   Re-membering the Living Past in Feminist Theory:
    Suzanne Lacy's *Crystal Quilt*   *112*

6   The Body in Depth: Kazuo Ohno's *Water Lilies*   *134*

7   Screen-Deep: The Beauty of Mortality in
    Margolis Brown's *Vidpires!*   *147*

8   Dolly Descending a Staircase: Stardom, Age, and
    Gender in Times Square   *163*

9   Conclusion   *180*

Notes   *187*

References   *205*

Index   *219*

1

Acting Your Age:
Performance and Performativity
in an Aging Society

For almost two centuries to become "old" in the United States has been largely regarded in terms of loss. To become old is to lose beauty. To become old is to lose power, both financial and physical. It is to lose one's independence and to lose one's flexibility and potential for growth. And now, with the specter of Alzheimer's haunting those over eighty, to become old is to risk losing one's very self. These are the myths that feed the reality of the house of old age that America built.

That house is being remodeled. Sixty years of social security, working in tandem with medical advances and widespread health coverage for older adults, is altering the floor plan of old age. Although health and life expectancy is still tied to race, class, and gender, there have been across the board increases in the length and health of American lives. As the large numbers of Baby Boomers continue to age, they are expected to carry their unique brand of social activism (a blend of consumerism and political radicalism) with them, further changing what it means to be old.

But amidst these changes, the way we value old age remains largely untouched. To be old is still negatively associated with loss. We have simply created more ways to avoid the label—and with it, the house of old age. There are countless ways to avoid becoming "old." There are hair dyes and protein drinks. There are estrogen and testosterone treatments. There is exercise, meditation, and Tai Chi. For growing numbers of men and women there is cosmetic surgery. There are books that tell us we are "ageless." There are even attempts to add length to our chromosomes in the hopes that we can "immortalize" our cells.

There is a fine and sensitive line between alleviating the physical and emotional pains of older Americans and further devaluing old age by recreating it as an imitation of young adulthood. If there is to be a real restructuring of how Americans value old age, we can not rely on technology and the Baby Boom to provide us ways to dodge the label. We must create an intergenerational effort to build the value of old age anew.

The Stages of Age looks at eight different theatrical performances that construct their own unique meanings of old age. Performance, in terms of how we perform ourselves in everyday life and in terms of theatrical representation, offers a way to imagine old age as a valuable stage of life; one that links generations, that is engaged in both the present and the past, and that is constantly changing. For older adults the very *act of acting* interrupts popularly held notions that old age is a narrative of decline and rigidity.

I was drawn to the study of aging and performance out of a double frustration with my work as a playwright and a scholar of performance studies. As a playwright writing predominantly older characters, I had been told by fellow writers and directors that audiences do not want to hear about old age, and that older actors are a rare and unreliable commodity. Professional actors tended to retire and training programs tended to focus only on young actors. The few roles for older characters that were available in local productions (then the Minneapolis/St. Paul area) tended to be performed by younger actors, sometimes in garish age makeup. In spite of large audiences of older adults, it seemed that theater was an art form *of* and *by* the young. The older adult performers in the chapters that follow suggest otherwise.

My frustration with the dearth of scholarship on aging and theater also drew me toward this research. As a performance theorist, I was surprised by the lack of recognition of aging in cross-disciplinary explorations of cultural difference and social practice over the last decade. Theories of social practice, including the ground-breaking work of scholars such as historian Michel de Certeau (1984) and philosopher Judith Butler (1990, 1993), tended to overlook physical and psychological changes inherent in the aging process. The following essays reflect just a few of the many performing groups of older adults in this country that provide models to counter the oversights of these pioneering cultural theorists.

This book is also a personal journey, one whose path has become more clear with hindsight. In 1989 my maternal grandmother, Alice Davis Cantwell, suffered a stroke that stole her ability to speak. I had always had a special bond with Alice. She was a remarkably strong-willed woman who had been the keeper of our family stories. Before, during, and after college, I would pilgrimage to the small northern Wisconsin town where she lived, take her to lunch at her current favorite restaurant (inevitably Perkins), and listen. There was always a long introduction, designed to catch me up with the second cousins and great aunts whom she insisted I knew, but whose names were only familiar to me in her voice. Then came the real stories—of growing up on a Montana ranch, of high-society adventures in Chicago as a young nurse, of her move to Wisconsin to be a mother and small-town doctor's wife. I loved these stories, even though I didn't always believe them—Alice seemed to become the hero in nearly every one. But I knew why she told them to me, and she knew I knew. I had been chosen the one most likely to pass them on.

After the stroke Alice refused to give up her storytelling. She would point and nod and stutter the same nonsensical word until the listener, one of her four children or twelve grandchildren, would guess what she was saying.

It was infuriating. I was angry at the loss of her stories; angry at old age and the stroke for taking them from me; angry at myself for not having listened more closely. But after a while, when our game of twenty questions became an almost zenlike state, I realized how much closer I felt to Alice after the stroke than before. I could no longer passively or selectively listen to her often rambling and repetitive stories. We were now engaged in a deeper dialogue—not one of words but of raw urgency. It was a dialogue bent on keeping stories, family, our relationship, and her alive.

I began researching and following the careers of older performers in 1990, just a year after the stroke deadened Alice's tongue. I now see this book as an expansion of our dialogue catalyzed by the stroke. Because the study of aging is a multidisciplinary endeavor, and because any study of old age must also be a study of youth and middle age, the dialogue that follows is many layered. It is a dialogue between personal stories and scholarly research. It is a dialogue between the cultural forces that shape us, and our thwarting of those forces through unsanctioned, everyday actions. It is a dialogue between a relatively young spectator (twenty-four when this research began) and older performers, both engaged in exploring the shifting meanings of aging and old age in this country at century's end. It is an imagined dialogue between my grandmother and me, between the young person I am and the old woman that I will be. Echoing Alice's urgency, these dialogues are bent on easing crippling fears of aging bred by the isolation of generations and devaluation of old age in this country.

Performances by older adult and intergenerational troupes, such as those I first encountered at the first Senior Theatre USA Festival at the University of Nevada–Las Vegas in 1993, quelled many of the frustrations that had first drawn me to the topic. Where nonprofit and for-profit theaters largely closed their doors to older actors, these performers started their own companies. Where theorists overlooked the performative nature of aging, these performers demonstrated that the transformative quality of performance—*the very act of acting*—can help shift popularly held notions that aging is a narrative of rigidity and decline. Where I had lost the chance to ask my grandmother about the emotional and spiritual terrain of old age, here performers and friends generously shared their experiences of loss, growth, pain, loneliness, comfort, hope, and passion. Sparked by the contagious enthusiasm of that first festival, I continued and expanded my studies of aging and performance to include experimental performance as well as mainstream theatrical representations of old age. These performances, of senior theater, experimental performance, and commercial theater, are the subject of the many-layered dialogues of this book.

The many stories of the many older performers I've met over the years have helped me to roughly chart the landscape of my own old age. Based on their stories and the view into heredity my grandmother gave me, I imagine that the age of eighty might find me with mild heart trouble, osteoporosis, stark white hair, and gnarled arthritic hands. That of course is barring major medical advances and assuming I'm lucky enough to get there. It's a difficult place to imagine from thirty-two, and to a great extent, to rehearse it is futile. When emotions cut too close, sometimes older performers and/or friends back away and simply say "you'll understand when you get older." But it's likely that I'll never understand in the same way they do. As aging is a biological and cultural/ historical phenomenon, the experiences of today's aged are unique. Their stories won't be mine. I'll never have first hand access to the fears, joys, pressures, and losses of my older friends who spent their childhood between the great wars. Similarly, my older friends' memories of youth differ radically from the tales of Xers that are too commonly dominated by broken homes, drugs, poverty, hopelessness, and cynicism. Life stages follow general parameters through which, if we're lucky, we will all eventually pass. But the experience of those life stages, my experiences of youth versus Alice's childhood for example, are historically unique. Conversations across generations can guide our growth in historical knowledge as well as inform our journeys across the life course.

The following chapters are linked by a desire to do just that: to bring generational voices into dialogue so that old age and youth might be imagined as unique and equally vital periods of the full life course. The performances, and my first person descriptions and analyses of them, are a dialogue between generations, across physical and psychological differences, and across historically constructed perceptions of age. My hope is that, besides presenting the wide array of contemporary meanings of age created in these performances, this research might also be valuable as: (1) a negotiation across differences of generation; and (2) as an illustration of how the consideration of the *whole* life course and the relationships between generations are critical if we are to dislodge ourselves from the narrative of decline on which American culture has run aground.

Since this research began, there has been a growing awareness of the need for reevaluation of the roles and treatment of the elderly in the United States. The aging of the Baby Boom population, who are now formulating their own retirement plans and caring for their aging parents, is likely the driving force behind more fully drawn, and increasing numbers of representations of older Americans in film, television, theater, and advertising. *Cocoon* began a wave of films aimed at older audiences, a wave that includes *Grumpy* and *Grumpier Old Men, The Cemetery Club,* and *The Grass Harp.* "The Golden Girls" and "Murder She Wrote" brought aging into prime time with complicated representations of saucy, but respectable older women. The successful 1995 Broadway run of Carol Channing's *Hello, Dolly!* is just one of several plays that season to feature older characters and actors. Eager to appeal to the changing demographic and what is largely a new and untapped consumer base, national advertising campaigns have begun to feature intergenerational casts. For example, a 1995 ad for Keds shoes showed women of all ages, from young children to a white-haired older woman, reminiscing about their first pair of tennies.[1] A 1995 Calvin Klein television ad included a bald, older man amidst the collection of waiflike young adults modeling Klein's line of clothing.

Simply increasing the number of representations of adults categorized as old, however, will not ensure improvements in the social status of older people. The devaluation of aging in this country stems from much deeper systems of domination than a few more movies, billboards, and thirty-second prime time ad campaigns featuring older faces can cure. While I believe that performance, in everyday life and onstage, offers a particularly valuable tool to reshape the meanings of old age in this country, one can not simply praise the increasing number of theatrical representations of age. Instead we must ask how each performance shapes its meaning of aging and old age by looking to all the choices that contribute to its creation: choices of costume, sound, movement, lighting, publicity, music, and text, to name but a few. Questioning the ways in which representations of aging and old age enter social space, the ways in which aging is performed at the nexus of everyday life and representation, is crucial as we negotiate our way through the dizzying increases in images of aging as the United States continues toward an "aging society."

Performance/Performativity

The line between theatrical performance and everyday life is mysteriously phantasmagoric, constantly shifting, and hotly contested. Metaphors of theater and/or performance have seeped into multiple academic disciplines as a way to describe seemingly given aspects of one's identity. One is now said to *perform* one's gender, race, and sexuality. Selections of clothing are costumes, home decor the set. In order to clarify and address both theatrical performance and theoretical performativity, my use of the term *performance* is based on theorists from both areas. My definition rests on two main ideas from Richard Schechner, perhaps *the* driving force behind the efforts to transform theater studies into performance studies. First, in *Between Theater and Anthropology* (1985) Schechner defines performance as "restored" or "twice behaved behavior" and includes everyday life and more formal theatrical pieces as part of a continuum rather than as separate entities.

> The difference between performing myself—acting out a dream, reex-
> periencing a childhood trauma, showing you what I did yesterday—
> and more formal "presentations of self" (see Goffman 1959)—is a dif-
> ference of degree, not kind. (37)

Second, Schechner emphasizes the transformative quality of performance.

> Restored behavior offers to both individuals and groups the chance to
> rebecome what they once were, or even, and most often, to rebecome
> what they never were but wish to have been or wish to become. (38)

In Schechner's continuum, which includes and acknowledges the differences between theatrical and everyday performances of the self, performance can be a powerful tool for transforming social behavior by
embodying memories of the past or dreams of the future. Such a continuum enables dual readings of the aged body onstage. The daily lived
experience of old age, with unique differences across race, class, and
gender, can be read as a performance, as can the more theatrical frame
in which the older performers appear as characters in a play. For example, one of the performers in the Geritol Frolics of Brainerd, Minnesota
is a former governor of the state who lived most of his life cautiously,
careful to maintain a pristine public image. In the Frolics, however, he
plays comic roles ranging from drag (he appears as singer Connie Francis) to the "straight man" in slapstick comedy. Another cast member, a
widow in her eighties, also plays comic roles, which she told me provided a wonderful change from a rather subdued life. In both instances
the two levels of performance each contain the potential for transformation in both the space and time of the theatrical frame and in the
overlap and extension of performance space into everyday life.

    In order to consider *aging* in performance, however, I must depart
from Schechner's model, for his transformable continuum does not
address the complications of time which make "twice behaved behavior" and the ability to "rebecome what they once were" impossibilities.
In order to account for changes that can occur with age which complicate the performative process, I also lean on Judith Butler's work on
gender as performance. Approaching performance studies from the
angle of feminist philosophy, Butler's *Gender Trouble* (1990) and *Bodies
That Matter* (1993) trace psychoanalytic searches for the origins of sex
and gender in a "prediscursive past," and expose such origins to be
socially constructed. For Butler one is not born with a fixed identity,

rather one congeals an identity through repeated performances or social practices across time. The differences between the two theories are subtle. Like Schechner, transformation is the hope of Butler's work as well. But where Schechner finds transformability in the repetition of behavior, Butler finds it in the impossibility of exact repetition. A continuum similar to Schechner's also emerges in Butler's writing, in which theatrical acts of gender parody reveal the performative quality of gender in everyday life. She writes:

> The parodic repetition of gender exposes . . . the illusion of gender identity as an intractable depth and inner substance. As the effects of a subtle and politically enforced performativity, gender is an "act," as it were, that is open to splittings, self-parody, self-criticism, and those hyperbolic exhibitions of "the natural" in their very exaggeration, reveal its fundamentally phantasmatic status. (1990, 146–47)

The excitement and power of live theater is exactly this "hyperbolic exhibition" and its potential for transformation, both in Schechner's terms through the embodiment of what one wishes to have been or wishes to become, and in Butler's revelry in the breakdown of established social roles.[2] The older performers in the groups I address in this book take on roles that expand cultural perceptions about what aging can be, using the transformative power of theater to disrupt stereotypes about aging. The Grandparents Living Theatre of Columbus, Ohio, for example, performs its show *I Was Young, Now I'm Wonderful* to incoming medical students at Ohio State University. The performers put human faces on older patients who will constitute a large percentage of these future doctors' patients and who are often treated as children or objects by the medical system. The 1993 Geritol Frolics featured a dance line of older women in short, sequined leotards and Las Vegas–style headdresses in an effort to prove their beauty and physical stamina, and to ridicule the assumption that old age necessarily entails rapid, thorough physical and mental decline.

The older performer, however, also falls out of the scope of both Schechner's and Butler's models, and demands a new consideration of what performance and performativity entail. Changes in both social and biological functions brought on by the passage of time alter the performance of one's identity. Children might leave home. Children might come back home. One might retire with a sense of loss, or one might take on a challenging second career. Illness or the death of friends or family might lose its sense of surprise and unjustness. Any or all of these events can significantly shift one's self-perception. Butler's model occurs in time, but without addressing the complications of age. If the impossibility of identical repetition creates potential for change, then aging itself might be regaled for its transformative qualities.

Instead, aging is generally regarded as a decline from the peak of youth.[3] According to this narrative of decline, we reach the peak of our physical, emotional, and intellectual development sometime in young adulthood. After this point, our actions are simply echoes of our former selves. Repetition breeds rigidity, and old age finds people set in their ways and incapable of learning new tricks. This story of decline paints older adults as distillations of their former, more flexible and vibrant youthful selves. The effect of stagnation is compounded if poor health or cultural biases keep older adults from the activities that previously enriched their lives.

According to the narrative of decline, visual markers of age are signs of shame. Hair on our heads thins or falls out, while on other parts of the body, hormonal changes often prompt hair growth. Women may get mustaches while men may sprout new growth from ears and noses. Bladders, muscles, bones, and skin lose strength and elasticity. Chronic diseases, incontinence, frailty, and deep wrinkles are realities of late life. In the techno-information culture of the late twentieth century, in which increases in speed and the manipulation of time reap financial reward, such visible signs of an aging body stand as symbols of technologies' (our) failure to stop the hands of time. The physical and psychological changes of aging are mourned as loss of control, as demonstrating time's victory over human beings.[4]

But performance entails taking on a role and transforming one's self through acting, both socially and theatrically. The ritualistic suspension of time in Schechner's model and the flow of time in Butler's, create a performance matrix in which meanings of old age can be questioned and potentially transformed. The older performer stands at the point of contradiction of these two senses of time—thick with potential, thick with time.

The aim of this study then, is to read aging and old age as performative acts, both on- and offstage. With overlapping lenses of theatrical performance and theoretical performativity I focus on eight performances that feature older actors and/or issues of time and aging. I read each performance as establishing its own meaning and value of age, each in its own unique context. These performances range in genre, from a one hundred–member vaudeville revue (The Geritol Frolics), to a two-man Japanese butoh dance (Kazuo and Yoshito Ohno's *Water Lilies*). The dual focus on performance and performativity also enables me to create dialogue between the embodied, everyday processes of aging and the larger social constructs of age, a conversation that questions both (1) the "natural" physiological processes of aging, and (2) the social construction of models of aging which are bound by persistent realities of physical and psychological changes and ultimately death.

Old Age Unsettled

Contemporary social constructions of old age in the United States are linked to recent changes in economic, political, demographic, and social structures, and reverberate with similar shifts in the past. My aim here is to trace a few of these shifts in order to sketch a general history of the construction of old age in the United States that provides a backdrop for the discussions of the performances that follow.

The modern life course, which emerged toward the end of nineteenth century, organized social roles of education, work, and retirement according to rather stringent chronologically defined age groups. Since World War II, these three stages of the modern life course (education, work/family, and retirement) have begun to erode.[5] In the contemporary postmodern life course chronological age has lost its potency in determining social roles. Yet the reduced value of the last phase of life, attached to old age even before the development of the modern life course, has not disappeared. Instead, as life expectancies increase, the heralded value of youth has been extended to include age groups that had once been considered old. Negative assumptions about what old age entails have not dissolved, but have instead been postponed and associated with later years. Definitions of who is considered "old" have shifted without significant changes in the status of those condemned to what remains a devalued category.

The period of industrialization and the burgeoning of the middle class after 1870 marks one of the most significant periods of transition for the meaning and value of aging in the history of the United States. Andrew Achenbaum is careful to note that shifts occurred throughout the country's history, but calls this transition "a watershed in which the overall estimation of old people's worth clearly changed" (1978, 40).

Howard Chudacoff (1989) marks this transition as the development and intensification of "age-consciousness." During this period, the concept of *time* itself became more fixed and central to the lives of Americans. In his 1983 study *The Culture of Time and Space* Stephen Kern suggests that technological changes during this period contributed to emergence of the concept of time as an external entity, existing independently of human activity. Daily schedules of industrial workers, for example, became regulated by the time clock, and in 1882, railroad companies divided the country into time zones (12). According to Kern, the modern industrial period generated a growing conflict between the external and overwhelming presence of public time and the personal time of individual experiences. Time, extracted from the body, symbolically took residence in clocks synchronized to Greenwich time. The once prominent agricultural life, which followed the fickle dictates of the weather, began to give way to an external clock that monitored industrial workers unceasingly, measuring and encouraging ever increasing levels of productivity.

In the late nineteenth century, the conflict between public and personal time coincided with a growing concern about the significance of time and chronological age for the human body, illustrated by changes in economic, educational, religious, and scientific structures. By the 1870s, the education system in this country had by and large adopted the age-graded system in which children were divided by age into separate classes (Chudacoff 1989, 36). As America changed to an industrial-based economy, workers became prized for their energy and productivity rather than experience, and youthful vitality won out over the wisdom and experience of older workers. Age limits for hiring and forced retirements began to increase the turn over of older workers for younger workers (Graebner 1980). Youth came to symbolize the regenerative power of a nation on the economic rise. With the growing emphasis on productivity, in tandem with the lingering effects of Victorian morality's split between positive and negative aging, "middle-class culture lost the power to envision aging both as decline *and* as the fulfillment of life" (Cole 1992, 170). Aging increasingly came to be associated with disability and loss, of both physical capabilities and of purpose.

Turn-of-the-century changes in the philosophies and practices of public health helped to reduce the rate of mortality among those under fifty. Sanitation and hygiene practices improved with the discovery of bacteria and the growing prominence of theories on how germs spread disease after the Civil War. Infant mortality and childhood diseases were the major contributors to the relatively low life expectancies for both men and women at the turn of the century (Achenbaum 1978, 53).[6] As childhood became defined by a growth in vitality, "normal" death and disease became increasingly associated with the elderly. Aging also became a target of the curative powers of proper hygiene. What Thomas Cole calls "prolongevity hygiene" (1992, 183) assumed that living properly could increase vitality in old age. To live properly meant to follow the morals of science and public health—a thin disguise for the lingering influence of Protestant ideals. Successful models for aging, illustrated in a growing number of books and articles about prolongevity, romanticized the simplicity of a hearty rural life and ignored differences of race, gender, and class on the aging process.

Throughout the latter part of the nineteenth century the field of medicine was turning from a general practice toward the recognition of diseases that affected particular age groups. By the mid-1870s doctors who specialized in the treatment of children began to be called *pediatrists* (Chudacoff 1989, 44). This paralleled a similar move in the formation of a medical specialization for the treatment of the elderly. Based on the research of French physician Jean Martin Charcot, who studied the elderly women residents of the Parisian psychiatric institution Salpetrière, American doctors began searching for normal as opposed to pathological aging processes. Charcot's *Clinical Lectures on the Diseases of old Age,* translated into English in 1881, was the major geriatric text in the United States until 1914 (Cole 1992, 200).[7] Modeling their research on Charcot, American doctors began to name diseases unique to old age, and to search for their cures. Scientists including Elie Metchnikoff, who coined the term *gerontology* in 1904, increasingly viewed aging as a problem itself and sought ways to increase longevity and slow the aging process (Achenbaum 1978; Cole 1992). The distinction between normal and pathological aging processes grew more obscure until doctors began to define aging itself as pathology.

In 1914 I. L. Nascher's *Geriatrics* became the new standard for the study of old age diseases. Nascher's dim view of aging identified many of what are now considered diseases of old age, such as osteoporosis, to be the result of normal aging.[8] The scientific approach to old age developed in the last decades of the nineteenth century generally came to view old age with a myopic focus on the negative pole Thomas Cole attributes to Victorian morality. No longer associated with God's grace or a higher moral plain, old age had become *obsolete*[9]—a functionless fall from the heights of health, productivity, and reproductivity associated with and valued in young adulthood.[10]

Despite relatively small demographic shifts in numbers of the poor, dependent elderly, the idea that the elderly constituted a problem for society continued to flourish. Individual states attempted to create their own pension programs for older adults throughout the first three decades of the twentieth century (Achenbaum 1978). In order to win support for a national program that would serve the elderly, advocates painted a bleak picture of old age that fed off the negativity of scientific discourse. Social Security legislation, finally passed in 1935, provided a monthly allowance for former commerce and industrial workers over the age of sixty-five—giving help to those described as being unable to help themselves. Thus, sixty-five became solidified as the gateway to a new phase of life—retirement. The exodus of the employed elderly from the work force created jobs for younger workers (Graebner 1980) and gave working class elderly, the majority of whom still lived in multigenerational households, the option of living independently (Gratton and Haber 1993).

The combination of age-graded education, a workplace dominated by young and middle-aged adults, and the newly created economic base for retired elderly now constituted the modern life course. Old age, by this time categorized economically, chronologically, and physically, became the focus of what has been variously called an "aging industry" (Cole 1992, 222) and the "aging enterprise" (Estes 1980)—the exponential growth of private and governmental gerontological societies, journals, conferences, and service organizations in the decades after 1935.[11] In an effort to reform their inhumane treatment of the elderly in poorhouses, Social Security refused payment to their residents. The move in turn prompted the emergence and increasing numbers of private rest homes (Achenbaum 1978, 144). This trend continued when Medicare, a national health insurance program for older Americans, was passed in 1965.[12] In the same year Congress passed the Older Americans Act, which promised to support projects that would secure better employment and housing options for the elderly.

The 1965 legislation emerged out of a radically different context than the initial Social Security laws of 1935. Proponents of the 1935 legislation relied on an image of aging that ran counter to demographics, while the push for the 1965 legislation relied on the support of the elderly themselves. Strong advocacy organizations of and for the elderly, such as the American Association of Retired Persons, the National Association of Retired Federal Employees, and the Gray Panthers, to name just a few, spoke out about rising medical costs, poor quality services, and discrimination by institutions and/or employers on the grounds of age. The "anti-ageism" movement also emerged amidst the swell of social upheaval in the 1960s and 1970s in which fights for civil rights and fights against racism and sexism ignited widespread social activism.[13] Those fighting ageism targeted negative stereotypes about the elderly that arose from decades of scientific pessimism and the categorization of aging as a chronic disease. While the anti-ageism campaign made great strides in mobilizing the aged as advocates for their own well-being, its methods ultimately sabotaged more significant change. Anti-ageism advocates aimed to replace the negative images of aging with "positive" images—a move that ultimately fails to question the strict division between these two poles (successful and unsuccessful aging), and which fuels a denial of physical and psychological changes in the aging process (Cole 1992, 229). Part of the reactionary polarization of the anti-ageism campaign may also stem from the fact that it emerged at the same time as Baby Boomers ignited the youth movement in the late 1960s. As yet, however, there has been little examination of the relationship between the emergence of the youth and anti-ageism movements. The two movements' uses of language, representation, and political tactics certainly merits more investigation.

The anti-ageism movement began to rattle the three stages of the modern life course that seemed to preclude any meaning or purpose to one's later years. During the same time period, the scientific models of the life course established during the early years of gerontology came into question for their predominantly negative tone and their lack of consideration of spiritual and emotional development. In the mid-1950s and 1960s developmental psychologist Erik Erikson offered a new model for the life course. Erikson divided life into eight stages, each of which held a unique challenge and reward for the individual.[14] In the final phase of life Erikson believed that one sought to overcome despair by *integration,* a process of coming to grips with both one's past and the inevitability of death. Successful integration yielded "wisdom," and offered the aged a new purpose and cause for respect from younger generations.[15] Erikson's linear prescription for the life course has been criticized for universalizing the aging process across gender, race, and class (Woodward 1986). But his work remains one of the few models for finding meaning and purpose in old age and reestablishing a view of aging as *both* positive and negative (Kivnick 1993; Moody 1993). Erikson's model of the life course became a valuable tool for anti-ageism activists, including Maggie Kuhn, founder of the Gray Panthers and Robert Butler, whose Pulitzer prize–winning *Why Survive?* (1975) popularized the tenets of the anti-ageism movement.[16]

More radical revisions of the life course have emerged among the major economic, technological, demographic, and philosophical changes in the last three decades. Fueled by shifts in technology, post-modern culture marks a shift from industrial based economy to a postindustrial, information and service-oriented, multinational, and media-driven economy. Time and space continue to shrink as people, products and information travel at faster and faster rates across fiber optic wires linking the most remote parts of the world. It seems that on our current course, postmodern culture is headed toward the ultimate elimination of space and time altogether. For example, architect and cultural critic Paul Virilio's study of war and its relation to the desires that lurk behind the invention, development, and proliferation of cinema suggests that the technological inventions of the modern period reflect a yearning for the ability to see and be everywhere at once (1989). Such a yearning continues in the race to link cable, computer, and telephone technology to create a virtual reality world in which consumers need never leave the comfort of their homes, making physical movement itself unnecessary.[17] The increasing speed of culture, the rapid flow of the processing of future into past, creates an illusion in postmodern culture that time has been conquered and transformed into a perpetual present.[18]

In addition to representing a unique economic and technological moment, postmodernism is also associated with the demographics of a particular generation. Increases in life expectancy, begun with advances in public health and medical treatment at the turn of the century, have continued at varied paces across gender, race, and class categories throughout the twentieth century. In addition to increases in life expectancy, recent decreases in fertility rates and the aging of the enormous number of post–World War II babies has shifted the United States from a country identified and predominantly populated with

youth toward a society of the aged.[19] The implications of an aging society for the American economy are potentially quite great. By the time
the Baby Boom generation, those born between 1947 and 1962, begin to
retire, the ratio of the number of workers to the number of those dependent on them for financial support will decrease considerably.[20] As the
first Baby Boomers inch toward retirement, forecasted to begin in 2010,
major concerns are being raised over how the American economy can
survive such a sharp change in the dependency ratio.[21] The number of
people over the age of sixty-five is expected to increase from twelve
percent of the population in 1986 to over twenty-one percent in 2030.
The number of people *below* twenty years of age is expected to decrease
by the same percentage. The issue is further complicated by skyrocket-
ing health care costs and medical advances that promise to continue
increasing life expectancies—extending the period of life most dependent on the health care system. The battle for limited financial
resources has encouraged a rise in verbal generation bashing, illustrated by the emergence of literature on "Generation X" and groups
such as Americans for Generational Equity.[22] The generational tensions
are in large part attributable to the widely rumored, impending bankruptcy of the Social Security system when it becomes responsible for
the large number of aged Baby Boomers. This debate, couched in terms
of federal deficit reduction, echoes early-twentieth-century arguments
that decried aging and the aged themselves to be the ultimate problem.
The obvious difference is that today the aged are depicted as selfishly
ripping off the system created as a result of earlier debates. What this
viewpoint overlooks is that social security was also designed to ease
the financial burden on the adult children who previously often had no
choice but to care for their aging parents. The many and varied meanings of the term *generation,* as well as how generations might interact,
are among the issues explored in chapters 4 and 5.

   Postmodern culture's demographic, economic and technological
changes exist simultaneously with a breakdown of (1) chronological
age, the social measure of time on the body, in determining social roles;
and (2) a new direction within the field of gerontology in which
research is questioned for its hand in shaping the value of and social
roles for the aged. The acceptance and use of postmodern theory within
gerontology is relatively new, but has already yielded considerable
changes.[23] Postmodern theory provides the tools for dismantling the
empiricism of the early twentieth-century research on old age that

equated aging with pathology. Some researchers use the basic tenets of postmodern theory to cast doubt on once respected studies by exploring how the researcher's methods produced the results. Betty Friedan, for example, devotes two chapters in her best-selling *Fountain of Age* to challenging studies that assume aging to be predominantly a mental and physical decline. Friedan points to limited samples consisting mainly of white men, institutionalized in long-term care or veteran's facilities, who were judged according to standards of emotional, mental, and physical behavior/performance of youth and whose results were generalized across race, class, and gender.[24]

Other researchers use postmodern theories to explore how the use of certain categories and vocabulary help mold perceptions of aging. For example, using the theories of philosopher Michel Foucault to support their theses, sociologists Mike Featherstone and Mike Hepworth claim that the term *life cycle* "implies fixed categories in the life of the individual and assumes a stable system" while *life course* "suggests more flexible biographical patterns within a continually changing social system" (1991, 386). The term *age* itself has been splintered in both popular and academic discourse, allowing for more complex and even contradictory descriptions of age. To be *old* might now refer to one's chronological age (number of years), biological age (rated according to one's health), social age (determined by social roles), or personal age (self-selected) (Laslett 1989, 7).

Observing demographic and economic changes in postmodern culture, gerontologists have also generated several different visions of the life course that continue to break apart the three stages of the modern life course—education, work, and retirement—social roles dictated by chronological age. Strict chronological divisions are now cause for suspicion. Instead, new formulations of the life course organize life stages around specific qualities and tasks that might occur at any age, but are typical of certain, general age groups. For example, Peter Laslett (1989) divides life into four stages: dependence/education, independence/maturity, personal fulfillment, and finally decrepitude and a return to dependence. Alternatively, Helen Kivnick (1993) emphasizes the simultaneity of life stages in her interpretation and defense of Erikson's theories. For Kivnick each life stage in Erikson's model involves a predominant theme, but is not limited to that single theme. Following this logic, Erikson's category of Older Adulthood is not strictly limited to passive reflection of one's past in the search for wisdom. Instead,

Older Adulthood becomes, in Kivnick's interpretation, a complex and dynamic stage in which all the challenges of the eight life stages are played out.

> Clearly, then, the notion of old age as a time to sit back and reap the psychosocial fruits of earlier efforts must yield to a more realistic view of ongoing, always dynamic reinvolvement, reviewing, renewing, and reworking. (1993, 15)

Bernice Neugarten's forecast for an "age-irrelevant" society was one of the earliest and most extreme interpretations of the effects of postmodern culture on the construction of aging. Neugarten was also an early observer of the growth of "middle age," a category marking mature, vital adulthood. As Baby Boomers moved into adulthood, and as health and life expectancy increased, Neugarten suggested that the boundaries previously marking old age were being pushed back by a prolonged middle age (1974, 1983). According to Neugarten, "age is becoming a poorer and poorer predictor of the way people live" (Hall 1980), and may one day become an irrelevant standard by which to determine a person's social status (1974). Similarly, Mike Featherstone and Mike Hepworth, who survey postmodern theories of the dissolving rigidity of the life course, conclude that "Adult life is a process—a process, we must emphasise [sic] which need not involve a predetermined series of stages of growth" (1991, 375).

The general tenets of postmodern theory have had significant effect on the reimagining of old age in the last two decades. Yet to date, very few scholars have wrestled at length with specific postmodern theories to tease out their implications on the concepts of time, the body, and the aging process.[25] Some scholars issue warning signs, cautioning against a hasty application of postmodern theories to age studies. Harry R. Moody, Mike Featherstone and Mike Hepworth, and Kathleen Woodward, for example, alternately rely on and question postmodern theory, leery that it seems to offer a deal too good to be true. They are right to be cautious. Taken in the extreme, postmodern theory destabilizes the chronologically ordered social roles and cultural values predominant for the last century until the very idea of age itself becomes irrelevant. If Virilio is right, and technology is moving toward the elimination of time and space, medical technology may continue its parallel move and aim to eliminate the traces of time on the body as well.[26] Jean-François Lyotard's observation that "master narratives" have been liquidated in postmodern culture, may also include the narrative of the linear life course that has, at least since Erikson and Robert Butler's work, provided some comfort and purpose to the last stages of life.

Much work remains to be done in exploring the ways in which specific postmodern tactics relate to the complex layers comprising the aging process—from embodied phenomenon to media representations. Too often postmodern theory, including the work of Foucault, leans heavily on constructions of social space, overlooking the importance and implications of temporality.[27] Yet to adhere to the modern project of emancipation and enlightenment as Harry Moody suggests is the aim of critical gerontology, is to accept universality, reject multiplicity, and fold postmodern theory's strongest hand before the bets are called. Aging is an historical, social, psychological, and biological process that has for the last century in this country, been constructed as a burden and a problem for society. Such large-scale social constructions touch the lives of everyone who journeys across the life course— my grandmother, my older performer friends, my own. Shifting these constructions should mean neither replacing them with a single, new, enlightened ideal, as the modern project would entail nor their magical and instantaneous dissolution as critics of postmodern theory would suggest.

Instead, postmodern theory can offer a vision of social space in which no single image or experience of aging is deemed "natural," "normal," or perhaps most importantly, "pathological." The aging body is the materialization of the various discursive constructions of age, be they fashion codes, health care regulations, or the rules that govern private retirement communities. It is also sagging flesh, deepening wrinkles, thinning blood, weakening bones, and faltering memory. To consider the body postmodern is not to slip out of these characteristics nor to shed the ever-changing skin of the aging body but to acknowledge the relationships between the body and cultural forces at large and to open a door to potential social and material change.

The use of postmodern theory is one thing. The larger question that remains is whether postmodern culture itself is an hospitable environment for aging and the aged. As my analysis in this introduction demonstrates, I believe on the whole it is not. Yet the study of performances of age in general, and the performances that follow in particular, suggests that a shift is not only possible but under way.

The Performances

The groups and productions I have chosen to include in this study represent a range of performance styles and outlooks on aging. Because I was based in Minneapolis during much of the research phase, there is a slight Midwestern bias to my selections. Suzanne Lacy's *Crystal Quilt*, Margolis Brown's *Vidpires!* and Kazuo Ohno's *Water Lilies* were all performed in Minneapolis. Rather than considering geographic ease, however, I chose performances that trigger discussion of major issues in— the mastery of the body in theatrical performance; reminiscence and the construction of life stages, models for intergenerational relationships; the generational relationship inherent in the practice of writing history; postmodern theory and the aging body; and the relationship between temporality, technology, and the aged body in mediated and live performance.

I continue to discover senior theater troupes, commercial theater productions, and experimental performances that address aging and generational relationships, and imagine that their numbers will only increase as the Baby Boom moves further into old age. I present the following eight performances then, not as the first, best, last, or only examples, but as emblematic of the wide array of constructions of old age. Each chapter follows a similar course. An introduction of the issues at play and a description of the history and context of each troupe's community and performance are followed by an analysis of how each performance creates its own unique construction of old age.

The second and third chapters focus on performances by two senior theater groups, the Geritol Frolics of Brainerd, Minnesota, and the Grandparents Living Theatre (GLT) of Columbus, Ohio. Both groups are influential members of the rapidly developing movement of senior theater in this country. Chapter 2 examines the Geritol Frolics' emphasis on physical dexterity and a communal, nostalgic reconstruction of the past through popular songs. The group's 1993 performance, a three-hour musical comedy review boldly challenged stereotypes of the elderly in physical decline. But their invocation of an unchanging youthful soul invites questions about whether, ironically, they devalue old age in the very act of its celebration.

The Grandparents Living Theatre show, *I Was Young, Now I'm Wonderful,* uses the oral histories of its members to chart a journey across the life course. Older actors embody characters from each life stage, from infancy to the century mark. Scenes range from biting parody to more serious reflections on the experience of aging. The politically activist aims of the troupe, along with their use of reminiscence, open inquiry about the construction of oral history techniques in gerontology. Specifically, this chapter questions the universality of reminiscence, its devaluation in postmodern culture, and its categorization as therapeutic. The Grandparents Living Theatre's goal for professional quality performances lifts reminiscence from the level of individual therapy, where its political implications can be easily dismissed, to the level of social action where these implications can be more easily recognized.

Two New York City–based, intergenerational troupes, Roots & Branches and Elders Share the Arts, are the focus of chapter 4. Both groups base their original shows on the input of young and old actors, who in turn perform them as well. This chapter looks most specifically at how each troupe defines generations, and how and if these constructions interrupt predictions for growing tensions between generations as their demographic numbers even out and their political interests diverge.

The fifth chapter places performance artist Suzanne Lacy's 1987 Whisper Minnesota project in the context of academic feminist theater studies. I explore Lacy's project, and *The Crystal Quilt* performance it featured, as a model for intergenerational connections in the field from which I emerged as a scholar, and as a divining rod for biases against the aging process within the practice of writing history. Italicized sections in this chapter refer to the 1994 Women and Theatre Conference in Chicago, Illinois, at which the group celebrated its twentieth anniversary, and at which issues of nostalgia, generational identity, and physical aging boiled below the surface of more theoretically oriented conversations. The conference coincided with that of the Black Theatre Network (BTN), at which the invocation of "spirituality" and "ancestors" clearly unsettled WTP's predominantly white, materialist feminist gathering. Lacy's emphasis on difference in *The Crystal Quilt* and Whisper Minnesota, which I read through feminist philosopher Maria Lugones' theory of "curdling," offers a model of intergenerational connection without the razing of cultural and historical differences.

Chapter 6 looks to eighty-seven-year-old butoh dancer Kazuo Ohno's performance of *Water Lilies* as a model of old age that semiotically spills over simple divisions of youth and old age, life and death.

As Möbius strips of gender, generation, age, and ethnicity turn in the performance, Ohno presents what dance theorist Mark Franko calls a "range of difference" across the life span (1992, 603), and what I call a model of the body in temporal *depth*. It is in this chapter that I most deeply question postmodern theory and its applicability to the aging and aged body. Although my reading of Ohno's performance adheres to postmodern theories of performativity, it also disrupts theories of the postmodern body that playfully spin past mortality or imagine death as the human failure to resist discourse.

Assuming Ohno's *depth model* established in chapter 6, chapter 7 troubles the relationship between live and mediated performance, and asks if a depth model of aging is actually possible in a media-oriented culture in which the screen appears to immortalize its stars. Humphrey Bogart for example, his image frozen in his youthful prime, is brought back from the dead to sell Diet Coke. Two performances are set in dialogue in this chapter. This first, by Stelarc, proclaims the obsolescence of the mortal body. The second, a multimedia movement piece *Vidpires!* by Margolis Brown, mocks the yearnings for immortality enmeshed in pop culture. Both performances provide the touchstones for questioning the value, or lack thereof, of the mortal aging body.

Is it the screen itself or the classification of stardom that stigmatizes old age among actors? Chapter 8 turns toward the recent reign of older women stars on the New York theater scene, in a season in which Julie Andrews, Carol Channing, Carol Burnett, Uta Hagen, and Zoe Caldwell to name but a few, were welcomed back by positive reviews that proclaimed their stardom as emblematic of what theater was, can, and should be. Focusing on Channing's recreation of Dolly Levi in *Hello, Dolly!* a role she originated thirty years ago and has performed over forty-five hundred times, I question the tension between "timelessness" of theater stars and the ephemerality of theater as a genre, and ask what role older women play in this compelling contradiction.

Each of these chapters is interrupted by italicized sections that explore my memories of the performances, my relationships to the older performers, the stakes of a young scholar, and of the narrative structure of any remembrance. These *memory sections* are a space for me to address some of the contradictions in my behavior with older people, and my participation in a ageist culture. They also serve as reminders of the ephemerality of performance which can only be described in terms of memory—as performances in the past. Finally, they assert the importance of human memory, faulty as it is, to both the performance of self and the writing of history.

In all, this project has four main goals. The first is to overlap theatrical performance and theoretical performativity in order to maintain a tension between aging bodies and discursive constructions of age, and to account for the social construction of aging without slipping into disembodied, postmodern fantasies of immortality. Second, the self-reflexive memory sections and my use of first person narrative assert aging as a relationship between present and past, and the necessity of intergenerational alliance in the fight to dismantle the narrative of aging as decline. Third, because scholars have collected so little information about the use of performance in the representation of age, I hope to compel further interest in the topic by providing bibliographic information and listing performance groups working in the field. Finally, by fully exploring several performances that trouble traditional Western constructs of aging, I invoke and challenge academic discourses of gerontology, feminism, and postmodernism, and offer diverse, hopeful, yet realistic alternative models for aging that account for the whole of the life course and are not predicated on comparative binaries of youth/age and life/death.

2

Feeling and Being Young:
The Geritol Frolics

✎ *Bright red lights bounce off a shimmering, silver curtain. The audience of no more than three hundred, talks casually as if gathered for a town meeting. I am seated between two friendly women in their seventies, who inform me that I am sitting where their good friend would normally be, if she weren't in the hospital. They ask me who I know in the cast. I have to reply, "No one." Our conversations dampen to whispers as the sound of a timpani shakes the auditorium. Over the growing drum roll, a male voice erupts from the speaker system: "Ladies and Gentlemen, Welcome to the 1993 Geritol Frolics." The sparkling wall of silver fringe parts to reveal nearly seventy performers who, perched on risers center stage, begin to sing:*

> *You're as young as you act,*
> *You're as young as you feel.*
> *You're as young as you want to be,*
> *So pick up your feet, and kick up your heels.*
> *Blow us a kiss, you're as young as you feel.*

After several verses, the music pauses. The emcee announces "Ladies and Gentlemen. The Geritol Dancers!" Nine women tap dance onto the stage in large, red, feather headdresses and short, gold lame body suits. As the emcee later tells the audience, these dancers and singers range in age from fifty-seven to eighty-seven. The emcee proudly declares himself to be eighty-one.

I first became aware of the older adult performing troupe the Geritol Frolics when we shared a chartered plane on our way to the first national Senior Theatre USA Festival in January 1993. The Frolics, based in the northern Minnesota resort community of Brainerd, traveled with a sizable and enthusiastic entourage of nearly 130. Each wearing a red Frolics sweatshirt and variously cheering the pilot's skills or practicing their songs, their presence on the plane was as overwhelming as their presence onstage the next day when they headlined the festival and kicked off the three days of workshops, performances, and panel discussions.

The Frolics' 1993 performance was a three-hour series of short skits in the vaudeville tradition, featuring solo and full-chorus song and dance pieces, short comic scenes, and a connecting narrative woven by a tuxedoed master of ceremonies. The show's theme song, "You're as Young as You Feel," encapsulated the tone of both the subject matter and enactment of the individual scenes. The rapid, constant costume changes and scene shifts, and the demonstration of physical prowess in the numerous dance numbers all combined to create a show that combats a specific cultural stereotype of the aged that age necessarily brings physical and psychological frailty.

After seeing the troupe perform in Las Vegas to enthusiastic senior audiences—there were standing ovations at intermission—I journeyed to Brainerd in May 1993 to see the show once more. I made the two-hour trip from the Twin Cities again in May 1994 to see their musical reviews *Memories of the Thirties,* and to interview fourteen Frolics performers. The performers, many of whom had been new to theater, talked candidly about the demanding rehearsal schedules, and their fears of falling or not being able to memorize their lines. But these stories were counter-balanced by their pride at being part of the troupe and the emotional support their fellow performers offered in the times of loss common to old age.

The performers' pride is well founded. The Frolics have been instrumental to the flourishing senior theater movement in the United States. Their aim for "professional" production standards marks a shift from the recreational, drama therapy–based approach to senior theater prevalent in the 1960s and 1970s, toward the development and training of older actors, and the insistence that older adults are capable of doing much of what younger actors can do. In addition, the troupe serves as a model for successful outreach efforts aimed at involving seniors in the activities of the local community, in the Frolics' case, catalyzed by their home institution, the Central Lakes College (CLC).[1]

Since its inception in 1986, the Frolics has transformed from a well-intentioned and hopeful vision to a financial staple for CLC's Theater Department, a model for multiple senior reviews across the country, and a yearly tradition with a cult following in the Brainerd area. Tickets for the roughly one dozen performances in the BCC's 284 seat house go on sale several months before their yearly spring and fall shows. Tickets consistently sell out in a matter of hours.

The Frolics' deep connections to their community, their successful marketing strategies, their high-energy, positive message, and their "professional" standards combine to yield a celebration of the joys performing can bring to old age. In this chapter I look to the 1993 Frolics in detail in an attempt to chart the ways in which the show removes old age from its association with physical and mental decline, as well as some of the potential drawbacks to the Frolics' positive image of aging. First, however, I examine the history of both the senior theater movement and the Frolics' place within it in order to sketch a context for the 1993 production.

The Senior Theater Movement in the United States

In the early 1970s the field of theater arts began to reflect changing attitudes toward the elderly and to examine theater's potential contribution to the fight against ageism sparked by Robert Butler's provocative call to arms in the early 1960s. Practitioners, who had been successfully using Creative Drama exercises with children for decades, began adapting their techniques for use among various populations of the elderly. In 1972 the Georgia Gerontological Society hired a professional drama teacher to lead a Creative Drama workshop for the elderly in Atlanta, marking what Ann McDonough, Director of Gerontology and Head of Senior Adult Theater at University of Nevada–Las Vegas, calls "one of the earliest recorded instances of utilizing Creative Drama with people over sixty-five" (1981, 3). According to McDonough, between 1974 and 1976, the movement of Creative Drama for the elderly spread in workshops across the country.

Non-profit troupes of senior performers began to form in the late 1970s. In 1976 Liz Lerman incorporated the Dance Exchange, a Washington, D.C.–based, intergenerational dance troupe that trains and features older performers. In Chicago in the same year Patrick Henry formed Free Street Too, the senior component of the children and teen-focused, community-based arts program, Free Street. In 1979 Stuart Kandell began StAGEbridge, a storytelling workshop for older adults in Oakland, California. And in 1980, Elders Share the Arts, a community-based arts program for the aged began in Brooklyn under the directorship of Susan Perlstein. Although Free Street Too, now led by David Schein, has significantly reduced its productions, Dance Exchange, ESTA, and StAGEbridge remain vibrant participants in their fields.

During the same time, three major theater associations also took notice of the movement. The American Community Theater Association formed the Senior Citizen Committee. The Senior Adult Theater Committee formed within the Children's Theater Association of America. And in 1973, under the direction of Vera Mowry Roberts, the American Theatre Association (ATA) launched the Senior Adult Theatre Project (SATP), a committee organized to investigate the state of theater for retirees. In 1979 SATP published *Older Americans on Stage,* charting the activities of senior theaters across the United States and calling for more research in the field. A handbook of models for senior theater programs entitled *Senior Adult Theatre* followed in 1981 under the editorship of Roger Cornish and C. Robert Kase, a member of the original SATP committee. Other handbooks published in the same time period were largely aimed at recreational therapists working with the elderly and focused on the benefits of dramatic activity for older adults' mental and physical health. Handbook authors reveal the power of Creative Drama and the subsequent Drama Therapy movement, to transform the lives of older adults who had internalized the hopelessness of institutionalization and narrative of decline common in Western constructs of aging.[2]

The handbooks of the 1970s and 1980s coincided with the reigning theories of developmental psychologist Erik Erikson that separate the life course into eight stages, each of which holds a unique challenge and goal. As I suggested in chapter 1, Erikson saw the last stage of life as a search for *integration,* a coming to terms with one's past in the face of death. Successful integration leads to wisdom, while less successful efforts may cause depression, sometimes severe. The Creative Drama work of the 1970s and 1980s absorbs Erikson's developmental theories, positing dramatic activities, particularly reminiscence work, as a vehicle for encouraging social interaction and personal reflection. More significantly, early handbooks for senior groups emphasize the therapeutic effects of rehearsal over the final product. Anne Thurman and Carol Piggins, for example, write succinctly that Creative Drama is recreation, not performance. "They [the actors] do it for each other, *not* an audience" (1982, 2). Several essays in *Senior Adult Theatre* also caution directors not to be rushed into production, urging them instead to stress discoveries made in the process of rehearsal. In another example practitioner Horace Robinson writes:

> A quality performance experience is desirable, but seniors should not be so pressured with impending performances that they cannot savor fully every moment of preparation for the production experience. Senior adult theater is at its best when it is truly process-oriented, so preparation should last as long as it is stimulating. (Cornish and Kase 1981, 19)

Handbooks such as *Senior Adult Theatre* and Thurman and Piggins' *Drama Activities with Older Adults* proved instrumental in the development of senior theater on the national scale. In 1986, when Frolics' founder, Bob Dryden, went searching for a group on which to model his new troupe, word of mouth led him to troupes of older adults all across the country, each of whose focus on the quality of the final production was secondary to the process. Of the groups gathered for the 1993 Senior Theatre USA Festival several directors attested to their roots in oral history or dramatic groups sponsored by local senior organizations that used models which paralleled the early Creative Dramatist's theoretical and practical work.

But throughout the last ten years, senior theater troupes have also undergone some radical changes. Creative Dramatics and Drama Therapy continue to be vibrant fields. Several senior performing groups, however, have molted their early internally focused models and have turned their focus toward final productions, financial success, and widespread audience appeal. The troupe directors at the first and second Senior Theatre USA Festivals described this shift as a turn toward what they called more "professional" theater, and suggested that some therapeutic models tended to lock older performers into negative, medicalized models of old age.[3] Instead, the majority of festival performers appeared in large-scale musical reviews designed and directed by established theater professionals. Where group interaction and self-integration are the goals of therapeutic approaches, "professional" senior theater aims to bring performers a sense of accomplishment through a show's financial success, and through the respect garnered for performers as theater artists.

Additionally, troupes that began with storytelling techniques among older adults with little to no exposure to theater are increasingly drawing retired actors, or those with considerable theater experience, to their midsts. It is now fairly common for older adults new to performance to take extensive classes in preparation for productions associated with universities, community colleges, or senior centers. The University of Nevada–Las Vegas, for example, now offers a Bachelor of Arts specifically in Senior Theatre. Theater troupes with professional aims and former, if not current, professional actors, both claim and demonstrate that the process-oriented, therapeutic standards for performance often underestimated the dedication and capabilities of older performers. The therapeutic benefits of the rehearsal process, the camaraderie, and self-worth fed by a sense of growth and accomplishment, are still evident in the larger-scale, production-focused, entertainment-oriented senior performances. But in the current generation of senior theater groups, such benefits are also commonly saturated by the desire for professional appearance, positive reviews, and financial success.

And there is money to be made. Troupes with a savvy marketing team find enthusiastic and often untapped audiences among senior centers, church groups, nursing care facilities, and retirement communities hungry for hopeful and positive images of aging. In 1995 the Silver Foxes of the Fox River Valley area of Wisconsin claimed to be the major tourist attraction in the region. The Geritol Frolics all but stopped their marketing program altogether in the third year of their existence. Because the troupe consistently sold-out their twelve to fourteen show fall and spring seasons to busloads of regional senior organizations, sometimes in as quickly as fifteen minutes, any additional marketing efforts became counter-productive.

Dependency on box-office sales for both the therapeutic benefits of performers and the financial health of the troupe, however, does have its costs. Activities directors for senior centers or nursing care facilities are most commonly drawn to shows that have positive, upbeat messages about old age, a fact that considerably limits a troupe's choices for subject matter. The Senior Star Showcase of the Essex Community College in Baltimore, for example, known for the high quality of their large-scale musicals, developed an original musical about a woman with Alzheimer's disease. After extremely low turn-out plagued the opening week, troupe director Arne Lindquist was forced to cancel the remaining performances.

Although some senior troupes stay within the bounds of positive messages to meet their goals of professionalism, others interpret professionalism to mean taking artistic and political risks. Troupes of this sort often address more troublesome issues involved in the aging process, such as illness, death, grief, financial hardships, or loneliness. Some such troupes present classical plays, commonly adapting them to foreground issues of aging. The Senior Players of the American River Community (SPARC), for example, adapted Shakespeare's *Macbeth* for one of their 1993 productions, setting it in context with the older women performers' struggles to land serious acting jobs. While Chicago-based Primus Players do not adapt classic texts, they select scenes from well-known plays that feature older characters or issues of age. Primus' repertoire includes scenes from plays by Lillian Hellman, Arthur Miller, Anton Chekhov, Susan Glaspell, and Tennessee Williams, a pronounced divergence from the more extravagant musical review format.

Still other groups with more political/artistic aims create wholly original pieces in order to incorporate performers' personal stories and opinions with large-scale social issues. For example, New York–based Roots & Branches Theatre (R&B), the focus of chapter 4, performs an original piece *Old Aids*, about an older couple struggling to come to terms with their grandson's illness. Like R&B, the Grandparents Living Theatre (GLT), the focus of chapter 2, also creates a portion of its productions out of weekly oral history workshops. GLT's repertoire includes pieces ranging from the sweeping musical *I Was Young, Now I'm Wonderful*, which traces the life course from birth to one hundred years of age, to the smaller-scale, intergenerationally cast *Woman: A Joyous Journey*, which follows the rites of passage throughout women's lives.

Groups like Roots & Branches and GLT, concerned with social issues and the artistry of final production, commonly share another characteristic: by drawing oral history from their members, they tend to focus on the local, specific conditions of aging rather than a generalized, universal aging process. R&B's 1996–97 project, for example, is based on the immigration stories of its largely Jewish cast members. In August 1997 R&B joined forces with Risa Jorasalow's dance company to produce *Encounters at the Border* in the Lincoln Center Out Doors series.

Encounters combined professional and nonprofessional residents of the Puerto-Rican, Jewish, and Asian immigrant communities of New York's Lower East Side in an intergenerational, community-based performance that aimed to build bridges between the neighborhood's three distinct ethnic communities through the common theme of immigration. Similarly, GLT hired a community liaison in 1995 in order to explore and nurture connections with Columbus, Ohio's African American community centers for the aged with the aim of expanding the troupe's diversity. Thus far, entertainment-oriented musical review troupes have tended to universalize old age; their positive messages about late life mask the differences that race and class in particular can have on one's experience of old age. Not surprisingly, perhaps, these troupes remain largely a white, middle-class phenomenon. Of the troupes gathered for the 1993, 1995, and 1997 Senior Theatre USA Festivals, only GLT and StAGEbridge had more than one performer of color, none were directed by a person of color, and few addressed differences other than gender and age.

Dividing senior troupes strictly into therapeutic- and final production-oriented categories is misleading, as there is certainly slippage in both directions. As I suggested, the large-scale musical reviews troupes also focus on the personal development of their performers during the rehearsal process, and groups once focused solely on process might also present artful final productions. Groups with an equal emphasis on process and product fall into a middle category I call *bifocal*. For example, Brooklyn's fifteen-year-old group Elders Share the Arts (ESTA), the focus of chapter 4, facilitates extensive, thirty-week oral history workshops among poor senior communities. The workshops culminate in a spring Living History Festival, which features short segments from each community's performance. ESTA's considerable efforts at creating trust, comfort, and challenge in the lengthy oral history workshops are balanced by the care with which their professionally trained theater facilitators shape and present the final productions, produced in 1995 at New York City's Public Theater.

The Artreach Players, based in Milwaukee, Wisconsin, also exemplify this bifocal, or middle range of senior troupes. Made up of twelve older women, the Artreach Players share their personal stories and anecdotes in an interactive relationship with audiences at nursing homes, senior centers, and centers for troubled children—audiences often overlooked by large, entertainment-oriented, musical troupes.

Milwaukee-based Artreach Players perform interactively with nontraditional audiences. *(Photo by Susan Makepeace.)*

Personal interviews with directors of the Geritol Frolics and GLT suggested that the professionally trained older actors were sometimes hesitant to play to nursing home audiences, finding the institutional conditions too depressing. For troupes whose demonstration of professionalism depends on audience recognition and response, it is

understandable that playing before audiences whose physical and cognitive abilities might inhibit such a relationship to the performers
would be less appealing, even frightening. In contrast, in a 1996 interview Sue Hill of Artreach described performing as:

> Definitely giving something. And the feeling you get when you give is
> that it sort of warms you all over. We are giving something to them.
> And perhaps some of them are limited and some of them can't get out
> [to a theater] so we bring our show to them. And you can see it. Some-
> body may approach and just say a few words and you know that you
> have touched their lives in a good way.

GLT's multitier structure, the only one I am aware of in the United
States, enables them to have a professional troupe and several less polished troupes who perform oral history pieces in nursing homes and
schools in a manner similar to the Artreach Players.[4]

As made evident by the crowded voice, dance, and acting workshops at the Senior Theatre USA Festivals in 1993, 1995, and 1997 and
by the growing number of senior groups and actors bridging both
mainstream and nontraditional theater worlds, senior theater is clearly
not just for recreational therapy anymore. The transition from insular,
personal integration-oriented models in the first phase of senior theater
to those of professional-quality theatrical productions has created a
wide range of groups with diverse goals and production methods. Perhaps because of the considerable costs of bringing troupes to Las
Vegas, the large-scale, entertainment-oriented, and more financially
stable troupes dominated the first two Senior Theatre USA Festivals.
The large casts of the musical review troupes supported the festivals
with registration fees, and workshops at the 1993 and 1995 festivals
tended to be tailored to their interests, including vocal and dance training. The third festival, however, included a much broader range of
groups. The grand-scale musicals, including the New Fogey Follies of
Minneapolis, the New Wrinkles of Fresno, California, and the Senior
Star Showcase of Baltimore, shared the main stage performances at the
1997 festival with smaller, less extravagant troupes, including Sacra-
mento's SPARC and the Third Age Theatre Company of Muncie, Indiana. Workshop sessions featured a wide array of performance techniques, including storytelling, intergenerational performance,
solo-movement pieces, readings of new, original scripts, oral history
techniques, and vocal training tips designed for those who have trouble

memorizing.[5] As the festival continues to evolve, it is increasingly representing the wide range of roles the aged can play in American culture, both on- and offstage.

Both groups I discuss in this and the following chapters were part of the founding festival in 1993. The Geritol Frolics was one of the early and driving forces behind the move toward professionalism in terms of entertainment, and GLT exemplifies the bifocal concern for both internal and external aspects of production. In this chapter and the next I take closer look at how the aims and methods of both troupes create their own unique construction of old age, and how these constructions inform more general shifts in the representation and experience of old age in this country.

Geritol Frolics: History and Context

The Geritol Frolics was initially born of a desire to link CLC (then Brainerd Community College or BCC) with a substantial local population of retirees through the development of an older adult performing troupe. With the support of a Bush Foundation grant in 1986, Bob Dryden, then Director of Theater at BCC, embarked on what would become an international search for a model on which to base the troupe. After several disappointments word of mouth led him to Hamilton, Ontario and the Geritol Follies. What struck him as different about Hamilton's Follies from countless other senior shows he'd seen around the United States was what he described as the musical review's "professional" quality. Dryden writes:

> I had witnessed too many instances when senior citizens wanting to put on a show, were merely given a performance space and then were left alone to fend for themselves. . . . a poorly executed live show can be painfully embarrassing for both audience and performer. Not only is the senior talent then presented in a poor light; worse, he or she may merely be perceived as "cute." (3)

After the Hamilton show, Dryden returned to Brainerd. With the help of senior volunteers and members of his Theater Department, including current Frolics' director Dennis Lamberson, Dryden wrote, designed, and choreographed what the original publicity called "a two hour variety show featuring side-splitting comedy, dance extravaganza, and spirited musical renditions of the old favorites" (Dryden 4).

Thanks to successful marketing to regional senior centers and sup-port from the Brainerd community at large, the first Frolics' production sold out weeks before opening and was enthusiastically received. The production's success prompted an invitation for the group to perform at the National Council on Aging (NCOA) conference in April, 1988.[6] BCC's and the Frolics' fund-raising efforts to send the group of over one hundred performers and support staff to Washington D.C. drew the attention of national television. Soon after they were invited to the NCOA, ABC's *Home Show* featured a segment on the troupe in June, 1988. Later the same year the McDonalds Corporation sponsored the Frolics' performance at the Senior Options Expo in St. Paul, Minnesota.

In addition, the Sears Roebuck Foundation invited the Frolics to apply for a grant to test the viability of transplanting their senior musi-cal review to other communities around the country. In 1988 the foun dation awarded BCC seventy thousand dollars to create test programs at three small schools in diverse geographical settings—Essex Commu-nity College in Baltimore, Maryland; Brookhaven College in Dallas, Texas; and Fresno City College in Fresno, California. By the end of 1989 each satellite had given its inaugural performance with varying degrees of financial success. Community responses in ticket sales sug-gests that the Frolics' success in Brainerd was not a limited, local phe-nomenon. Satellite profits ranged from Baltimore's five thousand dol-lars to Fresno's eighteen thousand dollars. In 1993 the Frolics and their satellite organizations (the Senior Star Showcase, the Platinum Follies, and the New Wrinkles Review, respectively) were invited to perform at the first Senior Theater USA festival in Las Vegas. Both the Frolics and Essex Community College troupe appeared at the 1995 festival as well.[7]

In an interview with Dryden in May 1993, he admitted that he never dreamed of the Frolics' overwhelming success, nor had he antic-ipated the enormity of the task. By taking a sabbatical over the 1992–93 schoolyear, Dryden hoped to recharge some of the energy lost in the flurry of the Frolics' sudden and exponential growth. But in 1994 Dry-den stepped down permanently and turned over the Frolics to the direction of long-time technical director Dennis Lamberson who cus-tom-tailored the show considerably. For the first time the 1994 show featured all new songs and comedy sketches (as opposed to the "great-est hits" formats of previous years) revolving around a single theme—Memories of the 1930s. The 1995–96 show, *Trips through the Good Ole USA,* continued in the direction set by Lamberson. The Frolics has maintained its box office success in the face of changes in leadership, format, and performers. Dryden's stepping down initiated what seemed a natural attrition, as a good number of the Frolickers who had been with the company for most of it eight-year history chose not to return.

Who Are the Frolickers?

Brainerd, located 125 miles northwest of Minneapolis/St. Paul, has a population of approximately 12,000, and is known as a state center for tourism and outdoor recreation. "Locals" versus "tourists" sentiments in Brainerd are typical for a resort community, and Frolickers fall some-where in the middle. Although the area's lake country attracts large numbers of tourists in all seasons, the Frolics draws its performers and the majority of its audience from the year-round locals. Many of the local performers, however, are recent converts, having recently retired from careers in the Minneapolis area to settle at their lake homes. Com-munity support for the troupe as a source of local pride is quite strong in spite of a lingering difficulty with ticket availability. For several years tour groups bought out entire seasons' worth of tickets in several hours, leaving local audiences in the cold. To address local concerns without losing the valuable financial support of the bus tours, BCC demanded advance payment for all tickets (to guard against bus tour cancellations) and ensured a Frolics ticket to all season ticket sub-scribers. Now, locals must either take their chances on the availability of single tickets, or buy full season tickets in order to attend the Frolics.

The ticket price for the show in 1995 was ten dollars, twice as expensive as the tickets to the other main season shows at the CLC. Founder Dryden firmly believed that a professional quality senior show should command professional ticket prices. According to Dry-den, underselling the Frolics would cheapen audience expectations. Yet it may also reduce the number of local seniors, not part of bus tour groups, who are able to attend. Despite a discount for seniors and stu-dents, the limited availability and the price of tickets may still discour-age local attendance.

The costs of participating in the Frolics are also considerable and have a hand in creating a primarily middle-class troupe. Frolics mem-bers must pay for some costume pieces and for partial travel expenses, such as the trip to the second Senior Theatre USA festival in Las Vegas

Backstage at a 1993 Geritol Frolics performance. *(Courtesy of Dennis Lamberson, Central Lakes College.)*

in January, 1995. These expenses were not a problem for most of the performers I interviewed. Indeed, a group of nearly thirty Frolickers also spend winters in Dresden, Florida together. Yet some Frolics members are on more fixed incomes. Helen Molin said she tries to plan ahead for Frolics expenses, but the Vegas trip came up too quickly for her to be able to pay the lump sum. When asked if the monetary demands prohibit people from participating in the Frolics, performer Bill Smithburg said, "Yes, I think it does. We've had some people who have to pay $250 to go to Vegas. I think some of our widows may not be able to go, but Dennis [Lamberson, the director] has pretty much said we'll find a way to get you there" (1994). Installment payment plans and scholarship funds set up by the CLC help defray the costs for Frolics members on more fixed incomes. Of the performers I interviewed, the most common complaint was not of money, but of time commitments. Some performers, who live up to forty-five minutes away, spend most of their time coming and going from the theater. "We've given a lot to the Frolics, and we do it gladly," said Donna Diepolder. Although technically anyone can be involved with the Frolics, performer Ruth Meyer suggested that the time commitment kept many people away.

The majority of Brainerd area residents are Protestant and of Scandinavian descent. The Frolics' cast and performance reflects the town's Scandinavian heritage, with several standard Minnesota "Ole and Lena" jokes dotting the 1993 greatest-hits production. In an interview with Dryden in May 1993 he acknowledged that the Frolics has had difficulty getting grants because of their lack of diversity. "But in Brainerd, you're a minority if you're not Norwegian," said Dryden (interview 1993). Yet Crow Wing and neighboring counties are also home to several Native American Reservations. The community from which the Frolics draws support and targets as an audience clearly does not include the large, neighboring Native American populations. The Scandinavian humor, popular show tunes, and the Western philosophical view of aging most likely preclude the interest and involvement of Native American communities as either performers or audience members. When I asked Dryden if there had ever been any interest in including the Native American community, he said that he always has open auditions, and that any one can be in the Frolics. But he also acknowledged that the style of the show was such that it may prohibit their involvement.

In addition to the Scandinavian bent to the show, the early years of the Frolics tapped into Christian traditions. When Dryden first began recruiting members of the Frolics in 1986, he went to Brainerd area churches to find choir members who might harbor an interest in expanding their performing abilities. As one of the founding Frolics members told me, the original group had a very strong Christian element which has changed over time. Rather than sharing a common religious faith and inexperience in theater, the Frolics is now drawing retired professional singers to its midsts. "Now there's more people who have been more active in theater," said longtime Frolicker Donna Diepolder, "we just have to learn to adjust" (interview 1994).

Of the seventy performers in the 1993 Frolics forty-six are women. Twenty married couples made up the show as well. Women Frolickers sing in both the full chorus and solo pieces and constituted the Geritol Dancers. In addition to appearances in the full chorus and solo songs, male performers are predominantly featured in the comedy sketches, a division common among musical review senior troupes who tap into traditional gender roles reflected in musical theater.[8] The audience at the productions I attended were predominantly female. This female majority in both the cast and audience is less likely a result of marketing or the show's appeal, than a reflection of the ratios of older women to older men in American culture in general.[9] References to and displays of couples, and jokes about sex in the 1993 Frolics production were all based on male/female relationships. The lack of representation of single-sex partnerships in the show reflects an essentially conservative political community, and suggests that this cohort of performers formed sexual beliefs at a time when questioning sexuality was considered a private, not public, process.[10]

For the most part Frolickers appear in sound physical health. None of the cast members in the May 1993 performance used the support of canes, wheelchairs, or walkers. None of the performers even wore their glasses onstage.[11] To a great extent, then, the Frolics' positive, upbeat message about aging suspends physical realities of aging minds and bodies, and creates a purified, inspirational vision of old age for audience members. As performer Eleanor Bagne said, "I think it's a case of being proud of having our faculties and being able to participate in something as stimulating as this is. We're fortunate that we haven't developed Alzheimer's or something of that nature."

Dryden's book does outline rehearsal and performance techniques that consider special needs of older performers, including extra lighting in rehearsal spaces, extra seating for those not onstage, and extra water on hand to prevent dehydration. But Dryden is also insistent that his rehearsal schedule is as rigorous as any professional production, and that special treatment of older performers risks being construed as patronizing (77). This lack of special treatment also limits the range of performers who consider themselves capable of auditioning and performing in the Frolics. In receiving lines after the shows, performers told me they often hear older audience members say, "I wish I could do that." Yet performers insist that any one could be in the Frolics. Frolics dancer Pat Martinson said "A lot of people could do what we're doing if they tried, I mean I realize that people have arthritis, but they'll give them a comedy part or some speaking part." Still, Dryden acknowledged that on the whole, the Frolics reflects an image of the healthy aged, although he believes the show's message appeals to audiences across generations and levels of health.

In a country that isolates and hides its aged, a stage full of seventy well-trained performers between the ages of fifty-seven and eighty-seven is an extraordinary and powerful visual image. Although the lack of visibility and defined social roles among the elderly might also give older adults a sense of freedom, anthropologist Barbara Myerhoff's work suggests otherwise. Throughout the 1960s and 1970s, Myerhoff engaged in extensive field work in communities of older Jewish men and women in California and New York, finding that a lack of defined social roles among these older adults yielded a degree of freedom, but was also accompanied by a sense of meaninglessness that far outweighed any benefits. Borrowing terms from anthropologist Arnold Van Gennep, Myerhoff writes:

> The disadvantage of the lack of rituals for the latter part of life probably outweigh the advantages, for rites of passage are moments of dramatic teaching and socialization, occasions that a society constructs to inculcate and clarify, to make its members most fully and deeply its own. Rites of passage in later life could go far toward teaching the elderly and their juniors the meaning of their existence, the justifications for their continued being. (1992, 221)

The Frolics uses visibility in what has become a social ritual in Brainerd, to inspire confidence, self-worth, and a respect for aging among its performers and audience members—all aims shared with the much smaller-scale drama therapy practitioners. As emcee Don Forsberg said, "The cast took on the Frolics to prove on the stage that with our actions, our words, our songs, our dancing, our talent and enthusiasm, that older adults could do it just as well as the younger ones that are performing on the stage today." According to Forsberg, the Frolics has worked to improve the outlook on aging within the community of Brainerd: "Usually when you're old, you're out of it, you know what I mean? You walk around and they look at you like 'there's just another old poop,' you know what I mean? But now they say, 'Heh, I saw you in the Frolics.'"

The Frolics also provides an outlet for older adults to continue to challenge and develop their talents. Bob Holland, a professional musician before lip cancer put his career on hold in 1957, now plays in the CLC jazz band, the community concert band, and the Frolics band. Said Mr. Holland: "You read constantly about older people being set aside, they don't need them anymore whatever their talents may be. Well this certainly has given people an opportunity to use their God given gifts again and they don't have to feel left on the shelf." Vivian Holland, new to the Frolics in 1994, was a professional singer and comedian before an automobile accident in 1957. Because her disabilities prohibited her from singing or dancing, current director Lamberson cast Holland in several comic roles. Said Mrs. Holland,

> I thought in Houston when I had my wreck, I thought—this is it. I'll never have anything again in my life, and look at me—I'm going on sixty-five and I'm born all over again. I'm doing comedy, which is what I did when I was younger, and they seem to like it. I know I love it.

While most of the original members had no experience in theater other than church choirs and high school shows, the rigorous rehearsal schedules through the years have trained them in dance and breathing techniques. The professional quality of the show also gives the performers confidence that their efforts will be well packaged: "It's not the washboard strumming and ding ding dinging of a kitchen band," said singer Vivian Smithburg. "Instead," added her husband Bill, "It's something to be proud that we're involved in. We're putting Brainerd on the map." Clearly, the Frolics provides a venue for older adults in the Brainerd area to hone their performing skills, and to inspire audience members to view aging as a time of continued vitality.

The involvement of seniors onstage in the Frolics is mirrored in the troupe's back stage practices. The Frolics relies heavily on older volunteers to build sets, costumes, props, and to run the show. Older musicians make up the Geritol band as well. More traditionally aged CLC students of theater who might not otherwise encounter seniors, work side by side with Frolics members in the scene shop, back stage, or hanging lights during tech week. CLC is also working to integrate older performers into its main stage season where younger performers currently dominate, even in roles for older characters. Several performers I interviewed have also performed in the CLC season ranging from shows like *The Spoon River Anthology* to *Cabaret*. This integration of older and younger performers and stage hands demonstrates that while the Frolics features only older performers onstage, at its base it is an intergenerational project that counters the common trend of isolating older adults from families and communities.

My reaction to the Frolics 1993 show was split. On the one hand I deeply admired the production staff and performers' dedication and talent. The performance clearly benefited performers, the community, and CLC through the shows' intergenerational connections, its financial success, and the personal and civic pride it generates. Yet in their quest to establish the value of older people, the Frolics also set up a comparison between youth and age that risks perpetuating negative associations with old age in favor of a "youthful" frame of mind. The following sections explore how the Frolics' emphasis on physical dexterity, nostalgia, and parody might not radically shift the meaning of old age, but postpones it instead. The Frolics has changed considerably in the past four years. I focus on this 1993 production because it is a clear example of a very common coping method for those facing old age— the claiming of a timeless, youthful, inner self.

Midway into the first act, a single, tall, thin woman emerges from behind the silver curtain. She wears a brightly colored, form-fitting leotard and carries a red exercise mat. The audience is silent as she begins long, slow, yoga-like stretches. As she lays down and rolls her legs backward, over her head, my thoughts rush to both my grandmother's daily struggle to walk the length of her hallway, and to Michel Foucault's theories of bodily discipline. My seatmates and I exchange glances of amazement as performer Pat Pomeroy falls into the splits. I've never been able to do that. Incredulous, we shake our heads and applaud.

You're as Young as You Feel: Extending Youth into Old Age

Physical agility is featured prominently in the Geritol Frolics, from "Solace," Pat Pomeroy's choreographed yoga movements, to the tap dancing routines that pepper the entire production. The demonstration of mobility underlined the production as a whole, and was enhanced by fast-paced and multiple costume changes and smooth, rapid transitions between the numerous scenes. The emphasis on choreography reflects both the Frolics' variety show format and their aim to build the confidence of both performers and audience members by having performers tackle and master challenging, choreographed dance routines. Dryden writes:

> As we get older some of the physical coordinations get more difficult to attain so more practice is needed. . . . Because they worked so hard

and grew so much, the self confidence of the dancers skyrocketed, so of course the performance was improved. (84)

The haunting chorus of "You're as Young as You Feel" looms behind the choral tap lines and Pat Pomeroy's splits. In fact, the words to the opening and closing number suggest the Frolics' key move in redefining old age:

> Give us your attention 'cause we want you to know,
> We're here to entertain you with a crackerjack show,
> Dances to dance—songs to be sung,
> The body may be ancient, but the spirit is young.

(Dryden 34)

While the Frolics accepts, even boasts about the performers' advanced chronological ages, old age is actually downplayed in favor of a youthful spirit that resists the physical markings of age. Here the "youthful spirit" becomes an internal and eternal essence, a kernel of one's personality, formed in youth and encased in an aging body.[12] Biological and psychological aging are separated in the Frolics to display and defend the older person as a young person in an old body. While the soul is thought to exist *inside* the body, demonstration and control of that *inner* being is enacted on and by the aged body itself. Instead of the body containing the soul, in Michel Foucault's terms, "the soul is the prison of the body" (30).[13]

In this light, Frolics performers demonstrate their inner youthfulness through the carefully controlled choreography of the body, including both onstage movements from tap dancing kick lines to a fast-paced lip sync of the Village People's song "YMCA," and rapid, multiple, offstage costume changes. The contradiction between the inner being (here youthfulness) and the outer body (the aged body) subverts constructions of the older body as immobile or uncontrollable by cloaking it in the spirit of youth. In the Geritol Frolics youth is reified as healthy, energetic, and emotionally carefree, qualities that are superimposed onto the aging bodies of the performers through the many songs, dances, and jokes in the performance. In Foucault's terms the *soul* of *youth* is dislodged from the chronologically young body and encased in the body of the older performer, who then reveals it through movement. Pat Pomeroy's splits operate as a living contradiction between commonly accepted, culturally constructed categories of youth and old age—while simultaneously (and ironically) recreating idealized youth as the standard to which old age aspires.

The separation between the aged body and a youthful spirit is a common coping method for people of all ages who find the losses and physical changes of old age an oppressive, unjust punishment for humankind. The timelessness of the spirit or the mind is a common theme in popular self-help books aimed at improving one's outlook on aging.[14] Humanities scholars have also traced this phenomenon. Based on ethnographies of older men and women, Sharon Kaufman's 1986 *The Ageless Self* suggests that older adults commonly experience aging as something that happens to outer appearances, not inner personalities. Kathleen Woodward describes this rejection of one's own aging body in psychoanalytic terms as "the mirror stage of old age" in which, convinced of the eternal youth of her spirit, an older woman, for example, looks with horror at the older body she sees in her reflection (1991, 61–71).[15] The Geritol Frolics begins with such a separation of the aged body from the youthful spirit in the name of redefining old age. By the end of the performance, old age, purified of its physical and mental extremes, has been recast as a misleading physical sign—and a state of mind.

✳ *A woman with a large feather plumed hat, layers of over-sized sweaters over a house-dress, and tennis shoes, stands slightly stooped as she sings:*

> *When I was twenty-eight I was five foot ten,*
> *now I'm eighty-two and shorter than I was then.*
> *And everything hangs seven inches lower*
> *Than it did before.*

After she finishes several verses, the curtain parts to reveal a chorus of seven women with enormous, sagging, false breasts made of balloons wobbling under their bathrobes and house-coats. As the chorus repeats the original verses, the orchestra layers the music with the heavy pounding of a strip-tease. The audience laughs heartily, but I'm a little lost, a little embarrassed. As my neighbors join in the laughter, I write down on my note pad "parody of aging stereotypes—but are these men or women?"

What a Drag It Is Getting Old

Several scenes in the 1993 Geritol Frolics use parody to distance the older performers from stereotypes of aging. In act 1 eight women dressed in bathrobes, housecoats, feather boas, sagging stockings, and tennis shoes struggle to keep their "breasts" from wobbling out of control. The breasts are actually enormous balloons tucked into their robes. After the opening lines, the song continues:

> My eyes are puffed and now they're baggin',
> My knees are puffed and now they're saggin',
> And everything hangs seven inches lower than it did before.
> My wrinkles are getting wrinkles,
> My moles are growing hairs,
> My liver spots are multiplying, they're showing up just everywhere,
> I used to have such sex appeal,
> Now it's Geritol at every meal.
> And everything hangs seven inches lower than it did before.

Similarly, act 2 opens with a high-energy lip-sync medley by a handful of male performers. One segment features a male performer in a short pink dress and blond flip wig, singing the Connie Francis favorite from the 1950s, "Where the Boys Are." Several sketches later, the curtain parts to reveal several men in pink tutus, blond wigs, white tank tops with attached wings, white gym socks, and halos. The song, entitled "Nobody Loves a Fairy When She's Fifty," is a multilayered drag parody of both age and gender. The number ends as the performers sing, "Your fairy days are ending when your wand has started bending," and the silver stars at the tip of their pink wands fall limply in half. The three scenes, some of the few that directly address old age in the show, approach the topic of aging indirectly through parody and drag. Although the scenes certainly provide a release from what can be a dour subject, the Frolics' use of parody and drag in these scenes also invokes troubling cultural standards inherent in those forms.

I divide parody into two modes. First, to parody is to ridicule difference in order to reestablish a sense of normalcy. In this sense one's laughter at a parodic performance helps to constitute what is considered normal behavior. A parody is funny because it is *abnormal*. Frederic Jameson takes a similar view of parody. Writes Jameson:

> The general effect of parody is—whether in sympathy or malice—to cast ridicule on the private nature of these stylistic mannerisms and their excessiveness and eccentricity with respect to the way people normally speak or write. (Kaplan 16)

In light of this definition, "Seven Inches Lower" can be read as exaggerating the stereotype of older women's bodies as uncontrollable, even grotesque, in order to assert themselves as *normal,* controllable, even, dare I say, beautiful. The hyperbolic image of sagging breasts explodes stereotypes of older women's bodies quite literally when one of the performer's balloons pops at the end of the sketch. The scene declares that older women are in fact not such monstrous creations. Instead, they exist in the place of post–balloon popping, in the place of the deflated stereotype. In this same sense "Nobody Loves a Fairy" can be read as an exaggeration of the stereotypical emasculation of older men, whose "bending wands" are associated with both sexual impotence and, more metaphorically, with the cultural impotence of retirement. This mockery of impotence reestablishes these male performers' potency on both sexual and cultural levels. By exaggerating and parodying these gendered stereotypes of old age, performers in both scenes distance themselves from the stereotypes (of grotesque hags on one hand, and of sexual and cultural eunuchs on the other) and redefine old age according to what it is not, a potentially powerful tool in reshaping what are considered negative images of old age.

These scenes also work on another level of parody. In this second case parody is a comic release *not* based on reestablishing a sense of normal behavior. Instead, the pleasure of this type of parody lies in the realization that *the original standards are themselves illusions* (Butler 1990, 139). In this light all three scenes of parody aim their comedy at the very structure of gendered and aged social roles, opening a space for the creation of new roles for older adults. Such a vision of parody has enormous potential for shifting images of aging. The use of drag in "Seven Inches Lower," "Nobody Loves a Fairy," and the short Connie Francis sketch, however, is more complicated.

Parody may, in Judith Butler's terms, mock the notion of originality, but drag can also reestablish sex and gender norms. As Kate Davy suggests, male drag or camp "(re)assures its audience of the ultimate harmlessness of its play, its palatability for bourgeois sensibilities" (in Reinelt and Roach 1993, 244–45). Male drag is a safe excursion into the less culturally powerful position of "woman" as sign, a move which is not ultimately subversive. Rather than topple sex and gender stereotypes, male camp reinscribes them (Davy 238). In order to ridicule stereotypes of older men, "Nobody Loves a Fairy" derives its humor from the performers' safe crossing into the sign of "woman." They return from the cross with their masculinity re-pronounced. "Seven Inches Lower" works on a similar level, but rather than a drag of gender, the scene can be read as a drag of age. The older women re-pronounce their cultural status as "young" women by crossing into the less powerful role of "aged women." Davy notes that women playing men's roles does not yield the same comic release as men playing women's roles (1993). The cross from dominant sign to subordinate sign represents a comic fall in stature, with the comforting knowledge of a return. Similarly, crossing from the subordinate status of older people to roles of younger people reads as somehow grotesque (Woodward 1991), while crossing from youth to old age yields a comic fall with the promise of return. "Seven Inches Lower" taps into this aspect of drag, reestablishing the performers' status in their return from the exaggerated images of "old" women.

The cultural standards deployed in drag and described by Davy are by no means immutable. A closer look at "Nobody Loves a Fairy," "Where the Boys Are," and "Seven Inches Lower," reveals how older bodies can both reinforce and complicate Davy's models of drag, potentially tapping into the definition of parody as a mockery of originality. Both definitions of parodic drag depend on a clear differentiation between the layers of what one *is*, versus what one *is imitating*. On one hand, the contrast between the two levels empowers one over the other. On the other hand, the contrast between the two roles also reveals the "performative" quality of both: "they imitate the myth of originality itself" (Butler 1988, 138). In "Nobody Loves a Fairy" reading the performers as older men is essential to getting the joke, especially in the wand-bending finale. In "Seven Inches Lower" the distance between the performers and the stereotype of older women depends on reading them as women.

But were they women? Were the "fairies" men? Perhaps because I was an outsider to the community performance, I found it difficult to track the layers of gender and age in the drag sequences. In spite of my close relationships to older people, it's also possible that my own age kept me from a familiarity with physical changes in men's and women's bodies across time. But for a moment, the contrast between the wigs and makeup and the balloons bouncing in the oversized housecoats in "Seven Inches Lower" marked the dual masks of youthful femininity and an exaggeration of the older woman, while the performers themselves seem to slip away between the layers of costume and parody. Gender seemed to fold into age, and in so doing, undermined the clarity and power of parody. In "Nobody Loves a Fairy" the signs were more clear. White, ankle-length, athletic socks marked the identities of the performers as male, enabling their comic cross. Similarly, the performer in Connie Francis drag wore men's black slippers to mark his gender, and to clearly distinguish the layers of drag. Audience members familiar with the performers would most likely have less problems negotiating the parody and distinguishing between gender and age levels, especially since I later discovered that Connie Francis was played by a local political celebrity, a former governor of Minnesota and long time mayor of Brainerd.

My muddled reading may indicate a limited exposure to older bodies, or my outsider status in the community performance. But the Frolics' efforts to mark the "original" gender of the performers suggests their awareness of a physical blurring between genders that age can bring. This moment of blurring, born of my mistaken reading, has several. First, it falls within the second level of parody (Butler's model): parody as a celebration of the loss of originality. But, secondly, it also complicates Butler's model of gender as performative. For Butler "gender is in no way a stable identity or locus of agency from which various acts proceed; rather, it is an identity tenuously constituted in time—an identity instituted through a stylized repetition of acts" (1990, 270). In this light, as people repeat acts of gender, they develop a more solid sense of gender identity. Butler points to the impossibility of exactly repeating acts through time as the marker of both the instability of gender roles and the potential for social change. The process of growing older, both physically and culturally, further disrupts the sedimentation of gender identity through time. The recent proliferation of research on the effects of menopause suggests that gendered social roles shift significantly after reproductive capability ceases for women and decreases for men.[16] Alice Rossi, for example, suggests that an aging society will be increasingly androgynous as both physical changes and shifting social roles among the elderly put sexual differences on more equal footing (1986).[17] Similarly, generational or cohort characteristics influence how a certain generation will reshape aging. For example, the generation that came of age during the social upheaval of the 1960s and whose actions defined the youth movement, is expected to question accepted gender roles among the elderly. Such a move is less indicative of a particular political stance (for this cohort certainly contains a range of political affiliations), and is instead more representative of a generation associated with the youth movement carrying this label into later life stages.[18] The performance of gender then both solidifies and dissolves through time. If, as Butler suggests, the impossibility of identical repetition of one's identity creates potential for social change, aging should be regaled for its potential for transformation, rather than mourned solely as a process of decay.

Yet, as Butler and Davy are careful to point out, the potential blurring in drag and parody (in this case of age and gender) are not inherently subversive. Butler elaborates in *Gender Trouble:* "A typology of actions would clearly not suffice, for parodic displacement, indeed, parodic laughter, depends on a context and reception in which subversive confusions can be fostered" (139).[19] Throughout the 1993 production of the Geritol Frolics stereotypes of age are disrupted, while sex and gender roles remain firmly entrenched. In a scene called "Football Favorites," for example, the women cheer in the background while a man leads the audience in song. It is likely, then, that my reading of blurred gender roles and the potential freedom that blurring might bring, is an exception among audience members, and that the gender blurring in "Seven Inches Lower" and "Nobody Loves a Fairy" are not the sources of parodic laughter. Again, "Nobody Loves a Fairy" taps into a long-standing tradition of male drag, which tends to reinscribe rather than undermine dominant cultural sex/gender roles. In the Geritol Frolics the gay male camp tradition is ensconced in a heterosexual world. While the Geritol Frolics' scenes perpetuate what Davy describes as "harmless play" in regards to gender, they do emphasize the parody of age in which traditional stereotypes of age are revealed as constructions. Yet these scenes cannot be removed from their context in order to preserve their subversive potential. The variety show format of the Frolics presents a complicated entanglement of subversive and conservative images of aging and gender, relying on popular show tunes and "old favorites" to create an entertaining, nostalgic reconstruction of a white, middle-class vision of the power and beauty of youth. Purifying and borrowing from the past, the Frolics inject the present with a dose of vitality and hopefulness in the name of reshaping and revaluing the meanings of old age.

♪ *The emcee takes the stage in a black tuxedo and tails, spinning tales of long autumn afternoons and Minnesota Gopher football games. "Bouncy and vivacious pom-pom girls and peppy cheerleaders led us in cheers that rocked the stadium and when the band struck up the Minnesota rouser, 65,000*

people sang their hearts out." Performers, both male and female, enter in
cheerleading costumes with letters from several Midwestern colleges, and
invite the audience to stand and chant fight songs along with them. People
actually seem to know the words. I slouch back in my seat and cover my
mumbling with overly enthusiastic clapping as they chant songs from both
my alma maters. I look to my friends on either side apologetically, feeling
suddenly robbed of college spirit.

Re-membering When

Shortly after the Frolics' energetic opening and the emcee's welcome,
the entire cast of singers and dancers performs a medley of "Collegiate
Favorites" and songs of the 1920s. This segment is followed by a scene
in which cheerleaders and the Frolics chorus lead the audience in
cheers and fight songs from Midwestern universities including the
Universities of Minnesota, Wisconsin, and Northwestern in Illinois. In
both performances of the 1993 Frolics that I attended (in January in Las
Vegas and May in Brainerd) a great many audience members stood up
during their fight song and sang along with the cheerleaders onstage.

Nostalgia is much maligned. Frederic Jameson condemns nostalgia as a symptom of the inability of postmodern culture to address the
present, time, and even history (Kaplan 18). For Jameson postmodern
nostalgia is an essentially conservative and uninventive recycling of the
past for capitalist consumption. Anthropologist Renato Rosaldo
describes nostalgia as an imperialistic impulse to romanticize the loss
of what has been or is being destroyed in the present.[20] Rosaldo limits
his condemnation to a *type* of nostalgia, but Jameson generalizes the
characteristics of nostalgia to what he describes as the *nostalgic mode*. To
criticize nostalgia in general without acknowledging its nuances is
troublesome, particularly when considering its close association with
older adults.

Generally, nostalgia is characterized as a view of the past devoid of
pain. But nostalgia can also serve other functions that tend to be dismissed along with its conservative bent. As a narrative of the past, nostalgia is always in dialogue with the present. It is a creative act that
reveals as much, if not more, about the present than the past. Although
nostalgia can certainly entail the donning of rose-colored glasses, how
and why it is used need not be inherently conservative. As Fred Davis
suggests, for example, nostalgia can be used to (1) cement generational

The 1920s medley scene from the 1993 Geritol Frolics
production. *(Courtesy of Dennis Lamberson, Central Lakes College.)*

identity, and (2) to create a sense of individual continuity across the life
course, both of which can be useful tools in combatting the loneliness
and alienation common to the later phases of life (1979). For Davis nostalgia can even be considered a resistance to narratives of "progress"
that suggest that the future necessarily entails an improvement over
the past. My aim here is to neither demonize nor romanticize nostalgia
but to fully consider how the Frolics use it in their recasting of the
meaning of old age.

Davis separates nostalgia into several categories. He differentiates
private nostalgia, a more personal look into the past, from *collective* nostalgia, which taps into events on a larger, more communal scale, including memories ranging from media figures to wars. Davis also divides
nostalgia into three levels: *simple, reflexive,* and *interpreted.* The first
level, which involves remembrance without an acknowledgement of
the manipulation of the past, is the level commonly excused as conservative. In reflexive nostalgia "a person does more than sentimentalize"
and considers how the past is altered in the act of remembering (Davis
21). Interpreted nostalgia goes one step further by considering why one

might feel nostalgic in the first place. The Frolics use of popular songs, college fight songs, military anthems, and the vaudeville format taps into a collective nostalgia that may in turn trigger private memories for audience members. Although it is impossible to guess the levels of nostalgia of Frolickers or their audience members, the performance itself, by not addressing its own manipulation of the past, falls within the category of simple nostalgia.

Ideally, the show's simple, collective nostalgia can create a sense of community among the older performers and audience members. The Frolics' reconstruction of the past falls between two approaches to history, best described by Barbara Myerhoff's term *re-membering* and George Lipsitz's definition of *counter-memory*. In "Life Not Death in Venice" Myerhoff describes the power of rewriting the past for elders in a Jewish Community Center in California with whom she worked closely for years, sharing and compiling stories.

> Through their own ingenuity, imagination, and boldness, aided by outsiders who publicized their activities, they learned to manipulate their own images, flying in the face of external reality, denying their existential circumstances. They displayed and performed their interpretations of themselves and in some critical respects became what they claimed to be. (1992, 259)

For Myerhoff there is no doubt that the elders manipulate their memories. As she suggests, the mirror of experience often lies. Theater offers older people the potential to transform their own and the theater community's (performers and audiences) conceptions about the meaning of their individual lives and social roles of the aged in general. In "Football Favorites" the Geritol Frolics, for example, creates a physically active and emotionally carefree youth, and in so doing the performers embody, or *become* what they claim as their past. Yet, by seeing the past through a sentimental filter without acknowledging its current manipulation, the communal memory established in "Football Favorites" and the Geritol Frolics in general remains enmeshed in a dominant cultural narrative of history. In this case the differences between "re-membering" and "counter-memory" come into relief. For Lipsitz:

> Counter-memory looks to the past for the hidden histories excluded from dominant narratives. But unlike myths that seek to detach events and actions from the fabric of any larger history, counter-memory

forces revision of existing histories by supplying new perspectives about the past. (1990, 213)

Clearly, "Football Favorites" removal of pain from the past falls more into myth than counter-memory. The Geritol Frolics uses the old favorites variety show format to create a sense of communal memory, one that retains the stereotypes of age from the time period, and that sets white, middle-class, college-educated youth at the peak of the life span. The older bodies onstage transform in the face of this process, and seem to flicker with an inner youth that still remains. This process reshapes aging from a period of frightening decline to a period of vitality. But this tactic also risks projecting the negative assumptions about old age onto less youthful, less flexible, less healthy, less energetic older adults. In this light the romanticization of the past interlocks with the Frolics' emphasis on the physical prowess to invoke memories of youth as representative of an eternally youthful soul.

This returns me to Jameson's observation of the contemporary nostalgia mode. Addressing what he considered a proliferation of "nostalgia films," Jameson writes:

> It seems . . . as though, for some reason we were unable today to focus on our own present, as though we have become incapable of achieving aesthetic representations of our own current experience. But if that is so, then it is a terrible indictment of consumer capitalism itself—or, at the very least, an alarming and pathological symptom of a society that has become incapable of dealing with time and history. (Kaplan 20)

Although I find his larger argument about the moral vacuum of postmodernism problematic, Jameson's assertion that time and history have become troublesome bears more exploration. The Frolics' resistance to change and emphasis on the eternally youthful soul seems indicative of a culture ill at ease with time and history, especially in this case, as represented by the aged body.

If This Is Old, Then Call Me Old

The final moments of the 1993 Geritol Frolics encapsulate the performance's redefinition of old age by freezing the internal time clock of the soul, while acknowledging the external flow of time and the changes it entails. Just before the grand finale, which features the entire cast singing and dancing to "Anything Goes," "Lullabye of Broadway," and a reprise of "You're as Young as You Feel," an older couple exchange witticisms about the many changes they have seen in their lives. The acceptance of change and the maintenance of the ideals formed in youth constitute their re/definition of old age:

> W: What do you think a senior citizen is?
> M: I suppose it's someone who's sixty or there-abouts?
> W: Age is relative. No one grows old by living a number of years. People grow old when they desert their ideals.
> M: Are loving and caring old? Are truth and beauty old? Are faith and prayer old? Are hope and wisdom old? If all these are old, then call me old, for old is beautiful.
> W: Years wrinkle the skin, but to give up enthusiasm wrinkles the soul. So long as your heart receives from your head messages that reflect beauty, courage, joy, and excitement, you are young.
> *They kiss.*

In the Frolics' model the soul, separated from the body, can escape the effects of social and biological effects of time. Youth, constructed and preserved as abstract concepts of "beauty, courage, joy, and excitement," constitutes the ideal soul of the older adult. The Geritol Frolics removes aging from the chronological passing of years and in turn redefines old age as a state of mind, alterable by choreographed movement and changes of attitude. The method is an effective one, as suggested by the Frolics impact on the community and the performers themselves. "I'm not aging," said singer Donna Diepolder, "I'm sixty-four and I don't ever think about age. I think about how many things I can pack into one day and just do it."[21] Singer Joan Witham says she doesn't think about age either: "I mean, when I'm onstage, I just feel young. I really don't think of how old I am. I like this time of my life. I just feel like a kid again." Don Forsberg also sees age as a state of mind:

> Someone once said to me, "I wish I could grow old gracefully like you," and I said you don't grow old, when you cease to grow, you are old. Even if it's postage stamps, or some little thing, do things, don't start saying, "hey, I'm old."

The Frolickers had a deep impact on me. They graced me with their openness about the challenges of aging, and with their enthusiasm for sharing their craft and message with audiences. The physical presence of older adults onstage, in this case in great numbers, and the shedding of the oppressive stereotypes that saddle the aged with dim futures of physical and mental decline, create an immensely powerful performance that appeals to community outsiders like myself, and especially to insiders who can see their friends and relatives transformed onstage. Their hopeful message is one sorely needed in a culture that continues to live largely amidst stereotypes of old age as riddled with decrepitude and haunted by the specter of Alzheimer's disease. Yet in this particular production, the Frolics' enthusiastic community celebration also adheres to preexisting, oppositional definitions of youth and age. Rather than question the comparative model itself, the 1993 Frolics show expands youthful middle age until it obscures and even overtakes the boundaries of old age, pushing that category further down the life course. The show underplays physical and psychological changes in the last stages of life, in the name of retaining youth and establishing professionalism in senior theater.

3

Radicalizing Oral History:
The Grandparents Living Theatre

Joy Reilly, founder and artistic director of the Grandparents Living Theatre (GLT) of Columbus, Ohio, aims to shatter the myth of the kindly, conservative golden ager, fondly and passively reminiscing about the past. In the group's show *I Was Young, Now I'm Wonderful* an older woman responds to suggestions that she should live for others in her old age: "Like Hell I will, from now on I live for me!" In GLT's jazz musical *A Picket Fence, Two Kids and a Dog Named Spot?* Spot's search for the ideal family leads him, among other places, to a gay household. In an interview in April 1994 Reilly admitted that the scene startled their audiences, adding: "We like to stir things up a bit in Columbus."

GLT and the Geritol Frolics share several goals. Both seek to shift their communities' perceptions about old age. Both seek to develop and hone the talents of older performers. Both seek to present their older performers in a respectful, "professional" light—a light in which the performers can be appreciated as artists, not, as Bob Dryden suggests, condescended to as "cute." Their methods for achieving these goals, however, differ considerably for the two groups, as do the communities they serve. Based on the oral histories elicited from troupe-based workshops, GLT's performances address a fuller range of localized, specific experiences of aging across the life course. While not quite as extreme as their namesake, Judith Malina and Julian Beck's experimental Living Theatre, GLT's performance style does play with conventions of traditional, realistic theater. My aim here is to explore how GLT's relationship to its community, its approach to oral history, and its choices in performance style constitute their vision of old age—in which the later years stand apart as a unique time of life, linked to, but not limited by comparison with, the past. Although I describe GLT's full repertoire, my focus rests most specifically on an April 1994 production of *I Was Young, Now I'm Wonderful* at the National Council on Aging (NCOA) in Washington, DC.

The Emergence of the Grandparents Living Theatre

In 1984 Joy Reilly, then Assistant Professor of Theatre at Ohio State University, started an oral history storytelling group for older adults through the Columbus, Ohio Parks Board. Reilly partially attributes the idea to form the group to her encounter with the Oregon Senior Ensemble, then headed by Bonnie Vorenberg, at the 1983 National Council on Aging in New Orleans. The Oregon troupe created original songs and dance pieces based on the casts' memories and concerns. Reilly hoped to encourage her oral history group to take a similar direction, but her plan was thwarted when the Columbus Parks Board balked at her larger goals, insisting that the group remain strictly recreational. Shortly after, Reilly split with the Parks Board to form her own company. Her actors, a troupe of nine older men and women with little to no theatrical experience, went with her. After the first few rocky years, GLT grew into a multitiered organization of 120 members with a wide range of performing experience. Performers with the least experience begin with the Grandparents Education Outreach Program, which tours schools, nursing homes, and senior centers, and conducts workshops on how to tap and present the performers' memories. Other performing branches of GLT include Grandparents on Tour, the troupe that takes GLT's life history–based shows to national and international audiences; Grandparents Ensemble, an organization for adults fifty-five years and older that helps them to develop and perform their own shows; and the main professional branch, Grandparents and Company, which performs a full season of original shows in GLT's local theater space.

According to their promotional material, GLT's mission is to incorporate the stories of ensemble members into professional shows that provide creative outlets for older performers and that challenge audiences to see aging in a new light. With funding from the Ohio Arts

Council, corporations, foundations, ticket sales, and private donations, GLT has taken its message to audiences around the world. In 1991 GLT performed *I Was Young, Now I'm Wonderful* at the First International Senior Theatre Festival in Cologne, Germany. In January 1993 GLT's Grandparents and Company shared the headline with the Geritol Frolics at Senior Theatre USA in Las Vegas, and in April 1994, GLT performed for the National Council on Aging in Washington D.C. They have performed for schools, hospitals, women's prisons, and a home for developmentally disabled children. In 1994 they received a grant from the Batelle Endowment for Technology and Human Affairs to produce a video that questions the impact of medical technology on the aged.

More recently GLT received a grant from the Ohio State Board of Health to create and produce a show based on the testimonies of older women with breast cancer which targets audiences of working-class women around the state. In 1994 Reilly developed *Woman: A Joyous Journey* which addresses the changes in women's lives across the life course. GLT's 1995 season included: *Black Gravy*, a new play by Farrel Foreman, a four-generational production of Thorton Wilder's *Our Town*, and a reprise of their consistently popular touring show, *I Was Young*.

The troupe has faced a number of challenges in addition to demands of the Parks Board that led to the troupe's founding. The Columbus Arts Council offered support to the troupe, but only on the condition that the troupe file for nonprofit status and remain independent of Ohio State University where Reilly was employed. In 1992, after a nomadic phase, the troupe finally secured their own performance space. GLT shared a stage space with Columbus' only equity company, the Players Theatre of Columbus. But in 1994, the equity company suddenly and inexplicably folded, leaving GLT management scrambling for a new space. As of this writing, the GLT is still looking for a permanent home. Finally, in the summer of 1995, the company split in two, dividing cast members and productions in repertoire between Reilly and the troupe's former business manager. Reilly was forced to give up hopes of hosting the 1997 Senior Theatre USA Festival in Columbus, and instead devote her energy to rebuilding the troupe. The 1996 season saw a new managing director and new challenges for the group in their search for financial stability and a consistent audience base. According to Reilly, original shows draw younger audiences, while more traditional pieces, like the 1996, all-elderly productions of *Mornings At Seven*, and *Love Letters*, draw older audiences.

GLT's range of shows include elaborate musicals, Christmas pantomimes, the simple exchange of life stories, and plays by authors such as Harold Pinter and Arthur Schnitzler. Their major touring shows, *Spot, Woman*, and *I Was Young*, however, stem from the ideas and memories of the performers. The GLT ensemble holds weekly oral history workshops in which members exchange life experiences and views on aging. Taking common themes from these sessions, Reilly shapes and edits the stories into the skeletal structure of GLT shows that are then completed with the help of company choreographers and music directors.

I Was Young, Now I'm Wonderful is typical of this format. A large "Biological Clock" onstage guides the performers through stories, songs, and dance numbers that illustrate a wide range of experiences in each decade of life. Older actors perform scenes chronologically from infancy to one hundred years of age that address the follies and hard realities of life with both humor and poignancy. In 1993 GLT developed *A Picket Fence, Two Kids, and a Dog Named Spot?* a jazz musical comedy about the changing nature of the American family. The show was inspired by the troupe's observations of the contrast between the idealized families portrayed in "Dick and Jane" readers and the diverse shape of families today. The musical follows Spot the Dog's search for a new home, which leads him from famous families in history to a sampling of contemporary families including a super-achieving family, a homeless family, a single parent family, a nursing home family, and finally, his own unique family. Like *I Was Young, Spot* features all original music and lyrics, created especially for the troupe.

When creating a new show, GLT holds weekly oral history workshops on the topic to be addressed in the piece. For example, workshops on *I Was Young* asked that participants share their memories of unique characteristics of each decade of life. Reilly's oral history workshops are exactly what the name suggests—work. A facilitator asks participants to respond to questions or topics in writing, and then to share what they have written with the group. To free participants from worries about grammar, Reilly encourages them not to edit themselves. Her concerns are less for the authenticity of the responses than for the freeing of the respondents' creativity. In workshops I attended, Reilly was straightforward about the artistic process of writing and shaping one's memories, and in her own weaving of those memories into a performance piece.[1] From the written comments collected each week, Reilly selects pieces to be included in the show and edits them as needed. In order to emphasize the artistic process and separate the performers from their own memories, Reilly makes a point of putting the text derived from one actors' reminiscence into the mouths of other actors.

Among the groups gathered at the Senior Theatre USA Festivals in 1993 and 1995, GLT's oral history–based approach is unique. Most closely related to GLT among the troupes is Acting Up! a troupe based out of the Oakton Community College in Des Plaines, Illinois, which, along with its smaller branch, Acting Up Too! also features all original music and lyrics. Most common at the festivals, however, are troupes that use preexisting scripts or a compilation of musical pieces revolving around a theme such as the Frolics' *Memories of the Thirties,* the Essex Community College's Senior Star Showcase performance of *The Nicely Naughty Nineties* (singing and dancing from the 1890s), or Robert Morris College's tribute to Stephen Foster. University of Nevada–Las Vegas' combination of a bachelor's degree in Senior Theatre and an MFA degree in playwriting has yielded several new plays on the topic of aging. And in 1996 Dramatic Publishing and Senior Theatre in Renaissance cosponsored a contest for plays about aging. But, although new play texts dealing with aging are slowly emerging, they are as yet still fairly rare.

By focusing on the stories and perceptions of its members, GLT is able to present a range of experiences of the aging process. Thus, the troupe's oral history approach, combined with its diverse cast, yields a performance that departs from universalized themes of the larger musical review formats which tend to generalize the experience of healthy, white, middle-class, older men and women as representative of old age as a whole. In their efforts to expose ageism and build the self-confidence of both older performers and audience members, senior groups risk overlooking how class and race, for example, can significantly impact health care, social interaction, and job or volunteer opportunities for seniors in later life.

In an April 1993 interview, Reilly said that her attempts to diversify the membership and content of GLT shows have been multiple and ongoing: "We began in 1987 when a woman complained that the show didn't feature any black grandparents. We asked her to help us find a local community center with older African-Americans, and now she is on our board." Reilly acknowledged that she and GLT made many mistakes in their efforts to diversify, the key problem being GLT's expectation that minority community members would come to open auditions. "In order to get them involved, you have to go to them," said Reilly. "Go into community centers and get community backing. Put them on the board, in the production crew, in the oral history groups. Try to include people on all levels of the company." Retaining minority cast and crew members also proved challenging for GLT, and Reilly admitted that "We lost some due to racist reactions of the white cast and audience members." But GLT continues to prioritize issues of diversity by offering oral history workshops in senior centers that serve racially and ethnically heterogeneous communities, and by representing a wide range of experiences of aging in its shows. In 1994, for example, GLT hired a community liaison specifically to increase participation of African-Americans as performers and audience members.

The diversity of cast members in GLT's professional troupe also ranges across gender, class, health, and theatrical experience. *I Was Young*'s cast is made up of eight women and five men, some of whom were acting or music professionals, while others came to GLT with no theater experience at all. Some retired from careers in advertising and education, as teachers, counselors, even a principal. Others came to GLT from working-class backgrounds. Although none of the performers consistently used canes or wheelchairs, several performers appeared with them throughout the performance. While the jokes and references to sex and relationships in *I Was Young* were all heterosexually based, the final scene, in which couples emerged onstage in a tribute to life-long partnership, included a woman in a wheelchair and a female companion.

Several groups outside of the Senior Theatre USA Festival circuit share GLT's dedication to diversity and social change through oral history–based performance, including New York City's Elders Share the Arts, Oakland, California's StAGEbridge, and New York City's Roots & Branches. With the 1995 success of Emily Mann's Broadway adaptation of the Delany sisters' life stories *Having Our Say*, the cultural value and marketability of such shows will increase.[2] Methods of collecting and styles of presenting oral history vary widely, from official therapeutic formats to the wild, creative weaving of tales that have little to no basis in truth. Each of these methods creates its own vision and value of old age. How do GLT's oral history techniques compare to existing reminiscence theories? What kind of image of old age do they conjure? After a short description of GLT's April 1994 production of *I Was Young* for the NCOA, I measure GLT's approach to oral history against the founding literature in life review and reminiscence theory in order to ask how GLT and groups like it expand available models.

I Was Young, Now I'm Wonderful

On the second evening of the annual National Council on Aging (NCOA) conference, the main ballroom was transformed into a stage for GLT. To avoid scheduling the performance while other events were taking place, the conference slated GLT's show for 9:30 p.m. Even though the show was promoted as being free and open to the public, GLT directors worried that older audience members, to whom the show appeals most directly, would not stay awake for the late-night performance. Yet when I arrived at 9:20, the ballroom was near capacity. NCOA conference attendees, largely consisting of care providers for the elderly from across the United States, made up the majority of the audience.

Because *I Was Young* is designed to travel, the play's set was extremely simple. A black backdrop defined the performance space, which was bare save for a large, black, two-dimensional, wooden clock that stood in the left corner. Written in white on the face of the large, black clock are the words "Biological Clock," with decades of the life course from zero to one hundred replacing the expected hours on the clock face.

The performance itself was framed by introductions by an NCOA official and Reilly herself, both of whom declared their common goals to change people ideas about aging and to create the best possible circumstances for people in late life. Just after Reilly's preshow introduction, performers burst in to the ballroom. The pace was frenetic; actors rushed onstage from several directions, complaining about theater audiences' misconceptions about aging performers. One woman asked, "Is the audience any good?" Another said, "These old people can't remember their lines. Oh well, at least the show will be short!" Another performer complained: "Old people's shows are so sentimental. They only do it for therapy." In the hectic opening moments the performers didn't seem to be acting. The usual line between on- and offstage, between performers and audience members, was obscured. As the scene progressed, however, an actor wearing an engineer's hat and a

whistle around her neck began to orchestrate the litany of the performers' complaints, whose targets ranged from the audience to today's
younger generation ("you people!" or "kids today!"). In the scene's
finale the engineer coordinated a chorus of "If there's one thing I can't
stand it's that!" The moment mocks the stereotype that older people
take certain pleasure in complaining incessantly, but does so without
invalidating their anger. Where Reilly's opening remarks questioned
the audience's preconceptions about aging in general, the opening
scene more specifically questioned the audience's reaction to older
adult theater. At scene's end, performers set the Biological Clock in
motion, after which point the performance was contained in the con-
ventional stage space framed by the black-curtained backdrop.

The play progressed chronologically through the decades on the
Biological Clock, with the ensemble of older actors playing the full
range of ages. Transitions of famous quotes, poems, and songs divided
the scenes. The first segment, entitled "Power Play," illustrated
infancy. Several actors, dressed in bright, primary-colored smocks,
fought over toys and the audience's attention. The second scene, "Raging Hormones," advanced the Biological Clock to fifteen and focused
on the turbulent teenage years. Set in a high school "mixer," the scene
shifts from the typical, seemingly realistic awkwardness of teenage
social scenes, to a dance between sperm and an egg, costumed in fluo-
rescent green and pink respectively. When the "egg" first appeared,
the "sperm" scattered—all except one whom she cradled, his face to
her chest, in a moment of tenderness. The scene closed as a wedding
march played and a nurse, accompanied by a father, brought two
babies to the couple left onstage after the end of the teenage mixer. In
the final moment of "Raging Hormones" the wedding march transformed into a military march, and as quickly as he appeared, the father
was off to war.

In the third scene several male actors appeared in military garb.
Entitled "Loss of Innocence," the scene began as a fairly typical comedy
routine in which shy, young men have their first encounter with a drill
sergeant who barks out verbal abuses. When the sergeant accuses one
of the men of playing "pocket pool," murmurs of surprise at the sug-
gestive language ran through the audience. The bold comic content
came to an abrupt end when one by one, the young men began to share
their memories of war.

In the following scene, "Keeping Up with the Joneses," the Biological Clock is turned around to reveal a game show board that reads, "Consume or Die." A game show host and two married couples took the stage—one the defending champions, the Joneses; the other couple this week's new challengers. The unpredictable and humiliating game pits friends and lovers against each other, until the main contestant is reduced to groveling before his boss for a raise. Failing to grovel sufficiently, the man loses both his job and his wife. The scene ended with the man crawling on his knees as the suitably tacky game show host carried a tiny "money tree" just beyond his reach, and the GLT ensemble sang "You can't buy happiness" in the background.

Scene 5, "Midlife Crisis," depicted a mother who, having survived raising her own children, is exasperated at the continued demands of motherhood in middle age. Her daughter divorces and moves back home; her son makes an urgent call for her babysitting skills. Throughout the scene she sings a chorus of "Where does a mother go to retire?" In scene 6, "In Pursuit of Youth," the ensemble took the stage clad in leotards and exercise gear, and struggled to keep up with a frantically paced aerobics instructor, who, with his seemingly endless energy and brown, curly-haired wig was more than vaguely reminiscent of exercise guru Richard Simmons. The parodic scene was a clear indictment of the exercise industry whose battle to conquer the aging process departs from basic health concerns. Finally exhausted by the instructor and fed up with his unrealistic expectations, the class rushed at him, silencing his perky encouragements.

After a fifteen-minute intermission the show continued with scene 7, "Bridging the Generations." Again, the full ensemble of thirteen performers took the stage, standing in a semicircle, and each sharing an anecdote about "what grandparents are good for" from a child's point of view. As the Biological Clock is turned to the seventies, the stage cleared and lights dimmed. Scene 8, entitled "The Darker Side," featured four performers sitting on stools in pools of light, each addressing some of the more difficult challenges of the aging process including death, loneliness, and illness. The passages were stunning in their honesty and directness. Said one older man: "I came home and found my father on the floor, he was dead." One woman told of her husband's illness, admitting that "sometimes I want my husband to die. I see him suffering and I just wish it could be over." I discuss "The Darker Side," by far the most powerful scene in the show, at greater length later in the chapter.

As the clock is turned to the eighties, the energy of the show changed drastically. The scene, "Medication Rap," is a thick satire of the medical profession's insensitivity to older patients. Three older women in hospital gowns are chased onstage by seven doctors and nurses, ominously chanting an endless string of complicated drug names. The scene includes several songs and a litany of sex jokes that disarmed the audience at NCOA. The scene is a potent parody of the medical profession's consideration of aging as an inevitable decline in function treatable by increasing doses of prescription pills, and an indictment of the depersonalized nature of geriatric medicine that overlooks the patient for the disease.[3]

The final scene, "The Lighter Side," featured a couple singing "You're Like Champagne to Me," after which, couples, two by two, entered the stage space. When the entire ensemble gathered onstage, they shared stories about new freedoms and fears that being ninety can bring. The stories of the nineties, while poignant, were light of heart compared to the bald honesty of "The Darker Side." After a long standing ovation at show's end, the actors remained on the stage to introduce themselves, share stories of how they became involved with GLT, and to field questions from the audience about the performance. With no official break between the performance and postshow discussion, this final question and answer period was also part of the performance itself.

Complete with preshow and postshow blurring of on- and off-stage performances, the 1994, NCOA performance of *I Was Young* was much the same as I remembered it from the Senior Theatre USA Festival in 1993. The audience at the NCOA, however, largely made up of professional, young and middle-aged care providers rather than older adults (as the audience had been in Las Vegas), was more aware of the clinical and governmental constructs of aging that are the butt of the show's many parodies. The audiences of older performers in Las Vegas, audiences of the already-converted, and more focused perhaps on performance techniques, warmly welcomed GLT's sharp satires. The NCOA performance, however, rang with a raised tension, its parodies more potent, its political commentary more biting against this audience's heightened sense of and complicity in the rigidity of the roles for both care givers and receivers, prescribed by standards of government agencies, insurance companies, and medical institutions.

↳ *The facilitator of the oral history workshop asks us to close our eyes. We are a big group, forty or fifty, and I'm the youngest by at least thirty years. "Now I want you to think back to your first job," she says. "Think back," she says, "What did you wear? How did you get there? Did you give your money to your mother?" My assigned partner, a woman in her seventies, turns to me and tells me of fleeing Germany, living with relatives in London, and working full-time as a "very bad" secretary at the age of fifteen. She remembers the color of her dress, the song on the radio, even the brand of the pencils. She asks me for my story, but I just smile. I can conjure no details. "It's too close in your memory," says the facilitator, "funny how it works that way."*

Old Age, the Self, and Oral History in *I Was Young*

Troupes like GLT that use oral history as a basis for their productions most often do so with no specific training in or affiliations with official therapeutic techniques of life review. Still, in a country where self-help books consistently top the best seller list, the jargon, methods, and aims of reminiscence therapy no doubt inform even the most mainstream uses of reminiscence. My aim in this section is to present a cross-section of reminiscence theory—alternately called life review, and in the circles of academic humanities, oral history—in an effort to question the terms, limitations, and possibilities of clinical and performance models of life review/oral history.

   In his germinal article on the topic in 1963 Robert Butler links the process of the life review, or the purposeful act of remembering one's life, to *integration,* developmental psychiatrist Erik Erikson's marker of mental health in the final years of life. For Butler reminiscence is a universal, natural activity for those nearing the end of life who feel a yearning to order what can seem senseless events into a meaningful, coherent narrative.[4] Butler sees the urge to reminisce as particularly characteristic of older people, born of an innate fear of and proximity to death, and, oddly it seems to me, a propensity for self-obsession.[5] He describes the process as an active one that yields a wide range of emotions.

> In its mild form the life review is reflected in increased reminiscence, mild nostalgia, mild regret; in severe form, in anxiety, guilt, despair, and depression. In the extreme it may involve the obsessive preoccupation of the older person with his past, and may proceed to a state

approximating terror and result in suicide. Although I consider it to be a universal and normative process, its varied manifestations and outcomes may include psychopathological ones. (489)

Butler is careful to warn against the use of life review in clinical settings only to encourage positive memories. He remains adamant that the value of life review is often found in wrestling with regrets and fears: "I submit that the hospitalized aged, already disturbed, need honesty" (194).

Butler's work on life review encouraged major shifts in the conception of old age in the United States. It provided an instrumental step toward dissolving the medical profession's negative assumptions about reminiscence among the elderly, which had largely considered it to be an obsessive, if not annoying, preoccupation with the past. In addition, Butler proliferated Erikson's notions that growth and change were evident in all phases of the life course, not just in the younger years, and that wisdom is an ideal and potential product of the last phase of life in which one seeks to integrate one's past in preparation for death. Both Butler and Erikson assert the value of imparting such wisdom to successive generations as they journey across the life course. "For those who will listen there are rewards," writes Butler, "the personal sense and meaning of the life cycles are more clearly unfolded by those who have nearly completed it" (493).

For all the important work Butler's theories set in motion, several critical problems remain. His findings have been questioned by a growing number of critical gerontologists, and are a rather easy target for postmodern theorists (myself included) suspicious of the very possibility of and desire for coherence of narratives. Although he asserts the value of both positive and negative aspects of life review work and the importance of "honesty" (which assumes the possibility that memory can yield "truth") even in the face of despair and severe depression, the normative/pathological model remains the grounding framework. Wisdom is clearly the aim, and integration (more recently called reconciliation) and resolution of troubling memories are rewarded with both a sense of coherency of self and calm in the face of death. The desire to look back at the past, born of a fear of death, is posited as universal. In short, Butler's and in turn Erikson's models, dissociate the life course from the machinations of culture, remaining blind to potential outcomes their models preclude.

Anthropologist Barbara Myerhoff's work, although based on both Butler and Erikson's, envisions reminiscence slightly differently. Myerhoff's model accounts for the *fictional* quality of life narrative that creates a new past in the process of clarifying hazy memories, or perhaps even boldly, consciously fabricating new memories in the place of unpleasant or cloudy episodes of one's life. Her passionate and invitingly readable essays based on her field work in California and New York Jewish communities describe reminiscence as the development of a *personal mythology* (1992, 249). Myerhoff departs from Butler and Erikson by asserting that reminiscence work does not simply reflect the past, but rather creates a new self in the present. In "Life Not Death in Venice," for example, Myerhoff describes reminiscence as "self-showing."

> More than merely self-recognition, self definition is made possible by means of such showings [life histories], for their content may state not only what people think they are but what they should have been or may yet be. Evidently interpretive statements are mirrors for collectivities to hold up to themselves: like mirrors, such statements may lie, reverse, and distort the images they carry, and they need not be isomorphic with "nature." (1992, 257)

For Myerhoff reminiscence is not a passive process that ultimately reveals the essence of one's true self, somehow archaeologically retrievable by sifting through and ordering years of memories. Rather it is an active process of constructing a myth of one's life—a personal mythology. Like Butler, Myerhoff sees benefits for those who would listen to the stories of elders, but takes his cautious assertions a step further by suggesting that the stories themselves are created in the relationship between the teller and listener. For Myerhoff the exchange is more than a lesson for the listener, it is an act of mutual creation. Like Butler, however, Myerhoff considers reminiscence work to be prompted by a universal longing. Such a stance goes a long way toward naturalizing and accepting tendencies among older adults to look back into the past, but ignores the cultural conditions that create such tendencies—and their acceptance or devaluation—in the first place.

Like Myerhoff, Marc Kaminsky's early work in reminiscence *The Uses of Reminiscence* (1984), emphasizes the fictitious qualities of remembering one's life. Stressing the incoherence of much memory work, Kaminsky writes:

> The life reviews of most older people are not composed of an orderly progression of memories, organized into a coherent narrative. Life reviews are largely quiltwork affairs, a matter of bits and pieces all stitched together according to a not very readily visible pattern . . . life reviews are dispersed among a great variety of scattered fragments; it is difficult to collect all the pieces of reverie, fantasy and lyric outbursts, storytelling and contemplation, and to reconstitute the whole rare amphora they compose. (156)

In Kaminsky's model, the self in old age is a bit of a trickster, eluding an orderly chronology, sliding into hazy, half-remembered, half-forgotten events. His vision of reminiscence might entail more free-form, stream of consciousness tales that skip across history like a stone on still water, the unique patterns creating a self unbounded by more linear narrative structures or the expectations of the therapeutic community. His later writings, particularly his introduction to Myerhoff's collected essays in *Remembered Lives* (1991), underscores the importance of acknowledging the cultural context of reminiscence work. For example, Kaminsky points to the religious and political history of the Jewish activists, Myerhoff's subjects, that informed their own needs for and acts of re-membering.[6] Although Myerhoff insists that life history is a creation born of both teller and listener, Kaminsky expanded that relationship to include the forces of localized history and culture at large.

These ideas of life review—as an internal, reflective exercise in fulfillment, as an active, communal establishment of personal mythology, and as a free form weaving of memory shaped by local and larger cultural forces—borrow terms from medical discourse, and envision reminiscence to be a therapeutic activity. The very act of categorizing reminiscence as a therapeutic activity already limits its potential outcomes, be they positive, negative, or somewhere in between. As David Middleton and Kevin Buchanan suggest in their essay "Is Reminiscence Working?" (1993), categorizing reminiscence as therapeutic burdens it with expectations of engendering positive "within individual" change, to be analyzed in psychological terms. Benefits of increased social interaction, the formation of community, or potential negative memories and/or results, all fall out of such strict clinical, psychological accounts.[7] Even if these models of reminiscence (reflective and personal mythology) are used outside of therapeutic settings, expectations of positive results may guide what is considered to be healthy fodder in the hopes that reminiscence might produce wisdom, integration, and coherence of self.[8]

But does reminiscence always yield wisdom? A better question might be what exactly *is* wisdom? In the years since Butler's essay first appeared and helped legitimize what had been thought the doting memories of older adults, many scholars have analyzed the models, expectations, and values of reminiscence. In "Reminiscence and the Life Review" (1986), for example, Kathleen Woodward questions the assumptions of positive outcome born of normative models of reminiscence such as Butler's. Using playwright Samuel Beckett's disjointed *Krapp's Last Tape* as a point of divergence, Woodward points to Robert Butler's reliance on an Aristotelian notion that, to avoid a pathological outcome, reminiscence as narrative should lead to positive closure. In Woodward's example the lack of closure in Beckett's play would signify faulty or failed memory work. Woodward also suggests that Butler's emphasis on happy endings may affirm life at the cost of further removing death from a culture that already obsessively denies its reality: "Why should integration and reconciliation necessarily be valued or prized? And are our memories necessarily available to us, or to put it differently, is the continuity of the self itself a fiction?" (1986, 160). Bertram Cohler (1993) makes a similar point when he suggests that Erikson's and Butler's models may, ironically, assume that memory and life-story skills among older adults obey the same rules as they do for younger adults. Writes Cohler: "As the elderly come to a stronger sense of the finitude of life or experience a personalization of death, they may need to change the manner in which they use time and memory to order their life-story construct" (119).

To rattle the structures of developmental psychology and life review theories, to question how their models already shape and preclude potential outcomes (Woodward 1986, Cohler 1993, Kaminsky 1991, 1993) is not necessarily to fully reject their value or import. Nor does questioning linearity and coherence of life narratives necessarily mean that scholars who use postmodern theory wholly unmoor themselves from biology. Concerned that this may be the case, Anne Wyatt-Brown (1991) leans on the chronological biology of aging to support Butler's model of life review in the face of postmodernist criticisms.

> But his [Butler's] point is more valid than Woodward concedes. After all, real lives, unlike postmodern novels, have their psychic coherence.

They can display the Aristotelian characteristics of a beginning, middle, and end. Postmodernists may justly question our ability to find genuine meaning or provide a sense of psychological closure at all times, but even they cannot dispute all of Butler's clinical findings. (341)

But to dispute all of Butler's findings is far from the postmodernist point—at least far from my postmodernist point—that although space and time are culturally constructed modes of thinking, the physical body undeniably guides us through certain general steps from birth to death. In her defense of Butler, Wyatt-Brown underestimates the crucial, larger point, which is that normative models have a hand in forming the results they seek to find and are shaped by the historical moment in which they emerge.[9]

GLT approaches the gathering, shaping, and presenting of oral history as both an active production of memories and an expansion of the positive, normative strictures of the therapeutic model. Reilly's process of gathering oral histories reflects a stance similar to Myerhoff's; both use reminiscence to create a new present for the older adult. Reilly is up front about her role as editor. Her suggestions that the performers shape their stories as they repeat them to each other reveal that for GLT, reminiscence is a creative process. GLT's oral history workshops are also not bounded by the desire or need for positive closure. Memories triggered by the weekly sessions are not always positive. They may be joyous, angry, even depressing. When Reilly asked one of her oral history groups to bring in objects from home that had special significance, one man returned the next week with a turnip. Having grown up during World War I, turnips were all his family had to eat. "I hate turnips," said the man. Another woman brought in a dust rag. "I've dusted my whole life. You dust one day and the next day all the dust comes right back. I hate dusting."[10] Reilly actively encourages creative life review in her workshops, and edits and presents them in GLT shows without neatly contextualizing them into happy endings.

Departing from Kaminsky's suggestion that "the life reviews of most older people are not composed in an orderly progression of memories, organized into a coherent narrative" (1984, 156), *I Was Young*, presents the memories of its performers in a linear, chronological structure arranged from infancy to one hundred years. Like Myerhoff, however, Reilly's oral history workshops take reminiscence as a creative, narrative exercise. The linear form thus appears as another narrative construction, a convenient ordering of what can sometimes be scattered memories.[11] To a certain extent, the choice of a linear storyline participates in the desire to achieve integration and wisdom in later life, aims that have now been absorbed into mainstream through the continued publication of self-help aging theory books stretching from Erikson's *Adulthood* (1978) and Butler's *Why Survive?* (1975) on through to Deepak Chopra's *Ageless Body Timeless Mind* (1993), and Zal Schatcher's *From Ageing to Sageing* (1995).

Yet by including a wide range of emotions, *I Was Young* also departs from this therapeutic and now general focus on positive closure for which Robert Butler's (echoing Erikson) journey toward integration would strive. Four particular moments in *I Was Young* demonstrate the show's balance between joyful and somber memories. In "Raging Hormones" the comic awkwardness of the mixer was quickly cut by an ominous fear that besieged the teenage dance when the "sperm" surround a confused and frightened young girl. In the following scene vivid images and raw emotional memories of war interrupt the rote comic military routine. In "Keeping Up with the Joneses" the toothy game show host moves from being entertaining to sadistic when he dangles twenty dollar bills in front of the contestant who crawls along the stage floor trying to grab the bills in his teeth.

Finally, and perhaps most obviously, "The Darker Side" offers glimpses of death, pain, and loneliness. The forthrightness of the scene is rare among senior troupes who most commonly create positive images of aging in the hopes of relieving and inspiring those too familiar with its pains. In contrast, these four examples from *I Was Young* balance the show's more positive, fond memories of romance, children, grandchildren, and late life adventures. In the final lines of "The Darker Side," for example, performer Ella Richey Wells offsets this optimistic focus. "I'm tired and I hurt," she says, "I'm lonely but I don't dare say so." She continues: "I'm not lonely the way they mean. I'm lonely for the people that were and aren't now." The music turned somber as the woman tried to dance without the help of her cane. Finding it too difficult, she picked up her cane and embraced it as a dance partner. Slowly, the woman extended her arm and elegantly drew an arc above her head with her cane, as she said: "I'm older now, but I don't feel wise. I'm telling you, I see the world through lonely eyes, and it's not all wonderful."

Ella Ritchey finds a dancing partner in GLT's *I Was Young, Now I'm Wonderful. (Photo by Will Shively. Courtesy of Joy Reilly.)*

Although *I Was Young* ends with a positive look at the nineties and a playful hinting at what the centennial might bring, the show's use of oral history, its reliance on parody, and its choices in staging techniques prevent simplistic, optimistic, closure to a life stage rife with myriad and often conflicting emotions. GLT's methods of gathering, contextualizing, and enacting the oral histories of its members are unique among more clinical approaches to life review. The troupe's approach yields an image of old age as a unique life stage, replete with both positive and negative stories, sculpted by both the actions of the performers and the cultural forces through which they move.

✣ *As the older woman onstage lowers her cane from over her head and the lights begin to brighten, I lean back in my chair, relieved for the chance to absorb the intensity of the last scene. But a chorus of doctors and nurses chanting in what seems like Latin disturbs my reflection. The sudden change of pace makes it tough to position the scene. As the doctor remarks about the size of his nurse's breasts, my friend sitting next to me raises her eyebrows. When the doctor makes a joke about the size of his patient's penis, the woman in front of me gasps. Is this comedy gone bad? A case of badly misinterpreting one's audience? Or a vicious, biting parody?*

Staging (and Off-Staging) Age in *I Was Young*

Parody is a main component of *I Was Young*. Rather than realistically portray the group's memories of certain life stages, GLT exaggerates them. "Power Play" exaggerates the behavior of toddlers; "Raging Hormones" is a larger-than-life depiction of stereotypical teenage behavior. "Keeping up with the Joneses" ridicules the competitive drive to acquire material goods; "In Pursuit of Youth" mocks the exercise mania that sweeps this country; "Midlife Crisis" takes aim at the cultural devaluation of housework; "Medication Rap," probably the most bitter of the show's parodies, attacks the medical profession's treatment of the elderly.

The parodic scenes in *I Was Young* point their ridicule at the institutions that dominate the life stage to which each refers. For example, the parody in "Medication Rap" is directed at the medical profession for its insensitivity to the personalized needs of elderly patients. The sexual jokes in the piece and the exaggerated doo-wop chorus of doting female nurses gathered lovingly at the feet of a noxious, male doctor take the form of vaudeville doctor routines to ridicule today's medical profession. Similarly "Keeping up with the Joneses" parodies the materialistic impulse toward competitive consumerism. Taking the form of a game show, the parody reveals the humiliation and broken relationships that can appear as fallout of the need to reflect one's worth in consumer products. GLT's use of parody resists equating memories garnered from their workshop sessions with a true, or real past. Instead

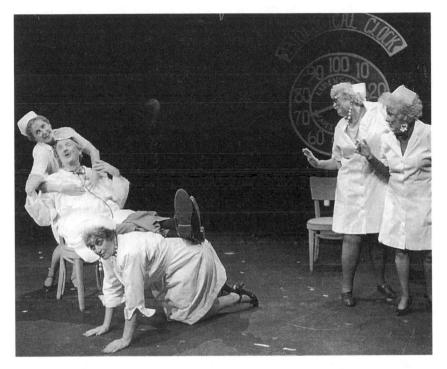

The Medication Rap in GLT's *I Was Young. (Courtesy of Joy Reilly.)*

they represent their memories in the context of the institutions that shaped them, sharply ridiculing the power of those institutions for their hand in creating age-appropriate social roles.

As a point of comparison, take the Geritol Frolics' "Seven Inches Lower" and GLT's "In Pursuit of Youth." "Seven Inches Lower" parodies a stereotype of old women, replacing it in the context of a performance that emphasizes physical agility and an internalized youth. "In Pursuit of Youth," on the other hand, parodies the industry that encourages people to look young, encasing the scene within a performance that reveals a range of physical abilities, and conflicting emotions about the aging process. The humor in GLT's parodies emerges from the characters' vulnerability at various ages during which their behavior is guided by their negotiation with the interests of cultural institutions—the military, advertisers, employers, the medical profession, etc. By using parody in this context, GLT does not replace the images they ridicule with definitive norms of age-appropriate behavior, but rather leaves life stages open to a range of new definitions.

In addition to the pervasiveness of parody in *I Was Young*, Reilly's use of nontraditional acting and directing techniques also shapes its own unique construction of old age. *I Was Young* opens with actors entering from backstage, side stage, through the audience, even through the doors to the theater itself. The scene, in which the performers complain about older actors as if they were the audience, jars the spectator from traditional theatrical expectations, that the performance will be contained within the stage space. The result of the thwarted expectations is a distancing affect of sorts, reminiscent of Brecht's *verfremdungseffekt*, or "alienation effect," the aim of which is to have the audience both empathize with and think critically about the performance.[12] To simultaneously empathize with and critically analyze the performance is to emphasize the links between (1) the internal world of the theater and (2) the codes that govern the audience's lives outside the theatrical frame. For example, when the performers in the opening scene anticipate what the audience members' preconceptions about older actors might be, they point to enculturated views carried into the performance space that GLT hopes to alter during the course of the show. This initial hope expands to a desire that the audience carry those changed perceptions with them after the show, not only in their treatment of older people, but in their awareness of how perceptions of age shape their own experiences.

The opening scene of *I Was Young* uses the full auditorium as its stage, and occurs before the theatrical frame defined by the biological clock is put into play. The result is a scene that invokes a space in between on- and offstage, between performance and everyday life, between theatrical performance and theoretical performativity, between empathy and critical thought. The "in between-ness" of the opening scene is paralleled by the postshow scene in which the actors formed a semicircle onstage and introduced themselves, some relaying their performing experience, others sharing anecdotes about their families or how being part of GLT has affected their lives. The scene took place on the stage, under the performance lights, after bows were taken and the biological clock had come to rest at one hundred years. The houselights came up after a second standing ovation at the 1994 NCOA performance, but the audience lingered to talk to the performers who remained onstage. Similar to the opening scene, the final moments of

personal testimony fall between theatrical performance and the performance of the self. By opening the performance space to include the
audience in both the opening and closing scenes, *I Was Young* invites
the audience, regardless of age, to consider how their own performances of age might change with shifts in perceptions of the aging
process.

Another of Reilly's nontraditional directorial decisions is to have
the older performers represent the full range of ages across *I Was
Young*'s biological clock. In contemporary American theater it is common practice for younger actors to don age makeup in order to represent older characters, and very uncommon, even in more experimental
theater, for older actors to play younger characters. Surprisingly, there
is little historical or theoretical literature on this practice. I take this lack
of literature to suggest both that the practice is so common as to be
unremarkable, and that the aged are largely considered unable (or
impractical in commercial theater) to represent themselves.[13] This practice of stratified age casting creates a mythical one-way street of aging
unique to Western culture, where youth can represent a full range of
ages, but older people, supposedly limited by the physical and psychological changes that aging incurs, cannot go backward to represent
youth.[14] GLT actors break this one-way pattern in the first several scenes
of *I Was Young*. They play aggressive toddlers, anxious teenagers, vulnerable young adults, and well-intentioned middle-agers. Tapping
their own memories of youth to create the roles of characters in the
early stages of life, the GLT performers emphasize a continuity in the
journey across the life course and simultaneously point to disjunctions
between the younger characters and the older performers.

GLT's casting choices and their send-ups of the disjunction between
age and youth establish aging as an embodied, material process, and a
social practice. Aging itself is a temporal process that disrupts the stabilization of identity over time. Material aging is *a process of change,* of
destabilization, a process that makes the efforts to exactly reproduce
one's social identity an impossibility. As the aging process continues,
as I pass, for example, from my twenties to my thirties, from my fifties
to my sixties, it becomes more and more difficult to believe in the illusory stability of my identity. Countless numbers of creams, dyes, exercise, and diet regimes are offered as tools to assist consumers in efforts
to mask the changes that aging creates and to hang on a little longer to
the illusion that exact repetition (an equation of *who I was* with *who I am*)

stabilizes one's sense of self. But the aging process and the changes it manifests, are part of the now, part of one's present identities.[15] We produce ourselves anew with each practice, each act, and continue to do so across the life course. The older performers in GLT play infants, repeating the actions of toddlers scrapping for attention, or teenagers tossed in a hurricane of hormones, but the exact repetition of these actions of youth are, due to the passage of time, impossible.

A certain, if elusive, continuity does exist. The performers' memories and experiences of youth help shape their lives and are imprinted to a certain extent on the bodies of the performers.[16] In a simple example, if one develops bad posture as a child, the repetition or reiteration of that behavior as a child will affect the experience of one's old age. Memories of past performances linger in the body. The youths of the older performers mark their bodies with memories that are filtered through the present moment and the physical aging process. In this case the Frolics' emphasis on the older body's containment of youthful experiences appears to ring true. But GLT departs from the Frolics' emphasis on internal and unchanging youthfulness by also emphasizing the disjunction between the younger roles and the older performers. I point to two specific scenes as examples. First, in "Raging Hormones," an older man plays a young boy primping excitedly for a "mixer." The young man reaches for his comb and, with great deliberation, makes a great arc with his arm and slowly sweeps the comb across his head. Reilly sets the moment apart and plays it for a laugh—the actor playing the young man is completely bald. The scene "In Pursuit of Youth" provides a second example. At one point during this parody of aerobics classes and standards of physical beauty, an older woman wiggles the loose skin under her bare arms and whines, "Now if I could only firm this up!" Her tone and facial expression underscore the futility of such an endeavor. The parody itself suggests that the ideal body, the desired effect of many exercise programs, is based on a youthful, "hard-body" model. The GLT parody, in which the aerobics students rebel against their instructor, both asserts the physical abilities and stamina of the older performers who play aerobics students, and simultaneously separates them from the standards of appearance upon which the exercise craze is based.

Aging then, as created in GLT's theatrical model whose staging techniques blur the distinctions between theatrical and theoretical performativity, is simultaneously a stabilizing and destabilizing process.

In the later scenes of *I Was Young*, as the Biological Clock ticks past the sixties, seventies, eighties, and nineties, GLT performs old age, once categorized as one immense life stage—whatever was left after retirement—as a richly varied time of life filled with learning, joy, and hope, as well as loneliness, despair, and death. By referring to memories of youth while acknowledging the differences of age, GLT removes old age from a comparative relationship with youth and demonstrates that one doesn't cease from performing one's self after retirement.

This aspect of performativity, its appearance at all stages of the life course, helps to dissolve the binary of productivity and nonproductivity that continues to fuel the devaluation of older adults (and younger people similarly viewed as disabled) despite the erosion of age-related social roles and the once prominent three boxes of life that separated youth from older adults in education and the marketplace.[17] Pierre Bourdieu recognizes this devaluation of the aged on these terms when he writes in *Distinction:*

> Social ageing [sic] is nothing other than the slow renunciation or disinvestment (socially assisted and encouraged) which leads agents to adjust their aspirations to their objective chances, to espouse their condition, *become what they are and make do with what they have,* even if this entails deceiving themselves as to what they are and what they have, with collective complicity, and accepting bereavement of all the 'lateral possibilities' they have abandoned along the way. (my emphasis; 1979, 110–11)

To "become what they are and make do with what they have," suggests that older people are encouraged to stop producing, stop growing, stop changing—stop performing themselves anew. By the time one crosses the threshold of old age, a moment determined by the social fields in which one "plays," the cultural assumption appears to be that the illusory stabilization process about which Judith Butler writes has run its course and the older person appears to have atrophied in his or her own repeated performances. To stabilize, then, is to no longer be capable of performing one's self: in old age then, one has no other option than to simply *be* one's self, now almost completely defined by physical changes.

The idea of finally *being* one's self has a certain promise to it, especially within a culture that exerts such pressure on finding, discovering, and mastering the self. But with this reward of stability comes a forfeiture of the ability to perform anything other than one's perfected role. Here the limited performance of the self links with cultural assumptions that older people, as nonproductive members of society, are physically and mentally unable to *produce* and care for themselves. Although productivity covers a much wider area of study, including Marxist economic theory, it has clear ties to gerontology and life review, fields in which recent theorists defend the elderly as productive members of society.[18]

The Marxist notion of productivity, equating the value of the worker with his or her labor, has long come under fire by postmodernists, including Jean Baudrillard[19] and feminist theorists focused on the devaluation of housework.[20] Within the field of gerontology, Harry Moody questions the binary thinking behind such theories of productivity when he suggests that American culture needs to reconsider the value of the contemplative life if the elderly are to find meaning in old age (1986). But reasserting the value of the contemplative life as Moody calls it, *temporarily* lends value to the aged within a system whose very structure defines aging as a loss of "productive" capabilities. Charles Fahey and Martha Holstein point to this paradox when they write:

> The recent emphasis on a productive aging society (see Moody 1989; Pifer and Bronté 1986) continues to present a partial and exclusionary vision. Even when generously defined, that is, severed from economic metaphors, it separates the "productive" from the "nonproductive" and by implication further marginalizes and negates those whom the "gatekeepers of ideas" (Epstein 1988) deem nonproductive. (Cole and Achenbaum 1993, 246)

Proving the worth of the elderly by emphasizing their ability to produce (often in terms that draw comparisons to young adults), is not the solution. Instead, dissolving the binary of productivity itself can help reveal the constructed nature of the mechanism that denies worth to the aged and the disabled alike. In the terms of performativity, if the very materialization of the body is produced by social practice, and this production continues across the life course, then the very idea of *nonproductivity* is a misnomer.

GLT's *I Was Young* creates a model of aging that blurs the sometimes subtle distinctions between the theatrical performance of characters and theoretical performativity—producing one's self in social acts. This blur is created in part by the bookend scenes of the opening and the final scene in which the performers introduce themselves, and by the cross-age casting that places older actors in the roles of younger characters—spawned of the oral history workshops and the memories of the performers themselves. Aging itself becomes a kind of performance in *I Was Young,* a performance bounded by the presence of the enormous biological clock onstage, and by the linear, chronological structure of the show. The use of parody in the show attacks the social institutions that determine age-related social roles, a move that underscores the idea that the self is performed at different life stages in negotiation with social forces. The physical movement in *I Was Young* includes a range of behaviors, from the almost hyperactive stamina in the parody of aerobics, the teenage mixer, and the spoof of the medical industry, to the more quiet, stationary moments, when, for example in "The Darker Side," actors sit on stools, and a single performer battles and accepts her dependency on a cane. Rather than come to terms with her "disability," the scene ends with the actor defining her own range of movement, drawing an arc above her head with her cane, and complaining of loneliness and physical pain. Similarly, the emotional range of *I Was Young* separates it from oral history models that prescribe positive results. The parodies of "Midlife Crisis" and "Medication Rap," for example, are light and happy on the surface, yet such a facade is a thin disguise for rather bitter cultural criticism. Fond memories of teenage dances are complicated by the fears that can accompany awakening sexualities. The "golden years," as they are described in the doctor's song in scene 9, combine new freedoms and joys of grandparenthood with cultural invisibility and physical and emotional pain.

The older actors in GLT's *I Was Young* both play characters in the scenes that expose the construction of age and proudly claim the label of old for themselves. While the Frolics associates old age with positive, timeless traditions, and dissociates it from physical decline, for GLT, old age is inclusive of a range of physical and psychological states. Through the blurring of theatrical performance and performativity in the opening and closing scenes, the powerful moments of oral history testimonials, and the parodies of institutional constructions of age, GLT unsettles existing definitions of aging and puts forth an image of age as a heterogeneous blend of mental, physical, and spiritual growth and loss. The direct address and the merger of audience and performer space in the opening scene theatrically creates a mirror phase of old age in which the audience is encouraged not just see their reflection, but to ask, *how* and *why* they see it.[21] The range of loss and potential for growth, and the embodiment of the past in memory in GLT's image of aging, make it possible to accept the reflection of age in the mirror without denying the shifting memories of youth that linger and continue to impact the present, aging self.

4

Generations of Change:
Roots & Branches and
Elders Share the Arts

Seventy-one years divide the oldest and youngest performers in New York City's Roots & Branches Theater (R&B). At ninety years of age the oldest performers have witnessed the opening and closing of the twentieth century. Their stories encompass world wars, immigrant life, and massive economic and technological changes. At nineteen the youngest members of R&B are just taking their first steps in the long process of self-definition. The differences between the generations are considerable. They are differences that sociologists, economists, and political pundits predict will fuel "intergenerational warfare" over the next forty years, as age groups vie for political clout and shrinking financial resources. R&B's weekly improvisation workshops, however, tell quite a different story. The workshops, and the performances they eventually become, are a place where generations can acknowledge and explore differences, find common ground, grow friendships, and develop as artists.

Like Roots & Branches, New York City-based Elders Share the Arts (ESTA) also creates performances out of intergenerational storytelling. Among its many arts programs for seniors, ESTA facilitators guide storytelling workshops between groups of seniors and elementary school children within the same community. These "Living History" groups share stories and create improvised scenes around common concerns that are then performed for their communities at large. While R&B and ESTA are both focused on process and production, in the tradition of people's theater, ESTA's main concern lies primarily with the empowerment of its actors.

By uniting young and old in theatrical performance, both R&B and ESTA cut through the haze of misunderstanding between generations today—misunderstandings bred by isolation and by ageism in both directions. Through the workshop and performance process, both groups create a space where friendships can bridge generational divides. R&B and ESTA are among only a handful of intergenerational performance troupes in the country, a genre that will become increasingly important and popular as demographics swing toward the later half of life in the coming years.[1] While the two groups reach similar goals, their approaches differ considerably, and provide valuable, distinct meanings of age.

This chapter explores the history and scope of both R&B and ESTA. Using interviews with older and younger members of each troupe and readings of their spring 1996 shows, I ask how each performance envisions the meaning of the term *generation* as well as the relationships between them.

At a party to mark the end of the Women and Aging conference I fought the butterflies and approached some of the scholars whose work had led and fed my own. That good girl / student thing is tough to shake, but the conversations were too charged to shy away from. Wine and words—of theory, political action, and personal journeys—flowed fast. Just as I was leaving, exhausted and buzzing, an elegantly dressed woman in her forties touched my arm. "Don't forget. You are a beautiful, young woman," she said.
"Excuse me?" I asked.
"Don't forget it."

Talkin' 'bout Generations

Predictions for rising antagonism between generations are a fairly common tale. The story goes that as Baby Boomers reach retirement age, they will cause a radical demographic swell in the number of older Americans eligible for government services. This highly educated, politically sophisticated generation is expected to maintain its current control of the interests of advertisers and increase its stakes in the political system, diverting funding for education and children's services in general toward the concerns of the elderly. Squabbles across age groups for economic resources are predicted to solidify generational identities and alliances, and to further divide a nation already deeply divided by race and class.

Warning cries about the inevitable bankruptcy of Social Security and Medicare sounded in the early 1980s. The mobilization of Americans for Generational Equity and the publication of books such as Ken Dychtwald's popular seller *The Age Wave* (1989) and Phillip Longman's *Born to Pay* (1987), set the tone for the slew of "Generation X" literature that emerged in the early 1990s. Much of this literature is rife with blatant hostility toward the "greedy geezers," who are commonly depicted as country-clubbing through their "silver age," while college-educated Xers vie for dead-end "McJobs" at mock-chic franchises like Starbucks and Kinkos. Douglas Coupland's *Generation X* (1991), for example, an early and driving force in this genre, includes a scene in which a young man destroys a car that flaunts the incendiary bumper sticker "I'm spending my children's inheritance."[2] After the first wave of Gen X literature appeared, some young people within the Gen X age lines insisted they bore no resemblance to these apathetic roustabouts that had actually been created by Baby Boomer advertising executives. Second-wave Generation X material, such as Geoffrey Holtz's *Welcome to the Jungle* (1995), and Wexler and Hulme's short story anthology *Voices of the Xiled* (1994), are more careful to represent the age group with statistics and the voices of actual Gen Xers.

Second-wave Xer literature comes much closer to sketching common characteristics of children born and schooled in a shared historical moment. Certainly, people who share common historical conditions in their formative years, such as national tragedies like the Challenger explosion, or major technological inventions like the growth in prevalence of computers, televisions, and air travel, will in turn be shaped by these conditions. But, even if we accept loosely drawn generational boundaries, several significant questions remain.

First, just what is a generation? Are there consistent and useful ways to draw lines between people born in different years? Second, it remains to be seen whether generational identities are necessarily antithetical to the forging of intergenerational connections. A certain amount of friction is expected between generations as young people define their individuality. But antagonism between generations seems to pervade Western culture—from Greek myths of Titans devouring their children to the early twentieth-century, American imbrication of

youth and *progress* to the current use of narrow casting among advertisers to create and isolate generations of consumers. Is this antagonism
necessarily a given? Or might generational differences coexist with
stronger, common concerns of the full life course? Third, and finally,
who gains by dividing and/or connecting generations?

As 1960s rock and roll stars continue to sing about "their generation" and as Xer's decry the none too flattering depictions of theirs, just
what has *generation* come to mean? Amid the changing structure of the
American family and age-related social roles, the term has become
ambiguous at best. In *The Changing Contract across Generations* (1993)
sociologist Vern Bengtson traces four definitions for it. First, it can refer
to one's position in family lineage; grouping siblings as one generation
and parents as another. Second, it can refer to a group of people born
within a span of five to ten years. Third, it can also refer to groups born
in a larger span of time, ranging from ten to twenty years. The fourth
common use of the term *generation* is to describe a group of people of
similar yet unspecified ages, mobilized around a specific social issue.

Generation can also refer to two loosely defined categories: horizontal and vertical. Horizontal generations are widely drawn groups of
people born within similar time periods who share formative cultural
experiences such as wars, economic shifts, fashion, and popular
music/arts. Vertical generations refer to one's order in family lineage,
such as child, parent, or grandparent. Confusion can arise when one of
these categories is used to metaphorically describe the other, forcing
horizontal generations, for example, into relationship in terms of universalized family structures.[3]

To add to the confusion, increases in longevity have led to the
emergence of four- and five-generation families. Delays in childbear-
ing, decreases in fertility, and/or voluntary childlessness have also
contributed to the appearance of "age-gapped" generational structures
in which more than twenty years exist between parents and children
(Bengtson 1993, 16). In both cases multigenerational families and age-
gapped families, chronological age is no longer indicative of one's position in the family. Grandparents, for example, are increasingly taking a
parental role with their grandchildren, whose parents are either
pinched by the demands of single parenthood or are struggling to keep
the two-income family engine running.

In spite of these complications, scholars have created several models of generational boundaries over the last decade. William Strauss

and Neil Howe's *Generations: The History of America's Future, 1584–2069* (1991) traces patterns in generational relationship and identity over six centuries. They define a generation as "a special cohort-group whose length approximately matches that of a basic phase of life (or about twenty-two years over the last three centuries) and whose boundaries are fixed by peer personality" (61). In their extensive historical research Strauss and Howe found that peer personality ("a common generational persona" defined by shared historical conditions) exists relationally to subsequent generations. For example, the Boom generation, as they call it, is an "Idealist" generation, the protected, and coddled children that emerge after an era of crisis. Drawing lines according to historical events, Strauss and Howe separate contemporary generations into the following categories, designated by one's year of birth: GI (1901–24), Silent (1925–42), Boom (1943–60); Thirteenth (1961–81); Millennial (1982–2003).[4]

In contrast, Susan MacManus (1996) draws significantly different generational boundaries according to major political events and political characteristics of different age groups. Basing birth-year distinctions on voting statistics, and the labels on key events, MacManus creates the following categories: World War I (1899–1910); Depression / World War II (1911–26); Cold War / Sputnik (1927–42); Civil Rights / Vietnam / Watergate (1943–58); Reagan (1959–73). In one system I am of the thirteenth generation (a "thirteener"); in another I am a Reagan baby. In still another I am part of the Baby Bust, and in popular-speak I am an Xer. While my voting patterns may be influenced by a reaction to the reign of Reagan, my own sense is that I share more of a kinship with children raised in part by television nannies—children, and now adults whose common cultural vocabulary includes all the guests and hosts on the Love Boat and Fantasy Island, and nearly every escapade of the Brady Bunch family.

At best, these multiple definitions and categories offer a variety of tools with which to dismantle, describe, and rebuild "generations." At worst, they oversimplify complex relationships within and between generations. And in the extreme they can be used to divide generations for political and economic gain. For example, investment companies and Fortune 500 companies with interests in mutual fund markets, are reportedly channeling millions of dollars into convincing America's youth that the only solution to fixing Social Security is to privatize it (Dreyfus 1996). By dividing young voters from old, convincing them

that Social Security is beyond repair, and encouraging increased political action, these companies stand to make billions of dollars by providing private, individual retirement accounts. Dividing the generations
can also arrest the downward flow of oral history. In *Time Passages*
George Lipsitz describes the separation of generations as a strategic
effort to keep lessons of the past from being transmitted to future generations. Using nostalgic television situation comedies as his example,
Lipsitz writes: "The social relations of the past are used to legitimate a
system that in reality works to destroy the world that created those historical relationships in the first place" (1990, 72).

Marketers' oversimplifications of generational division and identity are fairly easy to unravel; one need only to turn the model slightly
to see them as predominantly white and/or middle class. Pepsi's "Be
Young, Have Fun, Drink Pepsi" advertising campaign or Centrum Vit-
amins' depiction of older adults swirling past the television camera in a
dizzying waltz are rather obvious examples of advertisers efforts to
create an identity for a generation that may sell products but does not
necessarily ignite a fierce sense of belonging to any particular age
group. A recent article in *American Demographics*, for example, warns
advertisers and marketing specialists that only about one third of all
Americans consider themselves to be part of a particular generation,
and that even among that third, there is considerable disagreement as
to what that generation means (Russel and Mitchel 1995).

Still, ad campaigns like Pepsi's, and literature like Coupland's
Generation X are sign posts of the larger cultural emphasis on differences between people of various ages, rather than cultural imaginings
of the whole of the human life span. Potential connections across, and
relationships between age groups are made opaque by such stereotypical, over-assertions of difference. How do intergenerational theater
companies enter this fray, in which definitions and divisions of generations can yield enormous profit? How do they organize and enact generational identity?

_⋇ I was teaching a class on older women and the arts. The students were
mainly middle-aged. Four younger women in their early twenties sat in a
tight grouping near the door. One woman in her eighties sat in the very back
of the room. On this night, one of women in her forties was describing what
she called "the age-test." "You pull up the skin on her hand, let go, and count
the number of seconds it takes for it to get back to normal. All at once, every-_

*one pinched; the groupings of twenty-somethings, and the middle-aged
women throughout the room. A series of groans and laughter followed. My
eyes met the student's in the back row who sat perfectly still, patiently waiting for the discussion of that week's reading to begin.*

Roots & Branches

In 1984 Howard Pflanzer and Susan Miller founded the JASA Theater
Ensemble, a senior-only troupe primarily serving New York's Upper
Westside Jewish community.[5] In its first six years the Theater Ensemble
created original shows about the senior performers' experiences with
anti-Semitism, assimilation, and ageism within the health industry.
Arthur Strimling, R&B's current artistic director, joined the group in
1990 as a director. In 1991 he and New York University Professor Jan
Cohen-Cruz established an intern program that brought the first crop
of undergraduate actors to JASA Theater Ensemble's weekly workshops. The new intergenerational format demanded a new name, and
the merger of JASA's Theater Ensemble and the NYU undergraduates
became known as Roots & Branches.

Under the direction of Strimling, the first intergenerational show, *I
Am Acting My Age,* explored and exorcised stereotypes each generation
harbored about the other. Subsequent seasons featured more plot-dri-
ven, original pieces, including comic adaptations of Shakespeare's
Romeo and Juliet, Chekhov's *The Three Sisters,* and Brecht's *The Unseemly
Old Lady.* The overtly activist bent of early JASA ensemble pieces continues under Strimling's guidance. In 1993, for example, R&B's *Old Aids*
looked at how the different generations were coping with friends and
loved ones suffering from AIDS. The main thrust of the troupe's work,
however, is aimed at dissolving the isolation of generations in this
country. *Romeo & Juliet and Juliet & Romeo and Romeo & Juliet,* for example, R&B's 1992 production of Shakespeare's tragic romance, features
several intergenerational love affairs, including one between actor
Molly Seif, then eighty-six, and Matt Boline, a twenty-two-year-old acting intern.

I first met the performers of R&B in November 1995, when I visited
New York and attended one of their Thursday morning workshops.
Like other senior groups I have come to know, the R&B ensemble is
peopled with warm, dynamic, outgoing performers and staff. Older
members range in age from their early sixties to early nineties. This age

span includes two generations; the Cold War / Sputnik and the World War I generations according to MacManus, and the GI and the Silent generations according to Strauss and Howe. In spite of these differences, the older performers, some of whom were founding members in 1984, are a closely knit group. The first fifteen minutes of rehearsal are spent greeting, assessing health problems, and asking after family and absent performers, and social events outside of rehearsals, such as Molly Seif's ninetieth birthday party in November 1996.

While R&B has grown more diverse, Jewish members remain a majority. Most come from educated, middle-class backgrounds. Some older members are still working, and those who are not working for pay, commonly have a full schedule of volunteer obligations. Ninety-year-old Etta Denbin, for example, volunteers weekly as a reader at a Veterans Hospital. Only two of the twelve ensemble members are men, a fairly common ratio among senior troupes. Three of the twelve are young interns. Although they joined the troupe only a few short weeks before the workshop I attended in November, the interns were already included in the weekly welcoming ritual. When the rehearsal finally got underway, Strimling and his 1995–96 cowriter/director, David Schechter, led performers through improv scenarios based on the actors' varying conceptions of time. Out of this and subsequent workshops grew the troupe's spring 1996 production *It's about Time: A Political/Temporal Review*, a series of loosely linked scenes that present various meanings of and experiences with time.

The troupe's small size and cohesive, caring ensemble is strongly bifocal. With an eye on the performer's personal growth, Strimling creates a workshop atmosphere in which performers feel comfortable exploring memories and current political opinions. But, rather than directly address performers' personal issues, Strimling focuses on their artistic growth. For Strimling the individual needs of performers are inextricably tied to their potential for artistic growth. Setting a common goal of artistic excellence allows personal issues to arise as performers feel the need.

R&B's focus on the artistic excellence of its productions is clear. A professional set designer creates the troupe's playfully painted wooden backdrops, and professional playwrights, including Strimling himself, arrange ensemble members' creative oral histories into fast-paced, witty scripts. Unlike the Frolics and GLT, however, most of R&B's shows are unticketed and unreviewed. Yet the performers still take deep pride in the high-quality appearance of the show. The bifocal bent to the group is underscored in performers' comments during interviews I conducted over my year and a half involvement with the troupe. Three performers emphasized the therapeutic aspects of being in the ensemble, while others stressed the fact that R&B was one of the few outlets for them to be theater artists at an advanced age. "I came here exactly because it *wasn't* a therapy session," said Michaela Lobel. "Here, I can be an actress."

It's about Time!

In her perceptive 1986 work, *The Ageless Self*, Sharon Kaufman observes that all too often, scholars use preexisting standards of time and age to describe the aging process, rather than asking people for definitions of time in their own terms. *It's about Time!* heeds Kaufman's call, presenting a playful and poignant kaleidoscope of interpretations of time from both young and old. The meanings of time, going back in time, stopping time, time's pressures, and time's gifts: *It's about Time!* explores all these aspects of time with grace and wit born of the performers own experiences and honed by R&B's professional directors and writers. The play opens with Time as a character, addressing the audience.

> Hello. I am Time. No, I'm not *the* time, like 3 o'clock. I *am* time. I'm not behind time or overtime or making or wasting or, God forbid, killing time. I'm not measuring time or keeping time or losing time. I'm certainly not leisure time or free time. Not these days. No . . . I am time. How do you do? (1)

Throughout the play actors young and old take turns playing Time. The style is loose and playful. In one early scene, for example, the whole ensemble gangs up on Time until Time "runs out." In another section wordplay abounds and puns pile up, pun upon pun.

> *Millie:* Once upon a Time . . .
> *Richard & Michaela:* Time flies when you're having fun
> *Al:* Tempus Fugit! Time is Money!
> *Etta:* Excuse me, sir, do you have the time?
> *Al:* I wouldn't give you a New York Minute!
> *Etta:* Haste makes waste!
> *Michele:* Now is the time!
> *Richard:* Like sands through the hourglass, so are the days of our lives . . .

Michele: I don't have time for that.
(long pause)
Muriel: Oh! It's all in the timing!
All: It's About Time!

(2)

The lightness of the scene is typical of the production's fast paced, free-flowing movement, void of any linear plot development. More reflective moments hinge on performers' memories of different times in their lives. Several scenes, for instance, follow the life course of the human "race" which Time begins by shooting a starter's pistol. Ensuing scenes are reminiscent of GLT's *I Was Young,* and include brief looks at new-borns, toddlers, working women, and war.

R&B's intergenerational interpretations and representations of time remind the audience that all ages are swept up in its flow. Three scenes in particular encapsulate the wide-ranging meanings of time in the play, which reflect generational connections alongside their differences. In the first example, which occurs midplay, twenty-two-year-old Jen Johnson asks Time if she can go back to when she and seventy-year-old fellow performer Muriel Mervis were the same age. Facing graduation from college, and feeling conflicting desires to pursue a career and start her own family, Jen is eager to ask Muriel about her experience as a young mother some fifty years earlier. Did she really regret not having a career? Was being a young mother so bad? Yvette DeBotton, a professional actress in her late twenties, is also curious about the older generation's past, but is more focused on how dating, romance, and commitment have changed over the century. The two young women implore Time to send them back for a firsthand lesson.

Time is at first reluctant to accommodate the young women's wishes but eventually concedes and casts his spell: "Tickity Tockity, Fum Fo Fi Fee, Turn the Clock Back Endlessly. Watch your Swatch and Big your Ben, Then is Now and Now is Then!" (18). Performers turn in circles, clocks spin backward, and suddenly we are back in time more than fifty years. The performance style is self-consciously over-the-top, as the actors balance between character (themselves in time travel), and wry parody (themselves in the present, commenting on the scene). Muriel, seated on a bench stage right, doesn't recognize Jen when she approaches. On a similar bench stage left, Ida Hardon greets Yvette without recognition. As Muriel feeds her newborn baby, she tells Jen of her happy postwar life in a Quonset hut. The world of 1944 is quite foreign to Jen. There are no TV talk shows for daytime entertainment. There are, in fact, no TVs. There are no disposable diapers, no encouragement to breastfeed. When Jen asks Muriel if she misses having a career, Muriel's responds: "Uh uh! No Mam! I worked while my husband was in the army, and I'm glad I don't have to now . . . right now I'm happy enough" (27). Jen, who still "feels like a baby" herself, doubts she could have her own child now. But Muriel assures her that she still feels like a baby sometimes too, and that books (like the "new" one by Dr. Spock) and family have helped her to cope with the demands of motherhood.

Intercut with this scene is the encounter between Yvette and Ida, who tells her young visitor from the future about her dating habits. "I won't sleep with a man until I get married," says Ida (23). "That could take ten years!" responds Yvette, incredulous. Codes of behavior have clearly changed between the generations. Ida wouldn't kiss until the second date, and never paid for a meal. Back in the present, Yvette lives with her boyfriend in a world where romance seems to have disappeared. "I'm jealous of you," Yvette tells Ida, "It sounds more romantic in your time" (24).

In addition to considerable historical changes, the women's experiences also differ according to their family's class, religion, and cohesiveness, as well as the women's individual personalities. While Muriel was at home raising her family, for example, Ida was dancing in vaudeville shows. All of these differences are evident in the short, deceptively simple scene. But the historical changes in codes of behavior and differences in family makeup create no stigma among the women. Instead, their differences are overshadowed by a palpable sense of friendship and respect among the women, born of common attempts to forge meaningful lives through family and/or career. Rather than separate them, their differences link the women who are making, and have made, their way through their lives, negotiating pressures from family, the economy, and media images at large.

In a second example, near the end of *It's about Time!* Millie Gold, sixty-three, presents a powerful monologue that addresses one of the most frightening aspects of aging—illness. The intense monologue counterbalances the play's general levity, and links R&B's generations in a common struggle for survival. Based on her own fifteen-year battle with cancer, the monologue is driven both by Millie's persistent refusal to give over to the disease and her changing outlook on time. "Let me tell you about time," says Gold, "I know something about time"(33).

It's about Time! by Roots & Branches Theater.
(Photo by Fran Kaufman. Courtesy of Roots & Branches Theater.)

After returning to graduate school at forty-four, she discovered she had breast cancer. "But I'm a *shtarke*, the show must go on," says Gold (33).[6] She finished school, landed a job as a high-school counselor, and then, three years after the first mastectomy, her other breast was removed. A short six months later, Gold found another lump and was diagnosed with non-Hodgkin's lymphoma.

The last fifteen years of Millie's life have been a cycle of horrific discoveries, grueling treatment regimes, and slow recoveries. This cycle is symbolized in the monologue by Millie's routine of rubbing lotion on her dry skin—a soothing process which also leads to the discovery of more lumps. In short sections, linked by the former folksinger's powerful rendition of the Yiddish love song "Mein Hartz, Mein Hartz," Gold tells of her relationships with her doctors, her routines of chemo, and her exhaustion born of constantly having to gather strength to fight the disease. Rather than sensationalize Gold's dramatic story, Strimling, who shaped the monologue, links it to the play's theme by focusing on how her battle with cancer changed the meaning of time in Gold's life.

> I live for the moment—the moment is all I've got. I go to movies or shows you don't have to buy tickets for months in advance. I go out to dinner on a moment's notice. I relish every moment with my family and friends. My favorite time words are "moment," "instant," "now," and yes, "remember." I hate words like "later," "then," and especially, "future." I'm more selective now. I don't plan trips, I walk away from fools. Time, you have taught me what I'm made of. I would never have known if you hadn't dealt me this new career. But don't ask me to thank you. (34)

Millie finishes the monologue by changing songs from the somber "Mein Hartz" to the more upbeat "Dortn' Dortn'" with which she began the story of her disease. Immediately following, twenty-two-year-old Michele Minnick describes her own struggles to keep focused on the present and not obsess over the future. "These days . . . I find myself fuller of what I hope is a healthy suspicion of that strange place which I can so clearly imagine in its multitude of colors and forms, but in which I do not yet exist," says Michele (35). While Michele's speech can't match the potent drama of Millie's epic struggle with cancer, it does capture the fears of a young woman who struggles to envision and realize her as yet unfulfilled, and perhaps unfulfillable, dreams of the future.

Both Millie and Michele, in spite of differences of health and age, find pleasure in life by living in the moment. While this point of linkage between generations might potentially counter predictions for intergenerational warfare, it can also inadvertently strengthen its chances. "Thinking for today" tends to encourage short-term thinking rather than long-term consideration of the needs of future generations, be they economic, educational, or environmental. While Michele is careful to explain that she seeks to avoid thoughts of the future and worries over achieving her potential, the same logic of "living in the present," can also support those who are old age-phobic. In a context of mutual, generational support such as R&B, however, the two monologues' leanings toward the present align rather than separate the generations.

The third example connects the generations in common, direct, political terms. Following Jen and Yvette's adventures in time travel, there are a series of exchanges of complaints, in which actors begin: "It's about time that . . . ." In the first, Richard, a semi-retired actor, rails: "It's about time we recognized that not everything can be measured in dollars and cents! We know the price of everything and the value of nothing" (30). Al, a working psychoanalyst, follows with a complaint about HMOs, and Etta and Michaela follow him with a diatribe against the disposable goods mentality of most Americans. Says Michaela: "Things used to last. You bought something; it would just last forever. Now everything is made of ticki tacki" (31).

Molly Seif caps off the scene, bounding onstage with a call for political mobilization. "It's about time all of us elderly took some action!" shouts Molly, shaking a clenched fist. "Let's march to City Hall and Albany and protest all these cuts in our pensions and our Medicare and our Social Security!" Jen and Yvette flank her sides. "And at the same time," Molly continues, fists still clenched, "support these young people's rights to a good education and a good job and a good retirement when they get there!" Jen and Yvette add, "It's about time we joined them!" (32). The three begin singing "Solidarity Forever," and, after the first verse, are joined by the full cast. In both performances I attended, audience members joined the chorus as well.

The scene's railings against time and American culture are riddled with clichés. But set against R&B's iconographic, cartoon-like set, and presented in their tongue and cheek manner, R&B parodies the clichés without losing the urgency of their message. "Solidarity Forever," the trumpet call for unions and activists of Molly's generation, is a lofty goal for the relations between the young and old. As presented by R&B, however, it is also a motto and a plan of action that can get this country past the potential political stalemate of generational isolationism.

It's about Time! on Tour

In general R&B performs for JASA (Jewish Association of Services for the Aged) senior centers around the New York area, as well as at schools, other area community and senior centers, and their home auditorium. Audiences range from elementary age children to the frail elderly. Benefit performances draw mixed-age audiences with significant theatergoing experience. There were six performances of *It's about Time!* in 1996—three at JASA, two at senior housing complexes, and one at a Brooklyn synagogue as a benefit performance for both Roots & Branches and the United Jewish Appeal. I saw the show twice, once at an enormous, high-rise housing complex in Far Rockaway in early May, and again at the June benefit in Brooklyn. The two shows varied wildly. When we arrived in Far Rockaway, the stage at the back of the cavernous lunchroom (which had served nearly four hundred people that day) was in disarray. R&B had rehearsed the performance with three microphones. There were none. Several lights onstage were burned out. The wings were completely dark and cluttered with broken furniture and boxes of books. Strimling joked as I helped him set up R&B's portable wooden set. "Welcome to the world of New York Senior Centers," he smiled, "they're not usually this prepared for us." Strimling managed to locate two microphones, but had to quickly adjust the blocking designed for three and teach it to the hesitant cast just minutes before the lunch crowd cleared the room for showtime.

In nothing short of a miracle of organization, housing staff cleared the lunchroom tables and set rows of chairs in long lines across the room in just minutes. More than four hundred older men and women soon filed in and took their seats. The audience, made up mostly of senior housing complex residents, included many in wheelchairs and walkers who punctuated the long rows of chairs. Staff members watched from the periphery, perched on the lunch tables at the back of the room, or in chairs near the side doors. As is common with audiences of the frail elderly, reactions to the performance were difficult to read. Although the audience greeted the light-hearted script with only occasional laughter, performers later said they felt the crowd following them. Just the day before, they had performed for an audience of older Russian and Eastern European immigrants who spoke little if any English. In contrast, the performers felt that the Far Rockaway crowd was with them every step of the way, in spite of their stoic response.[7]

Post show responses supported the performers' intuition. The audience lingered, joking about certain lines, discussing or even singing songs from the show. Several women snickered at one of Michaela's last lines in the closing homage to good times past and present: "Thanks for chaste and oversexed times." When I walked into the lobby, one older woman, who I later learned had been a professional singer, assumed I was with the troupe, hugged me, and broke into a show tune. My reading of the audience's reaction to the intergenerational aspects of the performance is pure speculation. But the performance as a whole, particularly Millie's solo, clearly resonated with the largely frail, senior audience.

In contrast, the benefit performance for the United Jewish Appeal, R&B's final performance of the year, came off without a hitch. The audience, mixed-age and predominantly Jewish, laughed at every joke. While the script hit its peak with this audience, the performers seemed to bond much more in the face of the challenges of the Far Rockaway show. Both Frolics and GLT members suggest that common concerns about remembering lines, mastering blocking, and adjusting to unexpected changes draw the performers together. The same can be said of R&B's intergenerational bonds, drawn taut by the challenges of performing, particularly by those surprises that lay in wait in the often underfunded and always unpredictable world of senior centers and housing complexes.

The strong intergenerational bonds expressed in the performance through both text and movement, are also reflected in the personal relationships evident in workshops and interviews. On a bumpy bus ride after the Far Rockaway performance in May 1996, Ida Harndon, a petite, former vaudeville dancer in her eighties, steadied herself on the immense, green, school bus seat and told me that she loved watching the stereotypes dissolve as the old and young performers got to know each other.

They come to us with maybe a little preconceived idea of older people, and they are a little wary of us—they're ready to treat us like older people. We of course look at them as young people. What's beautiful is the way it melds. All of a sudden we're all one age group. We become family.

At a June 1996 interview Jen explained how her thinking about older people has shifted through her work with the older performers:

Elderly people used to be this far away thing—the aged. And now I just realize that every older person is as different from each other and from me as every younger person. . . . And there are a lot more similarities [between old and young] than you think, because we are all living in New York, in America, in the '90s and we're all interested in theater.

Although the bonds between older and younger performers are strong, interviews also yielded a significant difference in their outlook on aging. Both groups see performance as a way to be active in late life, to shift focus from one's health problems, to entrench one's self in the present rather than becoming absorbed solely with the past or the remaining future. But older performers also separated themselves from other older people and even rejected the term *old*. Younger performers, however, as yet free of the stigma of the term, use *old* freely, and often reverently in reference to their fellow performers. "I'm not conscious of my age," insists ninety-year-old Etta Denbin, "I don't think that we are an old group." Ida explains: "I'm just doing things I've always done. This gives me such an outlet to perform, because inside of me I haven't grown old." Yvette believes that R&B's performances can help all ages appreciate the aging process. Her wording is slightly different than her older colleagues:

In this country the elderly are sort of pushed to the side. It's a country of the youth and I think we lose out a lot. I think this [performance] is very positive and it should get out there, not just to old people, but to people with families, just people you know. Because you learn that it's just about life. (May 1996 interview)

In her late twenties Yvette has much lower stakes in the term *old* than her colleagues who live with its consequences on a daily basis. These lower stakes can potentially give younger people the freedom to imagine new definitions of *old*, preparing themselves for their own old age and helping to shift cultural expectations for the social behavior of today's older people. Creating multidimensional, meaningful social roles for the aged, then, is a collaborative process among all age groups. Intergenerational theater groups, in which multiple generations can play with performative transformation, are particularly well equipped for creating and disseminating this collaborative change.

⚹ "Is there a history of breast cancer?" my new HMO doctor asks. Yes, my mother. A rapid series of questions follow. Early fifties, mastectomy, clean— knock wood—bill of health. "You're 31? I would do exams every month, and start with the mammograms in four years." I know we're only talking precautions and early detection, from which there's a high rate of recovery. But I rehearse it like a diagnosis. My enormous mental calendar drops down to the next five minutes. Who would I call? How would I pay for it? Will I survive? Three years ago, before mom's diagnosis, before my odds climbed to higher than 1 in 9, I didn't even think I needed health insurance.

Elders Share the Arts

In the late 1970s activist/performer Susan Perlstein participated in an agitprop performance about housing rights in the Bronx. After the show, an older audience member challenged Perlstein to address the special housing needs of seniors. Shortly after, Perlstein visited Hodson Senior Center in the South Bronx, and led the first workshop of what was to become Elders Share the Arts (ESTA). ESTA is now a three-tiered, intergenerational, community arts program offering community workshops, community-based performances, and professional training services.

Throughout its seventeen-year history, ESTA has maintained both its agit prop roots and its primary focus on addressing community needs through the arts. Racially and ethnically diverse theater, visual, and literary artists constitute ESTA's staff, many of whom have enjoyed long tenure with the group. Diversity and commitment characterize ESTA. They serve only "underserved" areas, usually populated by poor minorities, and ask for a commitment to a three-year, thirty-weeks-per-year workshop program from each participating community.

Of ESTA's many programs, my focus here is on their newest creation, an intergenerational touring production of the original play, *Bushwick, Why Vote? Why Vote?* blends the stories of older African-

Americans who fought for and cherish their right to vote, with the stories of young Black and Latina high-school and college students, whose apathy, cynicism, or general lack of information about eligibility paralyzes their involvement in the American political system. Although all the performances in this book can be considered political, *Why Vote?* is perhaps the most overt in its call for direct, generationally allied intervention in the political system by registering audience members to vote in postshow discussions after each performance.

As I suggested earlier in this chapter, predictions for rising generational tensions over the next fifty years commonly describe a stratification of the voting block into older adults who vote and young adults who do not. Even if younger people do begin to vote, it is assumed that their interests will be cancelled out by the activism and consistent voter turn-out among older Americans whose desires for government spending differ from their own.[8] Perlstein's mission to educate and mobilize young voters can interrupt this stratification, provided both young and old are brought to empathize with, or even share, each other's concerns. Does *Bushwick, Why Vote?*, in its creation and performance, encourage generational alliance as it urges political involvement? And if yes, how?

ESTA: Structure and Aims

Each year ESTA contracts with some twenty-five communities in the New York metropolitan area to run its thirty-week workshop programs. These include intergenerational workshops, in which participants at a senior center are joined with neighboring schools; conflict mediation theater, in which a community's problems are worked out through representation and revision; and "special needs" workshops, in which, for example, hearing impaired elderly act as role models for hearing impaired youth. Each of these workshops, no matter what their classification, culminate in what ESTA calls a Living History presentation. Depending on the workshop's facilitator, presentations range from theatrical performances to art installations. At season's end in May, ESTA sponsors a Living History Festival, a sort of greatest hits of presentations, in which all workshops are in invited to showcase their work.

Over the years, several workshop groups have developed enough momentum to continue meeting past their three-year contract, and now, under ESTA's umbrella, tour their shows to schools and community organizations. These touring groups, along with the yearly Living History Festival, constitute ESTA's second tier of services: community-based performances. Out of Perlstein's original workshop at Hodson, for example, grew the Pearls of Wisdom, a group of women storytellers who, until the fall of 1996, were directed by long time ESTA artist Peggy Pettitt. Las Añoranzas, a group mainly of older Latinas, developed out of a 1988 workshop at the Gaylord White Senior Center. This workshop group, initially facilitated by Jorge Mercedes, bases their bi-lingual stories on games the older women played as children, and is particularly effective with young, Latina audiences. In addition to the Pearls and Las Añoranzas, ESTA now tours and promotes Discoveries, a multimedia collection of visual art by older adults.

ESTA is currently augmenting its third tier of services, the professional training program. Thirty-six hour training sessions, whose target audience includes social workers, educators, and artists, address the theory and practice of life review techniques, and models for the administration, supervision, and evaluation of life review programs. Based on a blend of theories by Barbara Myerhoff, Erik Erikson, Robert Butler and Augusto Boal, ESTA's professional training programs teach the importance of reminiscence and storytelling for the mental, physical, and spiritual health of individual older adults as well as their communities. Currently the only financially self-sufficient tier of ESTA, Perlstein hopes the training programs will eventually earn enough to support ESTA's workshop and performance tiers which are especially vulnerable to governmental budget cuts and the evaporation of arts funding.

Perlstein originally developed ESTA in the model of the people's theater movement, hoping to create a space for individual and community self-empowerment through storytelling. ESTA's emphasis on storytelling is evident from the very first Living History play *Three Generations* at Hodson in 1979, to the 1996 tour of *Bushwick, Why Vote?* In most ESTA performances, for example, props are minimal and sets almost nonexistent. Costumes are rarely more than the actors' own clothing. Music is most often live voice. Unlike the Frolics, GLT, and Roots & Branches then, a polished final production is not ESTA's main focus. Instead, for ESTA, theater is a convenient and effective conduit for self-empowerment; a device to strengthen community as they engage and involve both actors and spectators.

I find three main desired effects in ESTA's intergenerational community programs. First, ESTA's base of theorists (Butler, Erikson, and Myerhoff) suggest that ESTA is concerned with helping older adults achieve "integration" through sharing the stories that fill their lives. Second, ESTA grant proposals describe rather dismal lack of social and economic resources in the poor neighborhoods they serve. Such conditions often lead to the fracturing of family structures and a general disbelief among children that they will live into old age. By bringing old and young together in dramatic workshops, ESTA aims to provide children with role models for living full and meaningful lives.[9] Third, intergenerational relationships in poor neighborhoods also commonly mean intercultural relationships. As young people move on to find better lives, new waves of immigrants often leave older adults isolated in their own neighborhoods, unable to understand the new languages and customs. ESTA's intergenerational work also seeks to create a dialogue between cultures so that the old and young might create a new community out of shared interests and concerns.

Bushwick, Why Vote?

Frustrated with the conservative swing in recent New York city and state elections, Perlstein designed the Bushwick project in the hopes of dissolving both the apathy and mystery that cloud the voting records of the poor and minority neighborhoods her organization serves. By mobilizing voter registration intergenerationally, ESTA can begin to heal generational divisions within neighborhoods, and set the importance of voting in a historical context.

ESTA began the leg work for *Why Vote?* in the fall of 1995. The play emerged from weekly workshops of the Bushwick Intergenerational Collective, a group of roughly a half-dozen older women and one older man from Bushwick's Community Round Table for Senior Citizens; Thelma C. Lenton and Sue Friars, both students at the East Brooklyn Congregational High School (EBC) in Bushwick; Gabrielle Bayme, a twenty-one-year-old intern from New York University; and Vladimir Auguste, a nineteen-year-old sophomore at Long Island University.[10] Over the fall and winter the collective shared their memories and stories about voting in the days of Jim Crow. For those seniors who had moved to New York from the South, voting stories were fraught with fraud, covert and overt manipulation, even graphic violence. Younger members of the group told of their reluctance to vote, their doubts about its effectiveness, their lack of connection to the community in which they live. Throughout the spring group facilitator Peggy Pettitt created scenes out of the group's stories, using popular freedom songs as transitions between scenes. The result is a play that invokes the weight of the civil rights movement to remind young voters of the urgency of engaging in the political system on both local and state levels.

The ensemble is a caring, serious group, with strong Christian faith. With the exception of Gabrielle Bayme, the young, NYU intern and Carrie Raeford, one of the Pearls of Wisdom, most members have little to no training in performance outside of early school or church experiences. Health problems are common, but generally do not inhibit the performers. Randall Cherry, for example, who is nearly blind, is a regular at workshops and performances. Depending on health and scheduling conflicts, Ensemble members take turns playing various roles in the many performances. I attended two brush-up rehearsals at Bushwick's Round Table Senior Center in the spring of 1996. The collective's usual meeting room under construction, group facilitator Peggy Pettitt gathered the senior performers and one younger performer around a lunch table in the noisy, crowded common room. I strained to hear the older actors as we shouted greetings and introductions above the sound of "The Price Is Right" blaring on a television a few tables down. In spite of the noise interference, the rehearsal garnered the performers' rapt attention.

Pettitt led the group through an assessment of the last performance, song practice, a heated debate about child care, and a "giving" exercise, in which partners endowed each other with "gifts that money can't buy." During Pettitt's review of the performance several performers worried over mistakes they had made in the show. "We started talking and left the laundry on the floor. I know what I did wrong," said Sadell Coleman who had played "Aunt Jerry." Pettitt was firm in her response: "There is no wrong!" she said, "When you are doing the best you can and you fall short of it, that's not wrong. What's wrong is when you don't try." Pettitt continued: "The good thing about this group is that when you get into trouble, you get help. Professional theater is about individuals, and here we are a group."[11]

Interestingly enough, the Frolics, GLT, and R&B, all of whom adopt "professional" standards for their productions, are also extremely group-oriented and helpful to their fellow performers when things go wrong. But whether Pettitt's statement is true or not is beside the point. Her differentiation makes it clear that the group's main concern is theater as self-empowerment. Although performers are clearly intent on improving it, the show's outward appearance ranks a far second. Pettitt's directorial tactics echo this focus on community as well. Rather than give her own notes on the performance, Pettitt suggested that each person talk with their designated partner to figure out how they might improve their performances.

Bushwick, Why Vote? in Performance

During its run from April to November of 1996, Why Vote? played a wide range of venues, including elementary schools, two shows at Long Island University (LIU), one of which was broadcast live on campus, EBC High School, and several benefit performances. I saw Why Vote? as part of the Living History Festival benefit performance in early May 1996. Shortened to fit at the end of a long program of performances and award ceremonies, the benefit performance of Why Vote? was greeted by an enthusiastic audience of ESTA supporters and alumni.

The benefit performance of Why Vote? was difficult to read according to the show's own goals. Where other performances inspired up to one hundred people to register on a single night, no one was registered at the May benefit. Where other shows had lively, even controversial postshow discussions, no one at the May benefit engaged with the play's message outside of supportive applause.[12] My sense of Why Vote? then is based on interviews and the basic text as it was enacted at the May benefit.

Why Vote? is a collection of seven short scenes, intercut with four songs synonymous with the civil rights movement. "This Little Light of Mine" bookends the first two scenes—monologues exploring the importance of voting from two different generational positions. Vladimir or Gabrielle, depending on availability, follows the first song. Both of their monologues harken back to the activism of the 1960s as a model for student political involvement. Vladimir addresses the change in student activism:

Today, lack of understanding the voting process and general apathy keeps us slaves to the idea that our vote does not count. But, several generations ago students took it upon themselves to teach others how to participate in the democratic process of voting. (4)

Gabrielle fingers her generation's apathy even more directly. She recalls the frustration that grew from a recent class where students complained of social ills, but did nothing to solve them:

So we all just sat there debating and complaining about things that should change. Our teacher commented that "yeah, if this was the six-ties or seventies we'd be out there picketing or sitting on their doorstep!" We all laughed when one of us pointed out that maybe this is why the media has labeled us "Generation X" and portrays us as apathetic whiners. (4)

Carrie Raeford, who supplies the "elder's point of view" in the second monologue, recalls the days before the civil rights movement when she was forced to sit in the back of the bus. Angered by the humiliation she suffered as a child, Raeford explains that storytelling has become her way to stand up for herself and for her people. Four short scenes follow the framing monologues, and tell the story of a three-genera-tional family who learn the importance and process of voting. All three generations, a grandmother, two daughters, and two grand-daughters, live in the same Bushwick apartment building. The play pits Grandma and Aunt Jerry, the voices of political activism in the play, against Mom and her daughters Lisa and L. C., each of whom find various excuses not to vote.

Interviews suggest that the play accomplished ESTA's goals of building pride among its seniors, knowledge among its youth, and strong bonds of friendship between the generations. Mr. Cherry's sen-timents were common among the seniors. "I love to work with the young people," said Mr. Cherry, "because someone's listening to where we come from." Vladimir Auguste learned many lessons from working with the older performers, including how to plan for his own retirement ("I think I should save money, invest in the stock market for my retirement fund"), how not to waste time in life worrying about being cool, and how to anticipate change. Said Auguste: "Because I see my Mom and she's like, oh my gosh, they are raising bus fare to a dol-lar fifty. So I'm thinking to myself, I got to remember to keep in mind that by the time I'm like fifty, it'll probably be five dollars."[13] The bonds

Bushwick, Why Vote? Bushwick Round Table's Intergenerational Collective. *(Courtesy of Susan Perlstein, Elders Share the Arts.)*

of friendship are evident in the warmth and openness of workshop sessions, and in the young people's aspirations to continue visiting the elders even after the project is over.

The process of creating and performing *Why Vote?* is clearly tremendously effective in solidifying bonds between the generations and in fueling confidence among individual actors. In the actual presentation of the play, however, I found several things potentially troubling: the use of generational stereotypes to drive the plot; the sole use of family relationships as a model for intergenerational relationships; and the heavy focus on the past in order to compel present action.

Why Vote? draws some fairly stereotypical, generational depictions of its characters. Grandma tells the same horrible story over and over and over again. Mom loses her job and becomes addicted to soap operas. L. C. is a selfish teenager who is constantly on the phone. Aunt Jerry is the play's sage, and after an initial bout of cynicism, Lisa echoes Jerry's wise advice. These broadly drawn characters enable the Ensemble to move the play quickly and clearly toward its lesson: the urgency of voting. Grandma's graphic stories of lynchings, repeated over and over again, end up convincing L. C. of the need to be politically aware.

> Back then we didn't have choices. We were told what to do. So we voted for the right to choose. Listen to me. Don't be too sure it can never happen again: lynching, tar and feathering, burning homes . . . Read your history. . . . Read one of them books. (She pats J. C.'s backpack) There's nothing in there! You're just wearing that because it matches your clothes. When I was your age we children didn't have books and pencils and if we wore bags on our backs it was for carrying wood or coal. We worked hard. We didn't have the privileges you have today. (13–14)

Worn down by Grandma's exaggerations, repetitions, and chidings, L. C. finally offers to accompany her to the polls. Aunt Jerry's persistent lectures about voting eventually moves Lisa to register and Mom to admit that she doesn't know how to vote or even who is running for office. "Isn't it strange," says Mom, "I know who's doing what to who on those soap operas but I don't know who's doing what to who in politics" (16). While the play begins in generational stereotype, it moves toward more nuanced intergenerational relationships. Both Lisa and L. C. listen to and side with their elders, and L. C. is stunned by her selfishness in the face of her mother's job-loss. The danger of using stereotypes to move the plot is that the play may ultimately simply reinforce images of elders as being repetitious and obsessed with the past.

By depicting a three-generational family, *Why Vote?* borrows the intimacy associated with idealized family relationships as a model for building intergenerational relationships at large. Depending on one's vision of family, this approach can have conflicting results. Interviews with student performers show both the pros and cons of such borrowing. Sue Friars, who played L. C., speaks warmly of her experiences with the Ensemble in terms of an ideal home.

> When I first walked in, I thought I was going to be a stranger, but I had a warm welcome. Everybody said hello to me as though they knew me. And everybody saw me as like their granddaughter or their little niece and I felt really at home. . . . [T]he place was cozy, I felt safe, and I felt wanted. I don't know. They way they greet you, the way you feel is just very special. They make you feel like you're part of their family. They like adopted me you could say. (November 1996)

On the other hand, Vladimir Auguste expresses the same warmth, but on the grounds of friendship, rather than family relationship. When I asked him if he thought there was such a thing as a generation gap, he responded:

> I don't know. I look at some of my friends who have grandparents living in the house. Probably for them, it [the generation gap] would be mostly with their family. But for me, it's like we're friends, you know? I guess it's the same way it happened with my mom, she had friends that were older people. (November 1996)

Why Vote? demonstrates the possibilities for intergenerational friendships, something that Roots & Branches' *It's about Time* also makes clear. The sole emphasis on family models in *Why Vote?*, however, can also ensnare the play in familial patterns that may not be as respectful as friendships.

Finally, *Why Vote?* emphasizes the activism of the 1960s in order to compel action among today's youth. This in and of itself is not a bad thing. But a more careful assessment of how times have changed, and along with them, how activism, politics, and the condition of youth have changed in kind, would help acknowledge that recreating 1960s activism would overlook the lessons of the past and the uniqueness of contemporary social and political conditions.

Redefining Generations

R&B's and ESTA's productions significantly interrupt predictions for a pending war between the generations. Just what *is* a generation for these two troupes? Both loosely group older adults, generally past the age of sixty, as representing a generation, and those under thirty as another. R&B also has a third generation—those over ninety. Both troupes roughly echo Strauss and Howe's definition of generation as "a special cohort group whose length approximately matches that of a basic phase of life . . . and whose boundaries are fixed by peer personality" (34).

In R&B the generations have their own unique historical contexts and their own life roles. Older actors tell of their experiences of immigration, of World War II, of parenting, of living alone at an advanced age. Younger actors tell of disappointing their parents, of struggles to find romance, of the worries of a nuclear age. Members of the same generation have widely varied experiences, depending on differences such as class, gender, and health. Common aims for (1) artistic excellence, (2) political engagement, and (3) a long and fulfilling life offset the considerable differences across and within generations.

In the ESTA performance of *Why Vote?* generations are drawn with more sweeping strokes in order to ignite action among spectators. Young characters are depicted as lazy, self-centered, fashion-conscious, and without concern for community. Older characters are nosy, repetitious, even annoying. Both these stereotypes, however, begin to dissolve as the play edges toward its message. Invoking memories of the civil rights movement with songs like "This Little Light of Mine" and "If You Miss Me in the Back of the Bus," *Why Vote?* dissolves generational differences as they remind characters, actors, and spectators across all generations of their common struggle to build community in a country still rife with racism and oppression. A next step might be to update some songs in an effort to acknowledge the unique struggles that face the current generation of young adults, and to create a common ground between those who lived the history of these songs, and those who must forge and live with the songs' contemporary relevance.

Both troupes use contemporary political issues to unite the generations in a common struggle. In turn, the challenges of performing, from memorization to the physical stamina that rehearsals and performances demand, also unite the generations as they support each other in the task of representing their common political aims. Sharing common goals, however, doesn't guarantee the blossoming of intergenerational friendships. Individual personalities can certainly foil alliances.[14] But a supportive, respectful atmosphere can absorb differences of age, personality, and opinion without breeding division. Older performers in both R&B and ESTA do not preach their knowledge of the past, but rather apply their stories to the task of solving a common problem. Young adults are not asked to simply listen to and revere their elders, but to offer input from their own points of view. As a result, both R&B's and ESTA's intergenerational ensembles build alliances where stereotypes had been, and nurture an awareness of aging as a life long process among actors and spectators alike.

✒ *I surprised her. Since Grandma moved to the nursing home, I didn't call ahead to say I was coming, because it made her too anxious. The door was open, and I could see her roommate curled up on her side, asleep. I knocked softly and walked in. Grandma wasn't in her bed, and the bathroom door was open, so I peeked my head in with a cheery hello. With great force, it slammed in my face. She must have kicked it with her foot. Later, sitting together in the common room, I apologized. She looked me in the eye, put her hand on mine and patted it. What I didn't tell her was how reassuring the force of that kick had been.*

5

Re-membering the Living Past
in Feminist Theory:
Suzanne Lacy's *Crystal Quilt*

On Mother's Day in 1987, 430 older women ranging in age from their mid-fifties to mid-nineties, filled the atrium of the IDS tower, a high-rise office building in the heart of downtown Minneapolis. Sitting in groups of four, at tables arranged in patterns and covered in colored cloths, the women created a living quilt as they joined, crossed, and opened their hands. Director Suzanne Lacy orchestrated their movements from a balcony three floors above the women. A soundtrack featuring bits and pieces of the women's memories accompanied the living quilt patterns, and echoed the simultaneous conversations among the women at the tables. The commotion no doubt surprised some Sunday shoppers emerging from Minneapolis' extensive skyway system that connects the IDS Crystal Court atrium with countless nearby retail stores. Although the free performance was advertised, many of the audience members standing on the balconies above the Crystal Court were passersby. At the end of the performance, "stage hands" offered brightly colored scarves to audience members, inviting them down the escalators to the main floor where they could in turn offer their scarves to an older woman as an entree to conversation. "I remember it being very powerful," said Jean Quam, Chair of the Department of Social Work at the University of Minnesota. "I remember seeing women who had no idea about the performance, carrying those scarves down the escalators, lining up to talk to these older women. I had no idea it would be so powerful" (September 1994).

Suzanne Lacy's performance art piece, *The Crystal Quilt*, was the culminating event of Whisper Minnesota, a two-and-a-half-year project that sought to empower older women across the state as active citizens. *The Crystal Quilt* used the older women's physical presence and oral histories to interrupt the silence and cultural amnesia that shroud the elderly, particularly older women, assuming "out of sight" to be "out of mind." The show's scale, form, and subject matter question the tendency in contemporary American culture to dissociate the present from the past and to draw distinctions between generations rather than seeking out their common ground.

The last chapter looked at two examples of intergenerational performance to see how they defined generational difference, and how they created alliances in the face of those differences. In this chapter I look to Lacy's *Crystal Quilt*, a show enmeshed in the history of feminist performance in the United States, to see how its form in particular links various, generationally identified styles of performance. I read the performance as (1) challenging Western practices of feminism and writing history in postmodern culture and (2) as establishing older women as powerful embodiments of a *living past*—women with rich histories, deeply invested in the present and future. Guiding questions include: how might the ways in which history is written and categorized perpetuate a breaking with the past, a scrambling to draw lines between now and then, new and old? How might history and generational distinctions be reshaped to acknowledge links to the past, between women of different ages, within in the long lives of older women themselves? I address the performance in four sections. The first is a brief description of the immense structure of Whisper Minnesota and *The Crystal Quilt* as a whole. The second section looks to the unique qualities of the performance—including its public setting, its orchestration of nonactors, and its simultaneous embodiment of several forms of feminist theater—and their hand in shaping the performance's vision of aging. The third section interweaves contemporary theories of the practice of writing history with definitions of generational divides delineated in the previous chapter. The fourth joins the third, revisiting and reading *The Crystal Quilt* as a model of aging that asserts intergenerational connection and interdependency of the present and the past. Interspersed among these sections are my memories of meetings of the Women and Theatre Program (WTP), an active and challenging focus group of the Association for Theatre in Higher Education (ATHE), whose 1994 summer conference marked the group's twentieth anniversary replete with growing pains and nostalgic tales of a supportive feminist community and of heated and productive debates. Uneasiness around aging, both individually and as an organization, is not unique to WTP. Instead, I believe the WTP examples to be typical of generational tensions haunting the shifting women's movement today as it splinters into identity categories and struggles to maintain its antiestablishment image as its founders are embraced in the higher reaches of academic institutions. I include these memories here to grapple with my complicity in the generational structures within feminism(s) today.

✎ *In an opening session at the joint conference between WTP and the independent Black Theatre Network, African-American scholar Glenda Dickerson passionately invoked a long list of influential freedom fighters across many generations. When she finished, the room fell into a stunned silence. As I struggled to comprehend the powerful arcing of Dickerson's voice and the presence of the spirits she called to be remembered, Barbara Ann Teer stepped in to fill the silence. Teer led the two groups in what she called "honoring of the ancestors" who, she said, needed acknowledgement before anyone could respond to Dickerson's performance. The references to spirituality and ancestors seemed to unsettle the WTP (and some BTN) participants, the vast majority of whom, including myself, are middle-class, white, academic women. The joint conference with BTN was part of WTP's effort to re-imagine itself, yet exploring connections to the past seemed to ignite cynical doubts among the women scholar/practitioners. Spirituality? It seemed to preclude theory, to assume Christianity. Isn't spirituality another mystical meta-narrative? Doesn't it separate body from mind? Ancestors? Didn't many women struggle to break from abusive families? Didn't many lesbians lose their families by daring to proclaim their sexuality? Both Teer's and Dickerson's invocation of ancestors and WTP's effort to assess its own twenty-year history dredged issues of ethnicity, race, sexuality, and spirituality. Of aging, generations, and the past. Throughout the conference, discord also seemed to form between WTP scholars across lines of age. As an established scholar in her forties pointed out the neutralizing effects of the academic institution that generously pays her to "perform lesbian," a "twenty-something" graduate student reminded the group that she owes "a small house" to an institution that is rapidly downsizing her out of a job. I remembered the previous night's dinner gossip about a new Clinique product that magically erases wrinkles, and wondered how much this conference really might have to do with anxieties of physical aging and generational adjustment.*

Whisper Minnesota and *The Crystal Quilt*

In 1984 Suzanne Lacy transformed her whimsical vision of hundreds of older women wearing white and standing on the beach into a moving performance that was the genesis for what would become the Whisper Minnesota project. The 1984 performance, *Whisper, the Waves, the Wind*, featured 150 older women descending to the beach in La Jolla, California, from buses parked on a hillside above. The women, all dressed in white, sat at white-covered tables arranged in the sand. Their directions were simply to talk—to air what too often goes unspoken: fears and hopes, images and reflections on aging and death. Lacy's 1987 *Crystal Quilt* similarly created a bold visual image of older women and facilitated dialogue among them. The canvas of *The Quilt*, however, was considerably larger. Embedded in the Whisper Minnesota project, *The Quilt* marked the end of a two-and-a-half-year, state-wide recruitment of urban, rural, lower- and middle-class older women, the organization of older women into leadership groups, and the mobilization of a communication network that would link older women and provide an outlet for their concerns both during and after the project. The structure of Whisper Minnesota was a large part of Lacy's artistry. When I asked her if juggling the interests of all the organizations that took part in Whisper Minnesota had shifted her vision for *The Quilt*, she responded succinctly that "the artistic vision *was* to create a working relationship with them. They didn't limit it [the performance], they *were* it" (September 1994).

Five goals outlined in the Whisper Minnesota mission statement reflect the multiple levels of this project, particularly its "structure as art" bent. The mission of the project itself was "to bring visibility to the abilities, talents, and interests of women in their later years and to demonstrate their leadership in the public arena, through an innovative union of community activists, policy makers, and artists." The project's five goals elaborate the mission statement:

1. To raise public consciousness toward older women and their ability to make significant contributions to our society.
2. To challenge prevailing images of the elderly as frail, passive, and needy by providing new images of the elderly as important participants in society.
3. To engage new constituencies, particularly older women, in public debate of issues that affect the elderly and humankind.
4. To provide an opportunity for the collaboration and communica-

tion among individuals, groups, and institutions from a cross section of social, geographic, ethnic and professional areas.

5. To develop a model which demonstrates the potential interaction
of artists, policy makers, and community leaders.[1]

The project description, which contained the mission statement and
goals, helped inform potential funders and participants of Lacy's aims
and the project's structure. The structure itself was extremely
dynamic—almost chameleon-like—shifting to accommodate the funding requirements of various sponsors or the needs of various older
women's advocacy groups. Lacy outlined the complex structure of
Whisper Minnesota in the September 1985 project description, as
shown in figure 1. The executive committee was the main governing
body of the project, responsible for planning, policy decisions, hiring,
staffing, and allocating resources. Lacy assumed the role of project
director; Nancy Dennis, then working for the Minneapolis YWCA, was
administrative director; and Phyllis Jane Rose, then of At the Foot of the
Mountain Theater, was associate director. Committee chairpersons
came from the many sponsoring organizations of the project, whose
specific roles were also detailed in the project description, along with
three tiers of programming, Education, Analysis and Outcome, and
Community Events.

The educational tier of Whisper Minnesota programming included
a wide array of programming. In the fall of 1985 the Reflective Leadership Program of the Humphrey Institute for Public Policy sponsored
the Older Women's Leadership Series, a workshop for thirty older
women in the greater Twin Cities area identified as potential leaders.
Through a number of seminars, the goal of the series was to encourage
the women to develop their leadership skills and to continue their
involvement with the Whisper Minnesota project by aiding in administrative planning and recruitment.[2] From the fall of 1985 to spring of
1986 Minneapolis College of Art and Design (MCAD) sponsored an
"Apprenticeship" program, designed to develop student interest in
projects such as Whisper Minnesota. Lacy, then artist-in-residence at
MCAD, directed the program. The School of Social Work at the University of Minnesota offered a similar program under the guise of "Independent Studies," which encouraged student research in the area of
older women. "Consultations and Special Forums" provided opportu-

National Board

3–5 community representatives

Minnesota Board on Aging
Minneapolis College of Art and
    Design
Hubert H. Humphrey Institute of
    Public Affairs
3 cosponsors

Executive Committee

Committee Chairpersons
    Education Committee
    Analysis and Outcome Committee
    Community Events Committee

Project Director
Administrator
    Communications
Publicity Committee
    Staff
    Volunteers
    Transportation

Fig. 1. Organizational structure of Whisper Minnesota.

nities for Whisper Minnesota or Older Women's Leadership participants to share information on the project itself, or issues surrounding it
with interested organizations. In the Split Rock Arts Program, housed
at the University of Minnesota Duluth, Lacy and several collaborators
created a series of "tableau performances" of older women in four
scenes of Minnesota's changing seasons.[3] The tableaux were to increase
the profile of the Whisper Minnesota project, and again to encourage
recruitment of participants in *The Quilt*. Similarly, At the Foot of the
Mountain Theater, then the longest running feminist theater in the
United States, developed and launched a state-wide tour of *Ladies Who
Lunch*, a comic play featuring older women actors, which was used to
increase awareness of and involvement in *The Quilt*.

Like the project description, the program for *The Crystal Quilt* performance itself featured the project's structure as a main component of
its artistry. The program describes the show as "the culmination of
more than two years of artistic planning and community organizing by
a coalition of artists, public policy specialists, and concerned citizens"
and as "the most visible component of the larger Whisper Minnesota
Project." The twelve-page program served both *The Quilt* and Whisper
Minnesota, detailing individual and institutional roles in both projects.
Newsletters circulated monthly by the Whisper Minnesota project also

emphasized the multi-layered organization, featuring sections on each of the various education, community, and analysis programs, as well as encouraging involvement and/or donations of time or money.

At a WTP *conference several years ago a guest performer rolled across the floor as if in agony, expressing the pain that being woman entailed for her. A friend leaned over to me and whispered, "someone please tell her it's over, that movement's dead." The sentiment is familiar. I recall saying words to the same effect watching an Artaud-esque performance rife with young, screaming, naked bodies and fake blood. "How embarrassing," I say. "Someone tell them it's over."*

Presenting Aged Women

The intricate and expansive structure of Whisper Minnesota, and the project's continual self-reference to that structure, clearly suggest that the organization and mobilization of older women as leaders in their community was the project's main focus—a focus served by the performance of *The Crystal Quilt*. Like the Grandparents Living Theater, *The Quilt* tackled this social/political mission by blurring distinctions between on- and offstage, between theater and everyday life, and, most important for *The Quilt*, between public and private spheres. Still largely unaddressed by academic feminists, aging remains to a great extent in the realm of the private, passed over by the 1970s women's movement motto "the personal is the political." The threat of dependency, whether by economic vulnerability or physical frailty, veils the later years in fear and shame, in turn commonly relegating older women to an isolated silence. Even among older women active in a "public" life, those who provide the backbone of the large volunteer core of older adults in this country for example, invisibility and purposelessness still ghost individual and cultural perceptions of aging. As Barbara Myerhoff's work suggests, invisibility may have its benefits. As socially accorded gender roles are most stringently applied to women of reproductive years, older women drop out of standards of beauty and ideals of femininity based on younger women, leaving them both culturally invisible and relatively free of prescribed social roles. Yet the stigma of purposelessness, especially in a country mad for productivity, can be devastating. Myerhoff was careful to add that releasing older women from social roles can also reduce them to "nonpeople," an act of degradation that may contribute to depression and even suicide among older adults.[4]

Lacy steps into this fray, this flux of invisibility and lack of defined social roles, that greet older women. By staging a coup of sorts in a public space in the heart of Minneapolis' financial center, *The Crystal Quilt* asserts that older women can and do take an active and valuable role in the present life of a community. *The Crystal Quilt* is what Myerhoff calls a definitional ceremony for older women, declaring a purpose for older women by creating a ritual for their public expression. For a little over an hour those who might normally take no notice of older women except to step around them as they rush to work, became an audience— listening, watching, some even speaking with the 430 older women gathered at the tables in the Crystal Court's atrium.

Although GLT and *The Crystal Quilt* share common political missions, Lacy takes the blurring of distinctions between on- and offstage, between theatrical performance and the performativity of everyday life, to much greater lengths. *The Crystal Quilt* collapses these distinctions in order to create a sense of authenticity, a sense that the performers are real people, in order to then transform their roles in culture at large from forgotten dwellers in the private sphere to indispensable participants in the public sphere.[5] Lacy has several mechanisms for achieving this transformation: true stories of the women's experiences, an exposed theatrical apparatus, and universalizing imagery.

Throughout what can be considered a two-year preshow Whisper Minnesota emphasized the individual lives of several key participants in the Older Women's Leadership Series. Their stories provided the cornerstone for a video used to encourage funding as well as participation in the performance and/or administrative duties. KTCA, a Twin Cities Public television station, also edited the video clips of the women's stories into their live coverage of the performance. These same women were also featured in various newspaper and local magazine articles promoting the performance. The women and their stories are richly diverse: Muriel Vaughn was a former Irish Catholic nun; Bea Swanson, an Ojibway from Minnesota's White Earth reservation; Agnes Reick, a white woman raised in a rural area outside of Eau Claire, Wisconsin; and Etta Furlow, an African-American woman whose careers included nursing, factory work, and community activism. Each of the stories is presented journalistically as real, and as an asset to the women's communities, not only for their historical value but also to demonstrate their continuing leadership. Because their diverse real-life experiences were the focus of *The Crystal Quilt*, the women performers needed no particular theatrical skills; they needed only present themselves. Thus, even as they took the "stage," sat at the tables, crossed and opened their hands in a rehearsed pattern, the older women were first social actors and theatrical actors a distant second.

In addition to the presentation of the performers' life experiences, *The Quilt* also collapsed performance and performativity by fully exposing the tricks of the theatrical apparatus. The inability to control and disguise the theatrical illusion in *The Quilt* was partially a result of presenting a large-scale performance in a public space. With no traditional dressing room or backstage space, performers were visible as they readied themselves to enter the playing space. With no wings or light booth, Lacy, wearing headphones and a microphone, became part of the action as she stood in clear view of both the audience on the balconies beside her and the performers below. Although the space certainly dictated the performance style in some respects, the exposure of the theatrical apparatus was also a choice. In some of her past performance art pieces Lacy disguised the modes of theatrical production in order to bring into tension the distinction between art and life from a different perspective. In *Inevitable Associations* (1976), for example, Lacy, clad in black and wearing layers of makeup to look old, sat in the lobby of a hotel for four hours until she was joined by three older women friends, also dressed fully in black.[6]

In *The Crystal Quilt*, however, programs painstakingly described the efforts of countless volunteers and participating organizations. No black curtains veiled performers or stage hands. The sheer scale and striking images of the piece, with 430 older women at 100-plus brightly colored tables, hyperbolized its theatricality. Live television coverage of the event cut from Lacy's conducting to the performers in the playing area, to audience members, melting distinctions between the creators, the players, and the watchers. The extensive labor of creating the performance, from recruitment, leadership training, and fund-raising efforts acknowledged in the program and promotional materials, to Lacy's visible orchestration of the performance, became featured parts of the performance itself, in effect borrowing the transformative qualities of theatrical representation while subordinating its status as illusion by exposing it.

The Crystal Quilt performance by Suzanne Lacy, May 1987.
(Photo by Peter Latner. Courtesy of Suzanne Lacy.)

The theatrical aspects of the performance exposed in *The Quilt* also emphasized the real-life experiences of the performers by creating a common language for and a universal quality of older women's lives. Set on Mother's Day, *The Quilt* invoked images of a positive and universal Motherhood in order to lend respect to older women. One newspaper article, for example, quotes Lacy describing the performers as "the symbolic mothers of our culture" (Lacey 1987). The colors featured in the performance, namely red and black, borrow from myths of the goddess, a conglomeration of what Barbara Walker describes as the three phases of woman: the virgin, the mother, and the crone (Walker 1985). The colors corresponding to these phases of womanhood are respectively white, red, and black—colors that dominate nearly all of Lacy's work including *The Quilt.* In her 1988 article "Suzanne Lacy: Social Reformer and Witch" Moira Roth even suggests that the notion

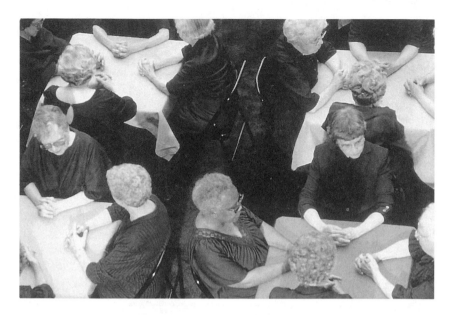

Older women sharing stories in *The Crystal Quilt*.
(Photo by Ann Marsden. Courtesy of Suzanne Lacy.)

of "whisper," upon which both the San Diego (La Jolla) and Minnesota
projects were based, might be traced to a medieval German legend of a
"triple goddess" from the "Valley of Wisperthal."

The Crystal Quilt also reinforced associations of motherhood with
nature and traditional women's roles, even as it staged its interruption
of stereotypes of older women in the downtown office building. The
urban setting was offset rather poignantly, and subtly compared to
Lacy's earlier works, by loon calls woven into Susan Stone's soundtrack to the performance.[7] The arrangement of the tables into a quilt
pattern designed by Miriam Schapiro, conjured connections not only to
women's communal work of sewing, but also to the gathering of
women in kitchens where they are catalyzed into community by the
acts of preparing and sharing food.[8] The ritualized, universal symbols
of motherhood and womanhood in *The Crystal Quilt* united the 430
older women performers in a common past and a common goal—the
struggle to assert their worth as citizens by sharing stories of their life
experiences.

The drawbacks of uniting women through such universalizing symbolism have been made clear by more than a few feminist scholars as the essentialism/plurality debates preoccupied the field during the 1980s and early 1990s.[9] Not all women are mothers. Not all mothering experiences are positive. *Mother* as a term and symbol has a range of meanings to a range of people, and not all necessarily elicit respect. Such cultural or radical feminist reasoning, depending on the feminist historian's categorical definition, is now considered passé, a simplistic, outmoded approach in these more complicated times. Yet such universalizing symbolism also serves/served to mobilize feminism in the 1970s and remains in the memories of women whose lives were changed by the women's movement. *The Quilt* tapped into this unifying power even as the women's diversity in class, race, age, physical ability, and geographic distribution (urban and rural), considerations of difference so prevalent in contemporary feminisms, simultaneously eroded the idealism of such unity. Lacy's inclusion of several performance styles, in turn indicative of several modes of feminist political thought, create an important link between the present and past— between generations of feminists. Before I explore these links, however, I turn to some of the machinations of writing history and of generational divisions that accomplish the opposite, separating the present from the past and fueling the already prevalent association of youth with "now," and age with "back when."

The reception for WTP's twentieth anniversary celebration was held in a cavernous banquet room. Amidst the overstuffed furniture and the dark wallpaper, Vera Mowry Roberts stood talking to other fellow past presidents of the organization. Their conversation fell into silence and I imagined walking around the long banquet table to talk to her. She is a vibrant, active member of the field with an invaluable view of its beginnings and its present. But what would I say? Does respect breed silence? Or am I just shy? The older women resume talking. I stay on my side of the hors d'oeuvre table and pick at the cheese cubes with my fellow graduate students.

History, the Great Divide

In *The Writing of History* Michel de Certeau asserts that: "Modern Western history essentially begins with differentiation between the present and the past" (1988, 2). The past, a dead and silent "Other" in de

Certeau's terms, is the raw material with which historians weave narratives that separate "the living" from "the dead" in order to clear a space for the historians' own "progress." Quoting Alphonse Dupront, de Certeau writes:

> "The sole historical quest for 'meaning' remains indeed a quest for the Other," but, however contradictory it may be, this project aims at "understanding" and, through "meaning," at hiding the alterity of this foreigner; or, in what amounts to the same thing, it aims at calming the dead who still haunt the present, and at offering them scriptural tombs. (1988, 2)

In contrast, de Certeau suggests that Indian culture, for example, embraces the past in a "process of coexistence and reabsorption" and the development of "new forms never drive the older ones away" (de Certeau 1988, 4).

It is fairly easy to see how the Western division between past and present might coincide with larger social fields in which the aged, saturated with past, are stripped of cultural capital and in which "youthfulness" in physical appearance and/or mental attitude comes to symbolize this country's ideals of productivity. Pierre Bourdieu (1984) for example, describes the aging process as an accumulation of capital throughout the process of maturity, and a loss of capital with the transition into old age.[10] After retirement, for example, an elderly man might be stripped of the cultural and symbolic capital that he may have enjoyed as a successful businessman. An older woman, no longer marked as physically desirable, can lose her capital as well, even if she remains gainfully employed.

The rapid rate at which historians assess the past further complicates the dubious cultural standing of the aged in this country. In a culture based on speed the present moment becomes flattened to an instant. Trends flash by at phenomenal speeds. Styles are out before they are in. Nostalgia shrinks from its twenty-year cycle to a fond yearning for last week's styles.[11] Applying de Certeau's theory to Paul Virilio's world in which time and space collapse as humans master the speed of light, the rate at which historians separate the present from the past would also increase. Although philosopher Richard Terdiman suggests that history is only written when the social memory of those who lived through the experiences begins to fade, I disagree (1993, 31–32). The past need no longer be pronounced officially dead before it is consumed and reshaped for the present, creating a culture, in de Certeau's terms, of the "living dead." The lists of what's in and what's out, usually reserved for the lead of New Year's Day newspaper entertainment sections, could potentially shame those deemed "out" on a daily, if not hourly basis. In such a realm the term *old*, usually reserved for chronological age, slides into association with *old-fashioned* or *out-of-date*, a confusion that can prematurely toll the bell for entire generations of people, regardless of political and social differences. The past is to be shed like so many dead skin cells—if not by exfoliation, then by face-lift. For an older woman to accept her physical age is to allow her body, marked with time, to be associated with past beliefs. For an older woman to accept her physical age is to risk slipping into the living-dead-zone of old age in which the quick-handed pickpockets of culture relieve her of what remains of her cultural capital.

Differences certainly exist between people born at different times. As Bourdieu carefully demonstrates, "social agents are the *product of history*" (1992, 136). Children coming of age in today's media culture, amidst high rates of child poverty and the continued threat of AIDS, have significantly different expectations of the future (if they fathom such a hopeful concept) than the children raised in the Depression or in the booming postwar years. Yet with scattershot definitions of the term *generation* and the changing shape of social roles across the life span, isolating differences between age groups proves difficult. In a culture driven by speed and technological advancement the pressure to keep up-to-date with the latest trends interlocks with the historical practice of separating the present from the past to construct generational identities whose uniqueness rest in their exclusion from other categories despite myriad differences among those born in the same year and similarities they may share with those born at a later, or earlier time.

You're Not My Mother/I'm Not Dead Yet

As medical anthropologist Margaret Lock notes (1996), the inculcation of numbers that so commonly introduce essays on the coming of the aging society bespeak the dangers of a country peopled by frail, older women who will deplete the economy and exhaust the social security system. Aging is certainly a feminist issue. Yet while feminists have begun to turn to the topic in general, little writing on ageism and aging *within* feminism has emerged. Barbara MacDonald's anger at this absence, republished in the first issue of the reformed *Ms.* in 1990, echoes unanswered—a battlecry sounded on a nearly empty battle-field. Despite Betty Friedan's *Fountain of Age,* aging and generational relationship within feminism remain relatively unexplored topics within feminist studies.

The sparsity of critical writing on age and aging within feminism is ironically countered by a considerable amount of stratification around age, as horizontal generations of feminists adjust to an uneasy coexistence. The symbolic grandmothers of first wave feminists, the real grandmothers of both the much maligned silver age and their daughters of the second wave, and now the young upstarts of the third wave, toss about in this swirling sea of very different historical locations and very common goals. Katie Roiphe's *The Morning After* and Friedan's *Fountain of Age* speak to widely divergent audiences of feminists who are just now beginning to see constructions of age and generation as unnecessary factors in their division and separation.[12] The lack of gender readings among cultural critics such as de Certeau and Virilio is met by a similar lack of age readings among feminist scholars, making my attempt to dialogue across these discourses both uncomfortable and necessary.

Do contemporary feminists also contribute to the segmenting of and confusion of generations? In an ever tightening academic job market, are established scholars reluctant to share what power they manage to secure? Do younger scholars polarize their work to what has come before in order to ride the novelty of their voices toward goals of publishing and securing increasingly elusive employment? I suggest they/we do, in several ways. First, feminists across generations fail to explore constructs of age and generation that perpetuate fears of aging between and among women. Second, what attempts have been made tend to conflate horizontal and vertical generations, using metaphors of parenting to analyze all generational relationships. Third, we continue to divide the feminist movement into categories that clearly, although often in unspoken ways, are devalued proportionate to hindsight.

The relative absence of scholarship on intramovement constructs of aging is especially evident in the light of the immense consideration given to differences of class, race, sexuality, and ethnicity. It may just be a matter of time. As second and third wave feminists come to coexist in academic and activist settings, their concerns and aims born of their differences in historical location will become more apparent. The

trick, as with other differences, will be to question how social constructions of age separate and divide women without either dismissing age
differences as somehow imagined, or concretizing them as unalterable
reality.

Another challenge will be to avoid the temptation to describe generational relationships between horizontally defined groups in the
terms of vertical relationships, particularly the problematic use of
mother/daughter analogies. Certainly my relationship with my
mother has a part, a large part, in teaching me patterns of interaction
with women older than myself in general. But transferring my relationship to my mother to that of *my mother's generation* masks countless
considerations of individual difference, and tends to polarize generations into stereotypical images of child/parent relationships.[13] For
example, Joannie Schrof's "Feminism's Daughters," which appeared in
the mainstream *U.S. News and World Report* in 1993, depicts young feminists ("third wavers") as the rebellious children of middle-aged feminists ("second wavers") who are in turn threatened by the energy,
audacity, and lack of respect of their "daughters." Schrof writes:

> "We hear all the time from older feminists that we're demanding
> ingrates," says Nadia Moritz, director of the Young Women's Project,
> a group that promotes political activism. "We're told how much we
> should appreciate, for example, that we now make 70 cents to a man's
> dollar instead of 33. But we're not about to celebrate that." Such talk
> burns the ears of older feminists, who after decades of activism know
> how gut-wrenching it can be to effect even minor changes. . . . Young
> women tell story after story of seeking the guidance of older feminists
> only to be told, "I'm not dead yet" or "That's my issue, I've been work-
> ing on it now for 20 years."

An alternative example comes from a 1995 essay in which several
young Italian feminist historians seek to define their generation of historians (Evangelista et al. 1995). Their definition indicates "neither a
bond nor a relationship dependent on biological fact . . . but points to a
strong link both within the profession . . . and to our awareness of being
women historians of one age group that notes a relationship between
itself and women historians of other age groups" (130). These young
historians carefully explore their unique historical location in terms of
intellectual thought, economic conditions, social roles, and family
structures. They connect themselves to the work of women who came

before them and question the models of "ascendance and descendance" within feminism, asking: "what kind of relationships could arise among three generations of women historians as determined by the different relations that women of different ages have and have had with politics and feminism?"(132) Where Schrof reads the waves of feminism in terms of familial roles, these young, feminist, Italian historians question the troubling connection between their personal relationships to their mothers and their professional relationships to the generation of feminists that preceded the young historians.

Perhaps it is a cultural difference. Perhaps the antagonistic tone of Schrof's article is the result of its appearance in a mainstream news magazine in which harmonic alliances rarely make headlines. Regardless, these two examples provide helpful markers for negotiating the way through the slalom course of generational relationships that will only increase in significance as more radical differences between the second and third wave emerge when the second wave enters "old age."

Another trouble spot in the growing consciousness of generational relationships is the way in which feminists categorize the past and distinguish it from the present. The temptation here is to disconnect one's self from the past in order to appear new, novel, and fresh, all qualities that "sell" education to students, books to publishers, and essays to journals. The danger here is in the slippery association between the ideas and the author, between "out-of-date" and biological age. Youthfulness becomes a desirable and unremarkable sign while old age marks the body with the past, with the weight of what was, making engaging in the present nearly impossible.

As an example, I return to the field of feminist theater studies, a field whose historical divisions provided the foundation for my early work as a "young" scholar. When I began my graduate studies in 1988, Sue-Ellen Case and Jill Dolan had both recently published books in the field of theater studies in which they applied Alison Jaggar's categories of cultural, liberal, and materialist feminisms to feminist theater practices.[14] Both scholars' ground-breaking works (Case's *Feminism and Theatre* and Dolan's *Feminist Spectator as Critic*) continue to resonate in the field today, and both were instrumental in my own development as a scholar and theater practitioner. The categories clearly oversimplify the wide range of feminist theater activity over the last several decades, as both Case and Dolan acknowledged at the time. Case includes a long

list of "strands" of feminisms of which people might identify with two
or three:

> A basic list might include radical feminism (sometimes called cultural
> feminism), liberal feminism, materialist feminism, socialist feminism,
> Marxist feminism, lesbian feminism, radical lesbian feminism, critical
> positions such as psychosemiotic feminist criticism, and l'écriture
> feminine (an application of French feminism). (Case 1988, 63)

After being criticized for asserting one good feminism and two "ugly"
ones, Dolan was careful to emphasize the debt materialist feminism
owes to the movements that preceded it, discouraging their facile dis-
missal (Dolan 1988, 10). In the last several years materialist feminists
(who created the division of historical categories) within theater studies
have begun to question the impact of their own methodologies on history, a step that acknowledges, in de Certeau's terms, a triangular relationship with the past rather than the oppositional relationship between
"the living and the dead." But to a certain extent, the separation of political approaches to the criticism and production of feminist theater seems
to have gone underground, exchanging overt criticism for a silence
around methodologies deemed to be "past," "over," or "out of date."
Gayle Austin's 1990 *Feminist Theories for Dramatic Criticism* extends Case
and Dolan's division of feminism into three basic political agendas by
also defining their chronological stages, the overlapping of which can
lead to the association of the past with passé, of old age with old-fashioned. Austin's stages of feminism read as follows:

1. working within the canon: examining images of women;
2. expanding the canon: focusing on women writers; and
3. exploding the canon: questioning underlying assumptions of an
   entire field of study, including canon formation. (1990, 17)

The categorical containment of political agendas into chronological
time periods explicit in Austin and implicit in Dolan risks suggesting
that only one political agenda exists today.

The uneasiness with spirituality and ancestors that rippled
through the WTP conference would seem to support this idea.[15] WTP in
particular, and the institution of academia in general, clearly accord
materialist analysis, which coincides with current cross-departmental
trends in cultural studies, with more cultural capital than earlier, and

what are often seen as more naive, movements. For those who owe the government a "small house" for funding their graduate studies, disconnecting oneself from previous generations of feminist scholars/ activists has more than nominal appeal. To remember or acknowledge connections to movements deemed outdated is to risk becoming outdated oneself. Fear of the "living dead" seemed to haunt the conference. Unexpressed and unanalyzed differences between generations and fears of joining the ranks of the "living dead," politically and/or chronologically speaking, limited WTP discussions of the material aging body to satirical quips and theoretical metaphors.

Moira Roth makes a similar point when she suggests that the critical writing on Lacy's *Crystal Quilt* ignores the spiritual aspects of Lacy's work. Roth writes:

> Recent discussion of Lacy's work generally contain no reference to subjects such as the Crone and the Witch or to the kind of powerful, discomforting ideas which they conjure up. Why the dearth of awareness and or recognition of these foundations in Lacy's art? I suspect that they would greatly hamper the increasingly broad appeal of her spectacles—most dramatically apparent in the state-wide interest in her Minneapolis project. Lacy herself makes less reference to this material than she once did; the art writers most interested in her work now are usually concerned with its over political aspects. (1988, 54–55)

In the last of a trilogy of articles on Lacy in *TDR* (1988), Lucy Lippard also suggests that the political aspects of Lacy's work overshadowed the spiritual. Lippard writes: "Because of the social form and focus of her art, prevailing dualisms within the art market have categorized her as 'political' as though political and spiritual were mutually exclusive" (73). But it is also possible that the spiritual side of Lacy's work is overlooked for its generational ties to an older, "out of date" cultural feminist movement. The local Minneapolis publicity certainly corroborates Lippard's observation. Of considerable coverage, only one article made brief reference to spirituality, outside of the profiles of participants who were active in their churches. A short description of *The Crystal Quilt* project in the *Star Tribune*, links Lacy to cultural feminism (without actually using the term): "The 'Crystal Quilt' is the brainchild of California artist Suzanne Lacy who believes older women should be appreciated for their wisdom and sensitivity, much as priestesses were revered by the ancients" (Best Bets 1987). The quote, taken from Lacy's film of the California *Whisper, the Waves, the Wind* performance, is the only reference made to spirituality in any of the promotional, publicity, and inter-organizational materials to which I had access.[16] Although Lacy's work has generally emerged from spiritual questions, and *The Quilt* resonates on this level as well, any discussion of the spiritual had been cleansed from support materials.

Willful amnesia of the inter-connectedness of the present and the past in feminist performance theory contributes to the myth of "post-feminism" that troubles women's studies departments and feminist scholars across the country. *Postfeminism*, as the term is used, suggests that the "second wave" of the women's movement is "over," its goals either accomplished or abandoned as politically naive.[17] Postfeminist schools of thought romanticize progress at the expense of the past—a past that is still lived by women whose lives have spanned several trends in theory. The concept of aging becomes devalued as such schools of thought struggle to cut the ties of time or to erase them completely. In a metaphor borrowed from Milan Kundera, the lightness of forgetting is preferred to the heavy weight of the past.[18]

The Crystal Quilt and the Living Past

How might feminists envision intergenerational connections in a culture with enormous economic stakes in perpetuating a fear of aging? *The Crystal Quilt* begins to dissolve the phobia of "the living dead" by focusing on aging women's contribution to the present and their connections to the past, and by creating a politicized, postmodern, self-reflexive ritual that uses oral histories to establish older women as active citizens rather than simply passive clients to governmental institutions of Social Security and Medicare. The seductiveness of "lightness" in Kundera's terms, and "transparency" in Maria Lugones', produce a yearning for a disconnection with the past, while the older women in *The Crystal Quilt* stand as symbols of the complexity and potential of thickness, of imagining the present past as "thick" (Lugones 1994, 463). One can trace the stages of life in each older woman's experiences, yet the women are clearly *more* than what they were at any single point in history.[19] They are symbols of the liveliness of history—the *living* past— resisting the confluence of old age and out-of-date; of quick, easy, and tempting associations between *old-fashioned* and *old-timers.* By providing spectators with scarves and inviting them to join the older women's conversations, the performance interrupted the silence that can encompass those saturated with the thickness of the past and marked as living dead. The performance's reallocation of cultural capital to older women offers a glimpse of how re-membering the living past might begin to untangle the associations between old age and old-fashioned that continue to feed the cultural frenzy to perform youthfulness in this country.

In addition, one can also trace a variety of historically situated, feminist performance styles in *The Quilt*, yet the performance is larger than any single category. In de Certeau's sense Lacy writes history with the living pens of older women, simultaneously breaking and a forging connections with the past. The ritual elements and universalizing symbols of motherhood and the crone stand in concert with the performance's far-reaching organizational artistry and the more materialist concerns for diversity. The thickness of the older performer's lives parallels a thickness of feminist performance styles. *The Quilt* blends historical forms of feminist performance that acknowledge and value the simultaneous existence of the *present past*, rather than conflating and eschewing old-age and old-fashioned in the name of an illusory, perpetual, postmodern present. Instead of fabricating a break between the present and the past as de Certeau claims is necessitated in the writing of history, Lacy's work *also* celebrates the living past in the form of older women, and in the overlapping lessons of contemporary feminist theater history.

As feminism in general, and feminism within theater studies in particular, continues to age as a movement within the context of an aging society, it will be increasingly important to recognize how discursive constructions of time and the past impact the political movement itself, the individual lives of women, and relationships across generations of all definitions: age groups, social movements, and family lineage. The increasing speed of American culture fuels the fantasy of lightness, stigmatizes the weight of the past, and encourages amnesia of the relationship between past and present. As life expectancy increases, and social roles across the life span shift, the multiple definitions of the term *generation* may yield connections across age groups, but may also contribute to stereotypes about age groups that fuse political stances and social roles. Although there is debate whether generational identities and alliances, and here I refer to the simplistic and sweeping borders between "Generation X," "Baby Boomers," "the

Tweeners," and the "Silver Generation," will swell into the intergenerational war that some gerontologists and political organizations predict, certainly the transformation of American culture to an aging society will demand more awareness of aging across the life span and of negotiations between age groups. Feminists need more fully explore how their methodologies, and how certain concepts of time and generation may unwittingly contribute to the kind of amnesia that separates the past and present, in turn cementing walls between age groups that might otherwise be permeable. Despite efforts not to create "two ugly feminisms" and one good one, and the strides toward self-reflexivity in materialist feminism, entanglements of political graveyards and physical aging were still evident in the discomfort with nostalgia and hesitancy to address spirituality and ancestors that loomed behind the 1994 WTP conference (as well as in my own trepidation at talking with past presidents of the organization). The self-reflexiveness of recent materialist analysis, which places it *within* the historical field rather than apart from it, need also acknowledge how it is constructed historically in terms of a generation mobilized around a political agenda, and how the construction of political and historical categories may over determine generational boundaries, obscuring potential links between them.

✷ In the final session of the July 1994 conference, professor of English at Kansas State University and active member in WTP Iris Smith asked why the invocation of spirituality in the opening, joint session with the Black Theatre Network had been so cavalierly brushed aside. Smith noted that the issue seemed to generate considerable reaction in small group meetings, but had been excused as somehow not worth pursuing in the larger group. A few people responded in support of Smith, in what seemed to me, as a younger scholar trained to identify and deconstruct radical feminism, a brave statement of a belief marked as passé in a rapidly changing field. But the topic faded as the discussion turned to more viable themes for the next year's conference. The resonance of Dickerson's, Teer's, and Smith's invocations of ancestors, however, lingered.

6

The Body in Depth:
Kazuo Ohno's *Water Lilies*

✣ I don't want to leave. After his fourth encore, and what seems a lifetime of bowing, Kazuo Ohno and Yoshito Ohno disappear behind the curtain and do not reemerge. I still can't move. My thoughts are back in grade school in Wisconsin, an experiment in Miss Bausch's class where after cutting one long strip of thick construction paper, I turned the paper with a single twist and glued the ends together. Following the curve of the paper with my pencil, I am startled when the end of my line reaches the mark from which I began.

On 30 October 1993, Japanese butoh dancer Kazuo Ohno and his son Yoshito performed *Water Lilies* in the intimate auditorium at the Walker Art Center in Minneapolis. At a private reception that followed, fans celebrated the elder Ohno's eighty-seventh birthday.[1] The performance entwined a series of Möbius strips of culture, gender, and age. In *Water Lilies,* a piece inspired in part by the Japanese gardens of French painter Claude Monet, both Ohno and his son performed male and female roles across extremes of the life course, including a scene in which the elder Ohno played an infant. A stage performer over the age of seventy is a rare sight in a country where the aged are commonly lifted and tucked or just tucked away. Whereas Carol Channing's 1995 Broadway run of *Hello, Dolly!* tantalized audiences with her ability to defy time in her nearly flawless recreation of a role begun in 1964, then eighty-seven-year-old Ohno's performance suggests quite another model— the possibility for a model of age that embraces change.

The devaluation of aging in the United States stems from deep systems of ageism complicated by categories of gender, race, and class. These systems are certainly shifting as the Baby Boom generation carries its economic weight across the cultural thresholds of middle-age. But to a great extent, shifts in the value of old age remain coded in terms of maintaining youthfulness and defying time—"Don't deny age, Defy it," says actress Melanie Griffith in her sales pitch for cosmetics. The aging process—the embodiment of time—is, ironically, maligned by the technological surge toward the elimination of time and space, the very (bio)technology that continues to increase human life expectancy. The same computer that can give an older person a previously unknown freedom of movement through virtual reality, can make human memory (the territory of value for many older people) appear faulty and untrustworthy in comparison to the wizardry of its externalized counterpart, computer megabytes.[2] The externalization of human capabilities of movement and speed creates a culture in which a hazy, golden filter shrouds the youthful body, encouraging us to overlook, even eliminate, what seem imperfections of aged and/or disabled bodies. Like a carnival huckster, technology tempts us with the ability to control time. "Contemporary culture," as philosopher Susan Bordo observes, "technologically armed, seems bent on defying aging, our various 'biological clocks,' and even death itself" (1993, 4–5).

Several key cultural values continue to perpetuate this country's obsession with youthfulness. The overemphasis on productivity as a measure of human worth creates young adulthood as the pinnacle of both the productive and reproductive life course. In such a system aging is inevitably mourned as a process of decay and increasing disability. When an older adult is praised or valued in such a system, it is for their ability to "still" appear or act youthful. Such binary divisions as productivity/nonproductivity, activity/inactivity, health/disease, and life/death also stratify the aging process into seemingly stable, independent life stages and disconnect moments of the life course from each other—separating, for example, the frail old person from the teenager, the infant from the adult, the young adult from the older adult. Rather than imagining the life course as a process, binaries set up, for example, productivity in opposition to nonproductivity, dividing life stages into opposite camps. In order to prove their worth in such a system older adults must perform and display productivity, activity, and health as characteristics of aging—a category that would otherwise bleed and deplete their cultural value.[3]

Detailed readings of performances of age (and aging as performance), can help to dismantle such binary systems by emphasizing the
instability inherent in the aging process, the body's production of time,
and the inseparability of life stages in the process of aging. Repeating
performances—social acts that define who one knows one's self to be—
creates a sense that, over time, one gains a clearer understanding of
who one "is." But aging itself is a process of change that makes identical repetitions of social acts impossible. The mirror phase of old age, the
moment when one recognizes and, most commonly, rejects one's
reflection as an "old" person, is symptomatic of Western culture's reifi-
cation of both youthfulness and the process of knowing, preserving,
and mastering one's "self."[4] Yet, when seen as performative, the aging
process entails continuous change across the entire life course.
Although the shame of old age is imagined to be the erosion of the
"self"—"she's no longer herself," said my father of my grandmother—
the seeming stability ("sedimentation" in Judith Butler's terms) of the
self is illusory. Not only does the self shift across time, but at any given
time, one is a complex amalgam of multiple selves. Who I am, who I
will be as an older person is not simply a shoddy replica of my youth,
but a vital stage in (and on) which to perform new selves.

This chapter consists of three sections. The first describes *Water
Lilies* in detail. The second section looks at *Water Lilies* as providing a
vision of the aging body that is spills over binary divisions of age, connecting points on the life course in Western culture that have throughout the twentieth century been disconnected in the name of increasing
productivity.[5] Based on Ohno's model, I explore the potential for imagining the body in *depth,* as irreducible to a single moment in history,
and question how the body in depth alters notions of both theatrical
performance and theoretical performativity, particularly in terms of
recent models of gender as depthless displays of surface appearances.
The final section asks whether postmodern theories of the body, which
are also predicated on dissolving binaries, support or undermine readings of the body in depth.

Water Lilies in Performance

Within the genre of butoh, Ohno is greatly respected as an innovator,
artist, and teacher. He shares with most butoh performers, a now
greatly diverse movement, the goal of merging the grotesque and the

beautiful.[6] Yet his style is also uniquely his own. Characteristics of his performances include: his unique brand of *onnagata,* the kabuki tradition of men playing the roles of women; his use of flowers; his representation of the fetus; his references to Christian iconography; and his blend of Japanese and European artistic traditions.[7] Ohno returned to dance in his forties after a short career as a physical education instructor and after serving in the army during World War II, and was fifty-three when he first collaborated with butoh founder Tatsumi Hijikata in 1959 on an adaptation of Hemingway's novel *Old Man and the Sea.* Ohno played the Old Man and his son Yoshito played the Sea. In his butoh work Ohno's age has to a certain extent then always enabled him to visibly and metaphorically blend age and youth—to dance on the precipice of life and death—a theme that recurs in his own writing on dance. "My dance," writes Ohno, "is an encounter with Mankind, an encounter with Life. But I cannot forget that we all sleep upon Death, and that our lives are carried by the thousands of dead that came before us and who we will soon join" (in Viala 1988, 26).

Water Lilies, or *Suiren* in Japanese, is a series of six scenes marked by changes in music and costume. The series builds from solo performances to a final duet in which father and son share the starkly lit, bare stage. The simplicity of the performance lends enormous weight of significance to the stage pictures. The props—a bright red silk flower, a parasol, a wooden staff, and elegant turn-of-the-century costumes—appeared slightly tattered despite, or perhaps because of, years of careful preservation. The dancers' movements were achingly slow, filling even the smallest gesture—the folding of a finger, the arching of a foot—with sharp intensity. The careful precision with which both performers moved through genders, ages, cultures, time periods, and life and death created an effect of "other-worldliness," obscuring clear distinctions of chronological time and space.

The performance began as the audience entered the Walker's small, steeply raked auditorium. Toward the right of the stage, a bald man stood completely still, his back to the audience, his head bowed slightly forward. Dressed in a modern silk suit, the man held this stillness throughout the lengthy preshow. As the lights shifted, intensifying the focus on his stillness, Kazuo Ohno appeared from the opposite side of the stage, dressed in a long, pale, Edwardian, gown. The wild shock of black hair that surrounded his lightly powdered face was shielded by a turn-of-the-century cloth parasol. His steps appeared awkward and angular, but landed with an eerie lightness. The mood was mournful as Ohno slowly traversed the stage in a serpentine pattern toward the stock still, contemporarily dressed Yoshito, as though this apparition of the modern era knew it was only a remnant of a time already disappeared. Schubert's *Ave Maria,* sung by Leontyne Price and Peter Schreier, underscored the delicate sadness. The scene's title, "A Woman Floating in Haley's Comet," encapsulated its tone. It is as if Haley's comet, which revisits the earth every seventy-odd years, connects all those it passes, creating a dense overlap of widely varying moments in history.

The second scene stood in sharp contrast to the delicacy of the first. When the elder Ohno left the stage, the pulsing, industrial sounds of Pink Floyd's *Speak to me/Breath in the Air, On the Run* grew almost unbearably loud. Yoshito, still standing as he was at the opening, began to tremble. Almost imperceptible at first, the trembling seemed to emanate from a source deep inside him, seeking a desperate release. With hands clenched, he rose his arms slowly until his entire body appeared to vibrate from what seemed uncontainable frustration and anger. Suddenly the shaking stilled and Yoshito's movements echoed those of his father's in the first scene. He continued to move between the two states, mournful fluidity and angry staccato, as though moving through time (the turn-of-the-century to today); through gender (the "woman" invoked by Ohno's first scene and Yoshito's own sculpted, muscular body); through life stages (an angry adolescence to a more patient maturity).

The scene shifted in tone as Ohno entered wearing a heavy, pale yellow robe and leaning on a large wooden staff that guided him as if he were aged and blind. Yoshito exited and the music softened. The yellow robe, now open, revealed Ohno's eighty-seven-year-old body, wrapped only by a small, white girdle-like cloth around his waist. His movements were slow and stilted as he leaned on the staff for support with each small step. As he danced with the stick, power seems to flow between it and Ohno. At one moment he leaned on the staff as if he were a great burden, in the next he waved the stick in the air as though it were weightless. Dancing with the kimono as a shawl, then laying it down as a blanket, Ohno exposed his body, all save his narrow waist covered by the girdle. Resting the staff on the yellow kimono, Ohno's movements became more flowing, as though the staff symbolized the long years of life that weighed on the body that began the scene. His head tilted backward, he raised his arms gracefully above his head, exposing the length of this body to the audience. It was powdered white, infinitely wrinkled, achingly delicate, and forcefully strong, simultaneously invoking the images of an eighty-seven-year-old man, an aging woman, a young woman, a young man. Like the woman floating in Haley's comet, the image of Ohno's body, saturated by the past, can not be contained by a single time period, gender, or life stage.

Yoshito again provided the transition to the next scene. As Kazuo Ohno exited to the right, Yoshito entered in his silk suit from the left, racing across the stage with knees lifted high, upper body again rigidly still. The disruption suggested a change in time, gender, and life stage similar to his transition in the second scene. After a variation of these crosses, Kazuo Ohno appeared again, this time as a coy young girl playing flirtatiously with a red silk flower.

Water Lilies' play with time and gender is best encapsulated by the next scene. Here Ohno, again tightly wrapped only in the small waist girdle, danced with a long silk cloth which he eventually spread out on the stage floor. Throughout the scene, he shifted from an aged person to an infant, rolling playfully on the silk cloth. Resting on his back, as though looking up from a crib, Ohno's fingers reached out and his facial features widened with the curiosity of an infant. As he moved across the piece of silk, Ohno appeared to gradually age, until at last he returned to the aged body whose slow, determined steps began the scene. At the end of the scene, he carried the cloth reverently, as if aware of its power to transform. Again, like Haley's comet, the cloth seemed to exist in a density of time, a time that swallows and contains linear, chronological time—"our" time. Dancing with these symbolic objects, Ohno's body took on their expansiveness, simultaneously signifying multiple points of time.[8]

The final scenes continued the play through gender, age, and culture. Yoshito appeared in a long, maroon dress, cloth-covered buttons climbing the length of his spine. His body moved slowly and with a slight trembling that recalled his first scene. As in the other scenes of cross-gender play or *onnagata*, in *Water Lilies* no attempt was made to hide Yoshito's bald head. Instead, Yoshito's movements and costume created a clearly constructed femininity. After Yoshito's solo, Kazuo Ohno entered in the black tuxedo that has become one of his trademarks. The two completed the performance, dancing in the same stage space yet utterly alone in their own spheres.

The ebb and flow between cultures, genders, and ages provided the structure for *Water Lilies* itself. The music ranged from Schubert's *Ave Maria* in the opening scene and the pulsing bass of Pink Floyd's *Speak to me/Breathe in the Air, On the Run* in scene two, to *A Song of the River Goddess* by Shuichi Chino in scene three. The countertraditional movement of butoh, which borrowed from modern European dance, doubles back on itself in this performance by personifying an art work, indeed an era, inspired in part by Japanese culture—as Monet's *Water Lilies* was inspired by his extensive Japanese gardens that surrounded his studio in Giverny. Ohno's performance was inspired by Monet's drawing of the Japanese footbridge, thickly draped in flowers, arching a small pond hidden within his gardens. As Ohno reveals in his essays, for him the bridge is a symbol of the inseparability of youth and age, of life and death.

The gender play followed a similar doubling pattern throughout the performance. *Water Lilies* opened with Ohno dressed in an extravagant Edwardian gown, and ended with him in the final scene "Morning Greeting (The Drawing Walks)" in a black tuxedo. Yoshito, who began in a contemporary silk suit, ended in the faded, maroon gown, again in turn-of-the-century-fashion, and carries the same parasol with which his father began the performance. The Möbius strips of gender and generation turned circles as father and son alternately dance roles ranging from a coy young girl and a sophisticated aging lady, to a young man exploding with anger and energy and an older man barely able to lift his wooden staff. The complexity of the stage images compels a series of questions. What vision of aging do these twists on time, age, gender, and cultures create? What questions do these images present postmodern theories of the body?

The Body in Depth: Reimagining the Aged Body

As Ohno reaches his arms upward in scene two, lifting his staff high, stretching and exposing the length of his powdered white, infinitely wrinkled body, he reveals a relationship between time and the body that is much maligned. What is too often imagined to be the *ravages* of time on the body in Western culture, Ohno's performance recreates as beauty, not only in the present moment, but as an accumulation of the moments across the life course and across generations. As he rolls across the silk cloth in scene four, symbolically moving from old age to infancy and back again, Ohno demonstrates the inseparability of life stages in the process of aging. For me Ohno's performance was an exercise in seeing in *depth*—in seeing through the transparent layers of past performances and imagined performances yet to be within the bounded course of human life.[9] In *Water Lilies* Yoshito and Kazuo Ohno's bodies exceed binary divisions of youth and age, of life and death. Ohno's performance symbolizes *the death* of binary limitations of age systems. The apparitions onstage in *Water Lilies*—the woman floating in Haley's comet, the infant suspended on the (Japanese foot-) bridge between life and death—are, as Ohno suggests, "the dead beginning to run" (in Holborn 1987, 36).

By merging life and death, Ohno creates a poetic model of the human body in depth, using performance to imagine and embody past and potential changes across time.[10] Writing about similar images of aging in photography, Anca Cristofovici puts it this way, "the poetic body makes it possible to keep in touch with one's different ages or different age-selves." Simply put, to see the body in depth is literally to see time across space. It is to witness the event of aging, to anticipate the changes the body will produce, and to remember changes already passed. To see the *older* body in-depth is to recognize the wrinkles and age spots while also seeing the thick, pliant skin of a child. To see a *younger* body in depth, on the other hand, is to imagine the unchartable changes that the body will produce. This forward imagining is tricky territory. Conflicting contributions of heredity, medical advances, differences in class, gender, and race, and just plain luck make it impossible to do more than roughly sketch the old age that awaits the child or young adult. But a rough sketch is quite sufficient. The important thing is not to polish the details, but to acknowledge the almost certain (barring tragedy) links between youth, adulthood, old age, and all categories in between. Like John Dollimore's (1991) and Judith Butler's (1990) models of gender as a *depthless* display of surface identity, imagining an aging body in depth does not insist on the existence of a single, unchanging, interior "self." Instead, it layers the selves created throughout one's life, making it impossible to isolate a single sign of one's age.[11]

As a category of difference, aging is unique in that if one lives long enough, one will occupy the seeming opposites of the binary division of youth and old age. While medical technology, masquerade, economic changes, and shifts in context make it possible to occupy "opposing" spaces in gender, race, and class divisions, these shifts certainly entail more radical acts than the simple passage of time. Although *Water Lilies* demonstrates the range of such categories that a body can create, claim, and move through with a simple, at times stunning theatricality, the difficulty of such mobility, the stickiness of certain roles outside the theatrical playing space is not to be overlooked.

In other words, I do not want to romanticize the possibilities of such role playing outside of the performance space. Certainly the fact that Ohno is a man helped him achieve his considerable success in a field of Japanese dance in which very few women are recognized. The "exoticism" of his aged, Japanese body in a Western context, in which the nearly naked, greatly aged body is seldom displayed, may unfortunately contribute to his wide-spread popularity outside Japan. While these examples of gender, race and ethnicity demand consideration, they do not deplete the potential of the depth model of age to help shift strict divisions between life stages both in and out of the performance space (in the space of overlap of both performance and performativity), divisions that continue to feed the cultural devaluation of aging and the aged in this country.

Ohno addresses this blur between on- and offstage in a 1986 interview with Richard Schechner. When Schechner asked Ohno how he prepared for and "cooled down" from a performance, Ohno, his translators, and followers broke into laughter: "At the age of nearly 80, there is no more 'stage' and 'daily life,'" said Ohno. Japanese dancer Eiko, who was also at the interview, added, "He doesn't commute" (Schechner 1986). Ohno's blending of ages in *Water Lilies*, along with his claim that he finds no difference between the stage and everyday life, creates a powerful sign of aging, one that counters cultural constructions of old age as a period in which the self is considered merely a shadow of what one was, the youthful self, painted as productive, reproductive, and a valuable cultural asset. Although performing in a theatrical space also differs from performing in terms of everyday life, theatrical performance can act as a hyperbolic reminder that complex and many-layered performances of self do not stop at what are often constructed as gateways to old age, whether they be menopause, retirement, widowhood, selling the family home, or the transition to a nursing home.

To imagine age in depth also adds a significant spin to the expectations of theatrical performance that can, ironically, measure older actors' performances in comparison to standards set by youthful bodies. Kazuo Ohno and his son Yoshito, himself in his sixties, establish a model of movement whose main characteristic is its intensity rather than its dexterity. In the effort to isolate and celebrate life the smallest movements take on immense significance in *Water Lilies*. With the slightest tilt of his head or the bend of his finger Kazuo Ohno suggests his transformation from old woman to infant. Like much of the work of dancer/choreographer Liz Lerman's intergenerational troupe Dance Exchange, in *Water Lilies* older performers define their own range of movement rather than struggle to replicate movements driven by discipline and mastery of the body at what has been long considered its peak of performance as well as its peak of cultural value.[12]

Ohno's overflowing of binaries of youth and age in *Water Lilies* also comes into relief when considered in terms of parody, which works by ridiculing one standard of behavior in favor of another. Parody shifts meaning when binary systems are dissolved. In the depth model, in which Ohno performs beyond binary divisions of gender, age, and cultures, making himself *more* than either category, no clear norm or standard is reestablished through parody. Yet Ohno's Chaplin-esque style does seem on the verge of comedy in each scene. The faltering steps of Ohno's characters, in whom life emerges from the death that encompasses them, recall Chaplin's flawed, vulnerable heroes whose undying optimism emerges triumphant in a world that seems to plot against them. If there is parody in Ohno's performance, it is, as Judith Butler describes it, aimed at the notion that binaries alone dictate the possibilities for humankind (1990, 138). In *Water Lilies* Ohno assumes the roles of young women without attempting to erase or ridicule the presence of his own aging body, just as Yoshito makes no effort to disguise his bald head when he dons the long maroon gown in the final scene. Ohno's characters are not limited to stratified, binary age and gender systems. Instead Ohno exceeds binary divisions of age and assumes roles through a complicated process of poetic reminiscence rather than, as dance theorist Mark Franko writes, "polemical masquerade" (1992, 603).

✴ At the reception following the show, there are awkward introductions and reverential testimonies from former students and admirers. Someone hands out posters of Ohno, and after graciously receiving his birthday wishes, he kneels down on the floor to sign posters. I want one. But I don't. He's not going to live much longer. But, that's so— I put my poster on the table,

hoping to get him off his knees. He looks at me, smiles, and pulls the poster to
the ground and signs it in fast, sweeping strokes.

Postmodern Bodies and the Dance of Death

My reading of Ohno's performance is informed by a rich body of postmodern theoretical writings that imagine the benefits of a world not
built on a foundation of binary categories. Scholars of age studies have
entertained these theories before me, but have been understandably
reluctant to adopt them wholesale. For Harry Moody "the postmodern
culture of aging presents itself as freedom from constraint . . . freedom
[that] is actually a massive form of denial and an escape from history"
(1993, xxxvii). Kathleen Woodward draws a strict line between the
aging body and postmodern theory, claiming that the body in deep old
age, on the precipice of death, becomes the "bedrock of the real in
Lacanian terms"—from which no amount of postmodern playfulness
can provide an escape (1991, 19). Woodward writes plainly that "there
can be no postmodern poetics of the aging body" (57).

Moody and Woodward, among others, are right to be cautious
about postmodern theories that, with careful scrutiny, read like science
fiction fantasies of worlds perpetually frozen in glory days of young
adulthood. Indeed, eliminating binary thought does not guarantee an
improvement in the cultural value of aging and old age. Entertaining
the elimination of binaries seems to fuel fantasies of agelessness and
immortality that have very real consequences on how we value and, in
turn, provide social and medical services for people of all ages.[13] One
might recognize multiple layers of signs of age on the body, but still
treat that body as worthless. But the postmodern playfulness of eluding
binary divisions needn't be constructed as childishness or as solely the
realm of the youthful. The dissolution of binaries needn't imagine time
and its embodiment (in aging) as an entity to be battled and elimi-
nated.[14]

During *Water Lilies,* Ohno produces the effect of both the passage
of time, and the simultaneous existence of several time periods. The
juxtaposition of Ohno as the woman floating in Haley's comet with the
contemporarily dressed Yoshito creates a swirl of time, including the
coexistence of two centuries and two generations of performers (father
and son). As Ohno rolls across the silk scarf in scene four, transforming
from an old woman to an infant and back again, his movements pro-

duce a mimetic passage of time that invites a reimagining of how aging is written on (memory, physical changes), around (objects, props), and by the body offstage, or in terms of everyday life. Performativity in this case becomes an embodied, temporal process in which time is *produced by the body*, rather than the body being destroyed by, or being a victim to time.[15] To acknowledge the body's production of time through practice is to reclaim at least partial responsibility for aging and mortality, rather than strictly separating the life course from death and imagining aging as the body's betrayal of a stable, youthful soul. Rather than submitting to time, rather than being passively dissolved by the relentless progression of history, the body itself *performs* time through practice.[16] To imagine aging in depth is to insist that spatial discourse analysis acknowledge its temporal component, too commonly dismissed in recent postmodern theory as indicative only of a false sense time as progressive and linear.

Ohno's performance in *Water Lilies* exemplifies an *embodied postmodern poetics of the aged body*, one in which the body is irreducible to discursive binary divisions, and one which acknowledges the body's performance of time in/across the life course. By performing a range of roles of gender and age, Ohno's performance conjures a body that encompasses a *lifetime* of changes and possibilities at the dense point of overlap between theatrical performance and theoretical performativity. Ohno's body troubles the Western vision of the aged body as flat surface by enacting a dense layering of historical experiences from the moment of conception to deep old age. To create a body that exceeds binary divisions is not necessarily to fantasize a single, liberated, idealized aged body. Such an ideal would oversimplify the category of aging, once again prescribing what it means to be old. Instead, Ohno moves through a range of possibilities of what aging can be.[17] To create a body that moves through a range of ages and genders need not necessarily dream of eluding aging and death. Rather than expressing the shame of time's markings on the body, or seeking their elimination, Ohno's performance embraces and displays the embodiment of time and celebrates the life that emerges from its inevitable death.

The performative, depth model of aging recuperates a space for the aged body through postmodern theory in contemporary, technology-information driven postmodern culture—a culture rapidly accommodating and shaping the growing numbers of aged consumers, while rabidly erasing visual signs of old age amidst doom and gloom warn-ings of the economic havoc to be wreaked by the "aging society" that lies in wait just over the horizon of the millennium. Postmodern theories themselves are generationally connected to the youth movement as it emerged in the 1960s in Western Europe and the United States, their goals entwined with desires to overturn and/or dissolve cultural structures set in place by previous generations. Certainly more generational analysis remains to be done on the relationships between technology, postmodernism, and generations. Yet, when troubled, postmodern theory remains a powerful and helpful tool in reimagining the cultural value of aging, and need not be eschewed in the meantime. I do not advocate using postmodern theory to create fantasies of agelessness. The coming of "age-irrelevance" that Bernice Neugarten anticipated for its easing of rigid age-related social roles, would also erase categories of age, leaving a residue of age biases in both directions (age to youth/youth to age and all variations in between) but no vocabulary to express them (1974). Rather, envisioning age as performed across time creates a discourse in which performances of self continue across the life course dissociated from cultural values placed on productivity which create, assume, and devalue social actions deemed "nonproductive." In addition, a performative model of aging carves out a way to speak of both youth and the aged whom exist relationally, both generationally and within their own bodies. Ohno's *Water Lilies* demonstrates that there *can* be a postmodern poetics of the aging body, one that remains embodied, demands scrutiny of the values assigned to various stages of age, and acknowledges the body's performance of time across the life course, dreaming not of escaping death and aging, but of the powers of embodiment at all stages of age.

✒ A handful of Frolics members sit around the conference table, while I chase their voices with my mini-tape recorder. They were trying to be helpful, responding to my questions about variations between performances. "Oh it's so hard when there's a bunch of blue hairs," says one man, "The energy just drags." I feel a flush of heat and wait for the other performers to react to his disturbing comment. But they just smile and continue. "We like it when there is a young crowd. There's more to feed off of."

7

Screen-Deep:
The Beauty of Mortality in
Margolis Brown's *Vidpires!*

When I walked into the lobby of Minneapolis's Southern Theater in February 1994, I found it had been transformed. What used to be a fairly generic waiting room was now a circus encampment on the edges of some unnamed Transylvanian town. The images appeared to be lifted straight from old movies that I saw when I stayed up too late watching television with my babysitter. In the back of a candlelit alcove an accordion player filled the lobby with danceable, soulful laments. A young woman tiptoed by with a candelabra, as if tentatively searching for the source of telltale bumps in the night. I got my ticket and walked in, handing my poker chip (the Southern's unique recyclable tickets) to a tall, thin, dour-looking young man in white face-paint and thick black eyeliner. In greeting, he offered me an icy cold hand, the result of, I found out later, an ice pack in his pocket. On stage, in the shallow space between a heavy curtain and the audience, a man and a woman dressed as marionettes bounced on long bungee-like cords attached to their wrists and ankles. The cords both supported and limited their movements as they bent, bounced, and floated together from on top of a small, square, black box.

The scenes I describe here constitute the preshow of Margolis Brown's 1995 production *Vidpires!*[1] *Vidpires!* was a comic, multimedia movement piece whose central characters are two vampires stuck in the perpetual boredom of today's media culture which both fuels and mocks their sentence of immortality. The preshow, particularly the human-marionette dance, set the tone for the multimedia performance to come, in which performers were both slaves to and freed by the screen. Troupe founders Kari Margolis and Tony Brown trained in mime with Etienne Decroux in France in the early 1980s and founded their company upon their return to New York in 1982. Now in their early forties, Margolis and Brown are considered "old" among dancers who commonly retire in their thirties. The intergenerational troupe, which relocated to Minneapolis in 1993, also features dancers in their early twenties as well as long-time ensemble member Stephen Geras, now in his late fifties. Like Kazuo Ohno, Margolis Brown Company plays to small, specialized, usually young-adult to middle-aged audiences schooled in dance, theater, and movement. Unlike Ohno, the troupe does not commonly address time or aging in their shows. *Vidpires!* is a compelling exception, and I include it here for the ingenious way it encourages its relatively young audiences to question the fantasies of agelessness and immortality that underlie the perpetual present that media culture seductively sells its viewers and participants.

As Nina Auerbach suggests in her 1995 *Our Vampires Ourselves,* "every age embraces the vampire it needs." Margolis Brown's video/vampires diverge considerably from their more traditional blood-sucking cohorts. Vidpires don't feed on their mortal counterparts, but keep eternally youthful by visually devouring bloodless digital and celluloid images and by transferring their own bodies from the temporal realm of the stage where, as Herbert Blau (1990, 366) tells us, the actors are dying before our eyes, to the spatial world of the screen where actors remain frozen in time. These vampires are truly addicted to television. Withdrawal would mean death.

The depth model of aging represented by Kazuo Ohno's *Water Lilies,* provides a way to see the body across time and space, through binary constructs of age, gender, and culture, without fantasizing an escape from the mortal, aging body. The body in depth performs and produces time through its social actions. It provides a way to anticipate and account for the range of changes that the body generates across the life course. This chapter turns to the ambiguous and contested lines between stage and screen representation, between "live" and "screened" bodies. Using *Vidpires!* as a point of departure, I ask if and how a depth model of the aging body can occur on screen. Is the depth model possible without a live—or, in Blau's terms, a *dying*—body? In this age of interactive video what does *live* mean? Is the depth model, which reasserts the relationship between time and space in spatial discourse, simply nostalgia for the tangibility of skin and bones in a time when skin is synthetic and bone marrow transplanted? Is it mere nostalgia for a live body that seems to be morphing into a "thing" body—just one of many homes for the fast-moving fragments of human subjectivity?

In order to address the multiple levels on which these questions resonate, I divide this chapter into several sections. The first speaks to the theoretical underpinnings of screen culture. In the second section I discuss the performance of *Vidpires!* in detail and suggest that Margolis Brown's comic interpretation of screened immortality operates as a depth model on screen and stage.

✎ There was an IV in his hand. There was a long thin tube in his nose and a piece of white tape stuck to his face in order to hold it in place. It was oxygen. Only a few hours before, he was sitting up, telling me to pick up the (nonexistent) little green birds that lay dead on the floor. Then he asked me to get him some chop suey and gave me ten bucks. Not enough oxygen to his brain said the doctor. That long thin tube would correct that now. His uncharacteristic muttering scared me and I welcomed the doctors' reassurances. The next day, when my father told me that grandpa loves chop suey and hates hospital food, that one thin ten dollar bill felt like ten pounds in my jeans pocket.

Estate Sale at the House of the Soul

Vidpires! is a series of twenty scenes including solo and twelve-member ensemble movement pieces, interactive scenes with media, and "solo" media scenes. The performance centers on Desmodus and Diphylla, two vampires enamored of each other and of their eternal youth. Desmodus and Diphylla feed on film images to perpetuate their own immortality both on and off screen. The connections between filmic and vampire immortality are overt in both preproduction publicity and in the production notes themselves. "Addicted to eternal youth, they are like the celluloid stars of the Hollywood orbit, and will never age," reads a description of the show in the Southern Theater newsletter, "After a century of sucking up a host of cinematic and other pop cultural images they fervently continue their bizarre pursuit of the meaning of love and life."

In addition to visually ingesting celluloid images, Vidpires also gain immortality by transferring their images into video, escaping the mortal body for the safety of the screen. In the opening scene Desmodus tries to wake Diphylla from her "casket," symbolized by a door lying on the floor. Lowered magically from above, a small video camera hangs temptingly before Desmodus. He takes the camera and begins to film Diphylla, the results of which are projected on a small screen onstage. Caressing his lover with the lens of the camera, translating her body onstage into live video, Desmodus succeeds in waking Diphylla. The audience watches Diphylla rise from her sleeping position on the stage floor both onstage and on a screen suspended from the ceiling that plays the live video footage.

The flexibility of life on screen is quite appealing. Like photographs, the screen captures one's image in the present and houses it, keeping it safe from what can be frightening physical and psychological changes that come with age and ultimately death. Be it television, film, or computer, the screen is a world of exterior appearances and illusion. Unlike the photograph, however, the screen is becoming increasingly interactive. You can be all you want to be on the Internet, for example, with little to no correlation to your material body. As I suggested in the previous chapter, virtual reality offers great mobility to disabled people of all ages (Featherstone 1995). Donna Haraway and the school of "cyborg" scholars that have followed her footsteps (Hables Gray 1995), find tremendous agency in the shape shifting made possible by the porous boundaries between human and machine.

My own cautiousness about celebrating the screen as a new, interactive, and potentially immortal site for human subjectivity stems from my hesitancy to encourage any further denunciation of the material body among older people whose cultural value is largely defined by their physical health. "Anti-body" talk only fuels and legitimizes fears of aging and death. My hesitancy is supported and fueled by the writings and performances of several theorists in this area. In the field of critical theory French philosopher Jean Baudrillard condemns what he sees as the race to turn human beings into objects (in this case screen images), thereby replacing *illusions* of immortality with their *real-time* counterpart, lived immortality. In his 1992 *Illusion of the End* Baudrillard writes:

> In aiming for virtual (technical) immortality and ensuring its exclusive perpetuation by a projection into artifacts, the human species is pre-

cisely losing its own immunity and specificity and becoming immortalized as an inhuman species; it is abolishing in itself the mortality of the living in favour of the immortality of the dead. (84)

The desire to get "beyond the end" of mortality, a desire Baudrillard sees as the ultimate act of human narcissism, destroys the notion of individuality. The achievement of immortality Baudrillard describes signifies (1) the obsolescence of birth, aging, and death, and (2) an end to evolution. He sees the pursuit to perfect memory by lodging it in reservoirs of computer megabytes as rendering humans incapable of memory. "Paradoxically," writes Baudrillard, "by dint of this zealous effort forcibly to bring back into the present what we no longer even remember, we live in a world which is both without memory and without forgetting" (1992, 72). The world Baudrillard describes is one of self-sameness, one in which bodies are purely objects and metaphor, illusion, memory, and in turn individuality lie in state, flattened into binary code.[2]

Where Baudrillard condemns applying technology to the pursuit of immortality, performance artist Stelarc celebrates media and medical technology's potential to liberate human beings from their material bodies. His creations range from a collaborative dance with a large robotic arm, to "suspensions," in which he is pierced by multiple fish hooks and hangs naked in a variety of settings. In his most recent performances Stelarc tests the boundaries of "the body" (his chosen label for himself), questioning longstanding, and what he sees as nostalgic, sentimental attachments to an outdated, if not broken, casement for human subjectivity. "As supposed free agents," writes Stelarc, "the capabilities of being a body are constrained by having a body" (3). Stelarc imagines a future for the human body in which organ transplants are as common as teeth cleanings, faulty limbs are as disposable as contact lenses, and cases of immortality as numerous as today's excessive displays of death in film and television. Stelarc writes:

> Death is an out-moded evolutionary strategy . . . bodies need not age or deteriorate; they would not run down nor even fatigue; they would stall then start—possessing both the potential for renewal and reactivation. In the extended space-time of extraterrestrial environments, the body must become immortal to adapt. (4)

Stelarc's performances divide and reorganize control of his body in order to make palpable the interdependent relationship between bodies and technology. In a lecture/demonstration at the University of Wisconsin–Milwaukee in 1995 Stelarc attached electrodes to his stomach through which he could control the movements of a "third hand," a robotic prosthesis attached to his right arm. In turn a computer program fed random electronic stimuli to electrodes attached to his left bicep. The jerky movements produced by the collaboration of computer and Stelarc looked more like the stuttered images of early science fiction films than his chosen label of "choreography." But the daily reality of the concepts at the core of his work—of computer-assisted shared subjectivities (e.g., "chatrooms" on the Internet) and of a post-body world of prosthetics (e.g., pacemakers)—gave his performance an eerie, haunting edge. He is far from the off-kilter doomsday prophet Virilio makes him out to be in *The Art of the Motor* (1995). Stelarc's predictions of a deathless culture, or at least a culture striving for deathlessness, already seem quite real.

In November 1995 Stelarc expanded the ideas of the lecture/demonstration model to an international performance. His body located in Luxembourg, remote computer sites across several continents were linked via modem to the electrodes controlling his arm and leg. Through use of his stomach muscles, Stelarc controlled a camera that supplied live photos sent out to the remote sites via the World Wide Web. Although proverbial technical difficulties kept the site at UW-Milwaukee from accessing Stelarc's "Stimbod" computer program (local wiring was incompatible with European systems), the still photos of the live footage of his body on the large screen of the conference-call system in the UW-Milwaukee's Business School recreated for me that haunting effect that the ideas conveyed in Stelarc's writings are already reality. The body, now virtually disposable, has very nearly achieved complete object status. The body as we have known it is near to opening its doors as the house of the "soul," and is instead becoming a mere passageway to other more permanent and mobile homes.

For Stelarc there is no difference between his screened body and his live body: "Images are no longer illusory when they become interactive" (8). In fact, one might contend that the body is best, most functional in this techno-driven, environmentally contaminated world, as its image. The body as object is prone to breakage, fixing, and manipulation. Video bodies can be touched up and restored. Humphrey Bogart and Marilyn Monroe are doing Diet Coke ads long after their deaths. Broken, mortal object/bodies, or "thing" bodies as Husserl called them, are fading from being the sole seat of subjecthood. Instead, they are taking on the shameful status of, in Heidegger's terms, "the conspicuousness of the unusable."[3]

In this relatively new field of performance and technology, performance theorist Philip Auslander forges ground similar, although not quite as extreme as Stelarc. Like Stelarc's declaration that images become real when they become interactive, Auslander asserts that live and mediated performances are no longer distinguishable. Pointing out that Broadway shows are now staged with a television, video, or film adaptation already in mind, and that rock concerts are now designed to replicate music videos, Auslander rejects what he sees as the nostalgic separation of live and mediated performance. "I would argue," writes Auslander, "that the live and the mediated exist in a relation of imbrication, not one of opposition" (1994, 1). According to this logic, such separation imagines a simpler time prior to media, and a tangible, "real," material body. Auslander writes:

> Live performance thus has become the means by which mediatized representations are naturalized, according to a simple logic that appeals to our nostalgia for what we assumed was the im-mediate: if the mediatized image can be repeated in a live setting, it must have been "real" to begin with. (1994, 2)[4]

Although I agree that live and mediated performances overlap, there are certainly distinguishable differences between them. For one, the flexibility promised by the screen, by transporting one's image through fiber optic wires or by freezing one's image in film or video, is seen to have great cultural capital.[5] It is the imbalance that bothers me. It is the imbalance that feeds fantasies of mastering time and immortality—fantasies in which the unscreened are dead and the screened, the undead.

For it seems that being embodied within technologically driven cultures has become a drag. It slows us down, trips us up on our pell-mell journey down the Autobahn toward the speed of light. Our bodies, apparently, are killing us. Within the interdependent relationship between media technology and the body, between the mechanized object and the mortal subject, a discrepancy has emerged between the value of disembodiment versus embodiment, one that continues along the track laid long ago by Cartesian philosophy. Certainly the two states are ultimately inseparable. But they are culturally rewarded as if they were. To self-objectify one's body through technological means is to have acquired knowledge and savvy of medical, economic, and electronic information systems.[6] It takes money, education, and time. Spreading one's image and actions across fiber optic wires to computer ports separated by multiple time zones, oceans, and even wars, dissolves what is left of the notion of the stable subject, yet marks that dissolving subject with a certain power of flexibility inherent in the ability to shape shift. Aging and dying, as Patricia Mellencamp suggests, may soon become the mark of poverty, as only those without health insurance or the funds to fill in the medical gaps will continue along the Darwinian path.[7]

Since the image of the body has become interactive, can it replace the mortal body in the depth model, producing time through social acts while remaining free of consequences of mortality and aging? If yes, lines between the thing body and the living body, between mediated and live performances, would be, as Phil Auslander suggests, beyond distinction (1994). In this light the relationship between live and mediated performance becomes a rich ground of slippage between living and thing body status. The subject, dissolved and disjointed, spreads itself across the air waves, becoming immortalized as it is captured on screen. Objects, now made "real" and legitimized by their likeness to the "live," are possessed by ghosts of subjecthood and take on the status of what is considered to be, and naively so according to Stelarc and Auslander, the live body.

But this does not mean that images and bodies are the same. Slippage between states of liveness and thing-ness, between subject and object, between live and mediated, between the mortal and the immortal, also produces untranslatable residue. My asking "where are the aged bodies?" or "how are aged bodies valued?" may reveal a nostalgia for a "real" that I understand to be nonexistent. But it also *uses* that nostalgia to question the contemporary elision of mortality and unusability. Rather than demonizing nostalgia, I suggest disturbing its definition. Nostalgia need not reject current complexity of embodiment in favor of a simpler time. Instead, some kinds of nostalgia can help us ask how the past and present (and future) exist in relationship to each other. As Judith Butler suggests in her theory of performativity, "discourse has a history that not only precedes but conditions its contemporary usages" (1993, 227). In this light the body in technoculture carries both its history of social relations and a potential for change. It is ensnared in the web of information that seeks to locate it, and yet is, with every performative entrance to culture, unlocatable. Mediated and newly interactive images of the body carry with them the history of their embodied counterparts. Dreams of immortality forget any value to mortality and old age, and erase the residue of translation between bodies and disembodied images, namely, as Stanley Aronowitz suggests, the human labor of producing such images (1994).

When I shook the icy cold hand of the dour vampire who greeted me at the Southern Theater, I entered a space where screened/live bodies and fantastical notions of human perfection through attempts to eliminate aging and mortality are at play in rich and complicated ways. The following section explores *Vidpires!* in more detail, adding its images to the philosophical, medical, and artistic dialogue on the contemporary status of the live body.

⁂ I brought her a silk flower, unsure about allergies or germs or other evil-doers lurking in something organic. There was an IV but nothing more. The simplicity of her body in the metal bed surprised me. "Looks like the old ticker jumped the track," said my grandmother. She had looked me gravely in the eye a few hours before and said good-bye, just in case after they stopped her heart it didn't want to start up again. "Beating like a twelve-year-old's."

Vidpires!

The Southern Theater, where *Vidpires!* premiered in Minneapolis, is a small, proscenium theater dedicated to fostering and presenting the works of experimental, interdisciplinary artists. The eighty-five-year-old theater has a partially restored proscenium whose crumbling walls echo artistic director Jeff Bartlett's mission to chip away at traditional modes of theatrical representation. Billed as a "steamy, satirical, multimedia movement theater extravaganza," *Vidpires!* drew on Margolis Brown's local following, the Southern Theater's reputation for experimental performance, and the positive advance reviews of local theater critics. Each of the eight performances played to capacity crowds of predominantly young-adult and middle-aged audiences. I saw the show twice. First intrigued by the advance publicity and the performance of *Koppelvision* I had seen the previous year, I saw it again in the second week of the run to help unpack the wealth of imagery that flowed by at break-neck pace.

Vidpires! imagines a world similar to those described by Auslan-

der, Baudrillard, and Stelarc and presents it in comedic terms. The performers symbolically inhabit the world of immortality by quoting
campy stereotypes of vampires and placing them in the context of
interdependent relationships with media technology. These vampires
are immortalized by their objectification in film, through their evolution into image and their removal from the physical, mortal world.
Simultaneously, these vampires are embodied by actors, live onstage,
images made flesh. Lines between subject/object, body/media, mortal-
ity/immortality fade, coalesce, and fade again. The excessive, comic
presentation of these complex issues had several effects for me. At
times it disappointed, abandoning the difficult act of juggling the multiple layers of representation for simpler movement or comic effects.
But mostly it challenged the complex theories and questions surrounding the status of the body in media culture, answering them with comic
excess rather than easy solutions. I will address three specific effects of
the performance, then explore its implications for a depth model of the
body/image in technoculture.

First, *Vidpires!* exemplifies Auslander's description of live performance as inseparable from mediated performance. Live bodies
onstage, live video projections, and recorded video/film projections
overlap in individual scenes, circulating and fragmenting subjectivity
between bodies and images. Several scenes played with the interdependency and inseparability of bodies and technology, symbolized in
the show by film images and video and film equipment. In one scene,
entitled "The End," a small-screen television rested on the shoulder of
a man on bended knee. The heavy black curtain behind him set the
monitor's blue hue into relief. Dressed in black, the man took on the
liminal status of a Bunraku puppeteer, visible yet invisible. On screen
appeared short clips of death scenes from films ranging from award-
winning classics to shoestring budget "spaghetti" westerns; from
wholesome heroes of the early days of film to thickly mustached street
cops of the 1970s. Some characters fell to their deaths with the sudden
ferocity of gunshots; others seemed to fade with a single, dramatic
exhalation.

With my attention drawn to the rapid and comic juxtaposition of
these scenes, at first I did not notice their relationship to the what
seemed the "lacky Atlas," clad in black, holding up the world of the
small screen. But as I tired of the repetition of the clips, I began to see a
pattern. If the character fell to the right, the lacky Atlas shifted his body

and the television to the right. If the character fell with a heavy thump to the left, the man shifted with a similar intensity in the same direction. He accompanied graceful sighing deaths with a similar, elongated, gentle shift. The duo, man and screen, entwined in a comic, elegiac dance of death.

In addition to "The End" three other scenes in *Vidpires!* stressed the relationship between the performer's body and media. In the seventh scene, entitled the "Body of Love Video," a male and female dancer stood to the right of the stage with their backs to the audience, their naked bodies washed in the hot light of a hand-held video projector—the only light on the black stage. The video was another rapid succession of looted classic film images, this time of kisses rather than death scenes. As the performers moved slowly in unison, the film images contorted to the shapes of their bodies. The kisses ranged from a stiff passionlessness to a campy ferocity, the comic effect compounded by images' distortion over the performers' curving backs and buttocks. It was as though the film images created a vocabulary for the dancers' passions and actions while simultaneously being undercut by the context in which they appeared, both in terms of editing and the human screen on which they played.

The publicity image for *Vidpires!* was taken from a scene that also illustrates the show's merger of media and performer in the guise of immortal vampires. Seated on a chair down stage, Desmodus held a small screen television on his left shoulder. On screen was the image of a violin being played in "real-life" size. His right hand resting on the corner of the television, it appeared as though Desmodus was playing the violin on the screen. The sound of a violin, although separated from the television, corroborated this illusion. The fourth and final example, "Disney Pestilence," featured a man emerging from the left wings who appeared to be pulling a heavy load as he began to cross the stage. His movements were slow and exaggerated, his progress labored. Slowly, an old cart rolled onstage behind him. The cart, almost medieval in appearance, was piled high with televisions. On the screens danced some of Disney's first renderings of Mickey Mouse, a skinny, stick-figured, happy animal with bulging eyes, bouncing up and down rapidly, continuously, and seemingly without effort. Both images, the video violin and the incessant hopping of the gleeful Mickey Mouse, juxtapose human labor with technology; the former underscores the potential of technology to multiply "beauty" and/or "art" through reproduction of images, while the latter suggests the frivolity of much modern entertainment, built of human labor.

The final scene of *Vidpires!* underscored the inseparability of live and mediated bodies while also pointing to lapses between the various states of being. Desmodus and Diphylla stood at opposite corners of the stage space, facing their own video cameras. Two video monitors were lowered from the fly space above the stage, floating above the performers, side by side, center stage. The vampires' images were projected live onto the monitors above the stage, each filling their individual monitor. Onstage, the two vampires faced different directions, but their screen images appeared to be facing each other. The stage bodies implored the camera for touch, making the screen images appear to be speaking to each other, begging for physical contact. The image was richly layered. It suggests that video images also differ from their live counterparts—that something shifts in the translation of human to image. By having the live performers and live video of those performers within a single stage picture, *Vidpires!* presents the often invisible relationship between media technology and the performers, rather than erasing or disguising the live body and participating in a fantasy of bodilessness.[8]

Vidpires! emphasizes the human, embodied element of the technological by pointing to the labor behind its production. From the "lacky Atlas" with the screen on his shoulders, to the naked, human screen, *Vidpires!* exposes the labor of producing film and video images. During scenes in which video is featured without performers, the screens were slowly and mysteriously moved forward toward the audience and back again. The movement did more than just make the two-dimensional video scenes more dynamic: it also reminded spectators that video representations are never independent of the live body.

Third, the comic presentation of vampires reasserts the value of mortality. The campy fangs, the Gomez and Morticia costumes, and the melodramatic accordion and violins playing in the background, created a larger-than-stereotype, B-movie replica of vampires and immortality (vampires, ironically, are usually characterized as being impossible to capture on film). The performers in *Vidpires!* commented on fantasies of bodilessness and yearnings for immortality by symbolically and comically inhabiting immortality through the role of vampires. By exaggerating their roles, they pointed up what Baudrillard calls the absurdity of achieving immortality in real-time,[9] simultane-

Tony Brown and Kari Margolis in Margolis Brown Company's *Vidpires!* in which media and the live collide. *(Photo by Ruby Levesque. Courtesy of Margolis Brown Co.)*

ously reestablishing norms and benefits of mortality. Examples of the excessive, comic presentation of vampires in the piece are many—including the performers' frozen facial expressions that act like a gestus of postmodern boredom. Frustrated by the meaninglessness of their immortality, and by their foiled desires for physical satisfaction, these were not happy vampires.

Several scenes reveal the enticing yet empty promises of this postmodern style immortality. Shortly after Desmodus succeeded in waking Diphylla from a dead sleep with his video camera, the two vampires tried desperately to keep their romance alive in a relationship of perpetual boredom. In this scene, titled "The 100 Year Date" and performed without media elements, Desmodus and Diphylla tried all the tricks of modern romance, only to have their props literally crumble in their hands. Desmodus courted Diphylla with flowers, but just as her face lights up, the flowers crumbled to sand. They tried feeding each

Tony Brown and Kari Margolis as video-vampires Desmodus
and Diphylla. *(Photo by Ruby Levesque. Courtesy of Margolis
Brown Co.)*

other chocolates, but as the candy neared their mouths, it dissolved in
their hands, sand running through their fingers. They tried smoking to
ease their frustration. Even the cigarettes crumbled.

In "Silent Movie Video" two screens were angled toward each
other on opposite sides of the stage. Desmodus appeared on one screen
dressed as Valentino, while Diphylla appeared on the other as Cleopa-
tra. Pleading with her for immortality, in silent movie-fashion text on
screen, Desmodus asked "If I can't live forever, what good is your
love?" Yet as the "100 Year Date" demonstrated, the immortality for
which Desmodus pleaded, now isolates them both in a world outside
of time. In effect, Margolis Brown Company re-enchant immortality in
Baudrillard's terms by returning it to the realm of illusion. Additionally, the performance gives meaning and purpose to both mortality and
aging and suggests that something *more* than the obsessive preservation of the material body as object is important to the human species.

Through its comic presentation of the immortal and its emphasis on the production of media technology, *Vidpires!* represents the complex interdependency between the body and media technology and the subsequent entanglements between mortality and immortality, "lived" and "thing" body status. While the show suggests the two states are indistinguishable, such indistinguishability does not demand the erasure of either the value of embodiment or our ability to address it. The mortal cannot get lost in the current love affair with the screened body in technoculture. To emphasize the live is not to reject the interdependence of the live/mediated, the living body/thing body, but to acknowledge and expose the human labor behind media technology. It is to reassert the value of embodiment, aging and mortality in a world eager to forget it.

The living (and dying) body is an important reminder of modes of production so easily disguised in electronic technology. But its presence does not always thwart efforts to pretend agelessness, as live bodies can also participate in the fantasy by erasing age, and older bodies can appear in contexts that further deplete their scant cultural value.[10] My reading of *Vidpires!* does not seek to establish a "nostalgic" vision of pure body somehow separable from technology, nor do I suggest that technology is somehow outside of time. Rather, I find that presentation of *excess* of the stage body (inseparable from technology) through the embodiment of a feigned immortality in both the use of video/film and the image of the vampire, uses nostalgia to demonstrate the importance of interrupting the amnesia that seems to beset consumers of virtual reality, remote control televisions, and film. It reminds us that we have a body parked at the terminal, on the couch, or the Milk Dud–encrusted movie house seat—a body that is aging and that will die. *Vidpires!* reminds us that the value of that aging body is its very mortality.

As *Vidpires!* demonstrates, the depth model can and does exist on screen. It not only imagines the body across time, but also across states of media/being. The depth model of the body should include the potential interactive images of the body, as well as the body's artifacts that trigger memories of its flesh-bound state. The depth model then is not at odds with media culture, but demands that the mortal, aging aspects of the subject not be forgotten in the celebration of its dissolution and expansion. Such a model enables us to address the body, liveness, and mortality without being excused as nostalgic or Luddite. It would have enabled Stelarc a way to push the boundaries of "the body" and come to terms with the polyp in this stomach that cameras found while he was performing an internal sculpture by resisting the gag-reflex and swallowing a tiny camera. It would have enabled Timothy Leary to fully explore the ironies of his recounting the options for immortality he outlines in *Chaos and Cyber Culture* while being diagnosed with prostate cancer.[11] It would enable us to address the complexity of corporeality and mortality without the shameful stigma of the "unusable."

I am at the nursing home for my weekly hour of "storytime" with a handful of the more cognitively with-it residents on the Alzheimer's wing. There are a dozen long, mock-wooden tables set in orderly parallel lines throughout the room, the kind on which I used to eat my brown bag lunches in seventh grade. A piercing alarm sounds every few minutes, set off by an electronic ankle bracelet whenever a resident wanders too near the elevator or door. Residents sit at their designated spaces at the tables. Some catch my eye and hold it. Some are slumped forward, their chins to their chest, sleeping. I gather up my story-tellers and we begin with the same introduction I give each week, the same one that will be forgotten only moments after I repeat it. As they share their interpretations of the picture I bring in this week, I relish their laughter and the brightness behind their eyes, a brightness that feels so fragile in this land that most consider to be the realm of the undead.

8

Dolly Descending a Staircase: Stardom, Age, and Gender in Times Square

It was a cold, bright November day as I walked up Broadway toward Times Square with my ticket in hand to the sold-out production of *Hello, Dolly!* with Carol Channing. As I walked the city, I had an inexplicable feeling that I was making a pilgrimage to the source. In my research over the past five years on performing groups composed of older adults, I've witnessed theater's transformative powers for those people our society believes to be beyond growth or change. There was the group of three women in their eighties doing tone poems with modern dance choreography. There was the one hundred–member vaudeville revue with a cancan–tap dance line of women in their seventies and eighties. And there was the tentative first steps into theater for many of a thirteen-women troupe, who, with script firmly in hand, shared their stories with an audience of severely developmentally disabled adults. With the exception of the vaudeville troupes, audiences for senior performances are usually fairly small, and their exposure limited to their immediate and largely supportive communities. They voice anxieties over memorization and falling onstage as commonly as they share their fierce pride and dedication to their craft. In many cases I have gone from observer to friend, enriched by the models my older friends provide for coping with fears and uncertainties about aging.

My pilgrimage to *Dolly* was born of a curiosity over the limits of the community-based model of senior theater. Would this model's transformative effects for actor and audience alike dissolve if their audiences grew? What if, for example, the Grandparents Living Theatre's *I Was Young, Now I'm Wonderful* played Broadway?[1] How is old age shaped in a performance on the level of international stardom? Is such stardom something that my community-based friends might benefit from in some way? Or does stardom, like Margolis Brown's *Vidpires!* suggests, somehow catapult a performer beyond the mundane realm of the mortal to the realm of the timeless and ageless? Can an aged star act as role model for those who face, or will face, the challenges of aging in a culture in love with ideals of youthfulness, and particularly for older performers who internalize those ideals and who doubt their abilities to memorize or to withstand the physical exertion of a three-hour show for days, even months, on end?

Seventy-four in 1995, Channing was the toast of the town. Reviews, interviews, and advertisements had set the scene. I expect jokes encrusted in glitz. I expect wrinkles, wobbles, and grace. I expect sentimentality and spectacle. It is Broadway after all. Before the show, I paused outside the theater to take in the scene. Broadway opened up into the triangular advertisers' battlefield that is Times Square. Flashing lights and enormous billboards vied for two seconds of a consumer's glance. Among them, a sliver of an adolescent waif pouted in her Calvins kitty-corner to a nearly naked, Barbie-legged woman lounging like so much fruit cocktail in a champagne glass. Helen Hunt and Paul Reiser, then television's current favorite happy yuppie couple, smiled down from a five-story, vertical banner. On that cold November afternoon, Times Square was fast, young, gorgeous, and white.[2] At least on the billboards. The consumers in the square—a rich blend of age, color, language, and gender—were worlds away from their two-dimensional counterparts.

A red banner tethered across the width of the Lunt-Fontanne theater welcomes Carol Channing back home to Broadway. Elsewhere in New York on that day, women in their fifties, sixties, and seventies were reigning over the New York theater scene. A few blocks away Betty Buckley starred in *Sunset Boulevard;* Zoe Caldwell in the *Master Class;* and Carol Burnett in *Moon over Buffalo.* Across the street at the Marriot Marquis, Julie Andrews played *Victor/Victoria.* Down in the village, Uta Hagen played psychoanalyst Melanie Klein. *Having Our Say,* the story of the real-life centenarian Delany sisters, was finishing its Broadway run and preparing for its national tour. Essayists and

Calvins and fruit cocktail in Times Square. *(Photo by Brad Lichtenstein.)*

reporters had picked up on the trend that countered the youthful face of Times Square. *Newsweek* columnist Jack Kroll attributed the return of the "divas" to a burgeoning gay culture (1995a).[3] Invoking Wayne Koestenbaum, author of *The Queen's Throat*, Kroll suggested that the reemergence of divas on Broadway is a sign of maturity in American theater, not a sign of senility. This is certainly a good thing. But older actresses are surely more than signs for consumption by gay male spectators. Critic John Simon suggested that the trend is predicated on rebuilding the reputation of Broadway. In a moment of bald boosterism Simon happily proclaimed that Andrews and Channing are "still the grandest grandes dames on Broadway." Ironically, Kroll made no mention of the potential for an interest in aging as a cause for the appearance of older actresses. Nor did Simon take interest in the accomplishments of the male costars of Channing and Andrews. The appearance of older male actors on Broadway, it seems, is common enough to be unremarkable.

Still a grande dame of Broadway. As I took my seat in the last row at orchestra-level, I realized that I didn't have the slightest idea what this meant. Never a fan of the American musical, I was not yet born when Channing debuted *Dolly* in 1964. From a bleary-eyed late night screening of *Thoroughly Modern Millie*, I barely remembered a hazy image of her. Instead, I more vividly remembered an imitation of Channing done in drag at the Baton Club in Chicago a few years back. Recently I had seen her on an entertainment news show. But, to be honest, I didn't understand why she was considered news, and feared she was being paraded, like Bob Hope and George Burns, as remnants of an era gone by. Like many of my generation, the glory days of Broadway are empty rooms in my memory. As with *Phantom* or *Les Mis*, today it is the show, not the star, that rises to catch the public eye.

My brief moment of reflection was broken by the growing intensity of the stage lights. The heavy curtain swung open and Channing floated onstage with the momentum of the ensemble. I craned my neck left and right, bobbing around the sea of craning, bobbing necks in front of me. My thirty-year-old eyes locked on her seventy-four-year-old body as Channing took the stage as a character she has played more than forty-five hundred times. Three rows up, a man who looked to me as if he were in his seventies rose to his feet and loudly, unapologetically applauded her entrance, leaving the audience, including myself, a bit stunned. I had expected a courageous display of wrinkles. I had expected sentimentality. What I had not expected was the audience's frenzied approval of Channing's morphed body in what seemed a confusing display of yesterday and today—a face fallen and lifted, a body hidden and revealed, time frozen and flowing. I had made a pilgrimage to—and was participating in—a theatricalized display of Channing's simultaneously aged and un-aged body. As Someone who works with older adults, often much older than Channing's "youthful" seventy-four years, I was saddened by the "inspirational" vision of old age that the performance celebrated. Channing provided a symbolic alternative to what Margaret Gullette has called the "decline narrative" of old age. But Channing was also frighteningly static. Having repeated this role over forty-five hundred times, she was stuck playing a symbol of the past in a revival that obsessively isolated her age. This chapter explores *Hello, Dolly!*'s spectacle of old age, the basis of stardom for older women who act onstage, and my own questions as a much younger spectator.

Give Me Stardom or Give Me Death?

Channing KO's Mortality.   —Jack Kroll, *Newsweek*

The cultural event of the 1994 national tour and the 1995 Broadway production of *Hello, Dolly!* generates conflicting images of older women, and echoes the shifting and contradictory status of older women in American culture today. Despite consistent living proof to the contrary, the narrative of aging as decline remains stubbornly persistent. This latest incarnation of Dolly Levi, a collaborative creation of Channing, the director of the production, the audience, and reviewers, soothes anxieties over individual journeys into old age. It eases concerns over the economic challenges marked by the coming of an aging society, one populated mainly by older women, by displaying the discipline and control of an older woman's body in a theatrical venue—a site that trembles with the unpredictability of live performance, and that, as Herbert Blau writes, "stinks of mortality" (1982, 83). To celebrate Dolly as spectacle, as the current Broadway tradition of peppering performances with standing ovations encourages the audience to do, is for all generations to celebrate their distance from the cultural marker of "seventy-four." Yet even as *Dolly!* assuages anxieties about aging, it also marks a dangerous and unruly freedom that aging can bring.

The anxieties over aging quelled by Channing's 1994–95 Dolly manifest themselves not only in terms of individual aging, but also in worries over the "aging" of Broadway. Laments over Broadway's narrative of decline are voiced in concerns over the unique status of theater stars as "authentic" in the age of multimedia pretenders. The yearning for authenticity here is a coded yearning for the seeming *realness* of youth. In Channing's case this is middle age, since she debuted Dolly at age forty-three, at time when talent/role/star merged.[4] Aging is imagined as mere repetition of that role, further and further from the moment of its utterance. The time trickery of repeating the same role over forty-five hundred times gives history an almost overwhelming stickiness, one that mirrors and feeds notions that people in their later years are merely distillations of their former selves, incapable of change or growth.[5] Because Channing has played the same role so many times, she is in a way the ultimate test of performativity theories such as

Michel de Certeau's and Judith Butler's. Reading the slippages of such an extreme example—Channing's use of her mask of a mask, and the newness that her age brings to the role—powerfully demonstrates the performative nature of the self across the life course, and call into question romanticized notions of a stable, former, and most importantly, youthful, self.

From its premiere in 1964 and reopening on Broadway in October 1995, *Hello, Dolly!* has always been a show that knows it is a show. *Dolly* is no mirror held up to nature. It proclaims no urgent political message. For someone drawn to the gritty side of theater *Dolly* is almost unbearably cheery. Its plot, based on Thorton Wilder's *Matchmaker*, turns on the manipulations of the charismatic widow Dolly Gallagher Levi, whose chutzpah is fueled by her strapped financial straits. Dolly can do anything it seems, but her forte is arranging marriages. By play's end, she has contrived several pairs: herself with stodgy, wealthy, Yonkers "dry goods" dealer Horace Vandergelder; his young niece Ermagarde with struggling artist Ambrose Kemper; and Vandgergelder's enterprising head clerk Cornelius Hackl with the lovely Irene Molloy, owner of a hat shop. Set in turn-of-the-century New York, the costumes, painted flats, and set pieces attempt neither realism nor meaningful symbolism. In the first scene a carriage rolls onstage drawn by two actors in a stiffly crafted horse costume, vaudeville style. In scene 4 the ensemble sings "Put on Your Sunday Clothes," dancing about the Yonkers' train platform in blinding, Day-Glo turn-of-the-century costumes, complete with matching chartreuse, magenta, or electric blue parasols. This is wink wink nudge nudge American musical comedy, aiming solely for entertainment through larger than life depictions of people and a time that certainly never were. Hirschfeld's now famous caricature of Channing as Dolly, one that was plastered over playbills, posters, sweatshirts, coffee mugs, and souvenir programs at the stand in the back of the Lunt-Fontanne in 1995, is more than just a handy logo. It perfectly captures the pencil thin lines of the show's plot and the director's vision.

Like *Gentlemen Prefer Blondes*, which propelled Channing to star status in 1950, *Hello, Dolly!* is a star vehicle whose plot and supporting roles are simply the trimmings on an elaborate costume designed for the title character. Winning ten Tony awards, the original *Dolly* played for nearly seven years on Broadway. Publicity for the show that opened in 1995 refers to a January 1950 *Time* magazine cover story on Channing's depiction of Lorelei Lee in *Gentlemen Prefer Blondes:* "On Broadway, an authentic new star is almost as rare a phenomenon as it is in the heavens. Perhaps once a decade, a nova explodes above the Great White way with enough brilliance to reillumine the whole gaudy legend of show business." It is this "authentic" Broadway star status that the 1995 production aims to replicate, an authenticity that reviewers both worry over and celebrate amidst the current wave of doomsday predictions for the death of Broadway. The structure and star status of Broadway shows have shifted since 1950, from an emphasis on star vehicles toward ensemble shows and pop operas like *Les Miserables* and *Phantom of the Opera*. In a January 1996 *New York Times* essay entitled "Quick, Name a Hot New Musical Star," Ethan Mordden first laments the lack of young stage stars today, then asks: "Do tourists really care who's playing Jean Valjean this week?" The answer is no, but they used to, that live theater with no retakes or editing, was the proving ground for "real" acting talent, and remains, as Barry King suggest, "the yardstick against which to evaluate acting on screen" (167).[6]

Of the older women on Broadway this past season, Channing is the ideal representative of this authentic stage star status. Unlike Julie Andrews and Carol Burnett, Channing's star status is largely contingent on two roles she created onstage over thirty years ago, even though she has appeared in some films and on several television variety show specials.[7] Channing has publicly mourned this fact, sharing her heartbreak when she was passed over for the film versions of both her famous roles. Marilyn Monroe came to the theater every night for three weeks to study Channing's Lorelei Lee, and Barbra Streisand took Dolly to the screen. The *Philadelphia Inquirer* quoted Channing on her reaction to discovering that the part had been given to Streisand: "I called up and said 'Is that true?' And everybody said yes. And I thought: 'All I have to do is open this window and jump out, and the pain will be gone. It will end it. You can take that sickness for just so long. Cancer is better. I mean, I can tell you—I've had it." (Klein 1995).

The 1995 production of *Dolly* along with the reviews of it recreate Channing as an authentic theater star in several ways. First, reviews and essays on Channing repeatedly pointed to her unique status as a star of the stage. Jack Kroll described her variously as "one of those pure theater animals without whom there would be no theater at all" (1995b), and "the most indomitable theater animal in our history" (1995a). Octavio Roca of the *San Francisco Chronicle* wrote: "She belongs to the stage. Dolly's back, Channing's home, and the American musical is alive and beautiful." The production itself reestablished Channing's stardom by almost completely replicating the original show. Original costumes, blocking, set design, songs, and choreography, were all recreated here—and all were under the supervision of the original composer, Jerry Herman, and the direction of Lee Roy Reams, an actor who played Cornelius Hackl to one of Channing's early Dolly's.[8] Promotional materials proclaimed: "This 1995 *Hello, Dolly!* recreates all the Tony award winning elements. The show features new sets and costumes—based on the award-winning designs—along with [Gower] Champion's inventive direction and choreography."[9] Everything is the same it seems, except Channing is older. By replicating the original, the *Dolly* of 1995 isolated Channing's age as *the* difference between the first production and the new run, and *the* challenge to her stardom. Will she fall? Will she look old? Will her voice crack? If the answers are no, Channing emerges a star. Enabled by her face lifts and "well preserved body" (which the reviews told us is due largely to a medically prescribed diet shaped by food allergies), Channing is an inspirational exception to an old age of decline. She promises us that with the right care and surgery, we too can stave off time and walk into old age with energy and vigor. This "inspirational" model is clearly a large part of the show's success and the audience's, myself included, generosity with standing ovations. But at what price inspiration?

For women, whom American culture ages socially more quickly than men (Woodward 1994), passing as a star has increased pressures. To prove stardom, older women have two primary choices: either play an older woman star lamenting the loss of stardom, or deny your age. In this regard the 1995–96 New York theater season was typical. In *Master Class* Zoe Caldwell played Maria Callas at the end of her career, sharing stories of her golden past. In long monologues from which spill memories of her fame Caldwell/Callas refers to herself in a distanced third person. In *Moon over Buffalo* Carol Burnett played Charlotte Hay, a would-be diva of second-string touring productions of standard comedy classics. In the course of the play her alcoholic acting partner and husband is offered a long dreamed of and too late chance at stardom as a last minute stand-in in a Frank Capra film. *Sunset Boulevard's* Norma Desmond (Betty Buckley) is arguably one of the most infamous theatrical has-beens, an actress particularly condemned for trying to play younger roles. If an older actress chooses to deny her age rather than

lament missed opportunities or the loss of stardom, she must not only
disguise the marks of age, but must also recreate the essence of youthful femininity which was, in many cases, the foundation of her stardom
in the first place. Culturally, the older star's successful masquerade of
youthful femininity functions to ease anxieties about the potential
unruliness and economic drain of growing numbers of postmenopausal women freed from restrictive social roles and fallen away
from standards of beauty set by young women.[10]

Amidst attempts to visually replicate the original, this latest incarnation of Dolly also differed from the original to offset Channing's age.
Dolly is sexier now, as Channing was quick to point out in interviews.[11]
Still, the triumph of the show and the proof of Channing's stardom, rest
in the negation of change. Does establishing the sexiness of an older
woman create Dolly as a feminist icon? Or does the production recon-
struct a certain type of femininity in order to re-root the older woman
into premenopausal systems of value? Vincent Canby's comment was
perhaps the most blatant in revealing the pressures on Channing to
perform youthful, or premenopausal, femininity. "Unlike some other
actresses of a certain age and unmistakable clout," Canby wrote, "Ms.
Channing remains utterly, almost naively feminine, even as she is rear-
ranging the universe. Celebrate her." Channing's display of (hetero)
sexuality proves her feminine in a way that could be, and was, taken for
granted during the 1960s, when she adopted the role of clown and
eschewed the role of "sex symbol." But cultural anxieties around aging
demand a shift away from her clownish stardom of the 1960s when she
rejected her femininity from within it. In 1995, in a woman's body no
longer culturally marked as feminine, Channing must first perform
femininity before she can spin away from it.

To assist Channing in her illusion of stasis and her rebirth as
feminine supernova, old age was exaggerated in both the reviews
and in the show itself. Indeed several reviews bordered on ageism.
Tom Shales wrote: "If Channing were the worse for wear, tottering or
enfeebled, the current revival of *Hello, Dolly!* would, of course, not be
the immense rewarding experience that it is." Pamela Sommers of
the *Washington Post* wrote: "If you are wincing as you conjure up a
wizened, enfeebled Channing tottering down the celebrated stair-
way, desperately trying to breathe life into the role of matchmaker
Dolly Levi, you couldn't be more mistaken."[12] In another particularly
brutal description, Kroll wrote, "If *Hello, Dolly!* were a title fight, the

septuagenarian Channing wouldn't be sanctioned by any athletic commission" (1995a). Like the Geritol Frolics parodies "Everything Hangs Seven Inches Lower" and "Nobody Loves a Fairy When She's Fifty," Shales and Sommers exaggerate stereotypes of old age in order to recuperate a space for Channing.

Several moments within the 1995 production itself also hyperbolize old age as enfeebling, allowing the contrast between imagined decay and Channing's disciplined body to create an "ageless performance" and a triumph over time. In the final scene of the first act Dolly, a long-time widow, stands before the dry goods store of her dearly departed husband. At the rear of the stage, an older woman—gray-haired and stooped as she pushes a cart—recognizes Dolly and asks after her. Even from my seat in the last row I could see the makeup that denoted lines of age and pale skin, an effect that exaggerates old age and separated Channing from that image of decay, even though Channing is as old as, if not older than, the character at the back of the stage. As the scene progresses, Dolly closes the book on her past with Ephraim and rejects this phantom of her future embodied by the ghostly older woman at the rear of the stage. Before "the parade passes her by," Dolly turns to a life of love, companionship, and mainly financial support by setting her sights firmly on her marriage to Horace Vandergelder.[13]

Another telling instance of the use of exaggerated age makeup occurs in the courtroom scene in the second act, in which a wizened judge attempts to sort out the facts behind the arrests of the previous scene's revelers at the Harmonia Gardens. The actor, wearing a comically large false nose and gray wig, feigns a wobbly voice and weak-backed posture. Like the phantom older woman, the hyperbolized representation of the judge as old distances Channing/Dolly from old age, and helps reinforce her ageless star status.

My point is that Channing's performance is no longer just about the antics of matchmaker Dolly Levi anymore. In 1964, when Channing was forty-three, Dolly was in part a model of an independent, strong, middle-aged woman.[14] In 1994–95 the successful masking of Channing's seventy-four years assures audiences that the authenticity of stage stars is still in tact and that old age among women can be controlled. Such masking also invites viewers to recreate their own idealized youth, something several reviewers do, and do with abandon. Vincent Canby, for example, found himself reduced to self-proclaimed "goon" status: "There I sat with some embarrassment as if chemically stimulated: helpless with pleasure and turned into a goon, wearing a dopey, ear-to-ear grin from the moment of her entrance through her pricelessly delivered remarks at the curtain call." (1995) Similarly, Ken Mandelbaum wrote: "There's little sense in feigning objectivity here—I was touched by the proceedings, marveling at the fact that something that was such a part of my youth was again available and still grand" (1995). The happy journey Canby and Mandelbaum describe fixes what was undoubtedly a time of turmoil (the mid-1960s) as "grand" youth, the departure from which can only lead to a frightening decrepitude—both in the metaphor of the lifelessness of Broadway, and in a personal narrative of decline.

But was there such a time? When stars were stars. When talent was somehow real—displayed and believed. From my generational location, I can not imagine a time like this. I can not journey back to the grandness of authenticity. I saw sweet, trouble-making, red-headed Danny Partridge become drug-addicted, bitter Danny Bonaducci, only to be re-born on national television as optimistic, seasoned-with-hindsight, talk show host—*Danny!* I knew, and could not have cared less about, the sham of Milli Vanilli before the powers that be started talking about what a disgrace they were and took away their little award. I was not yet born when Channing debuted Dolly. Perhaps I've read too much Baudrillard. I sat in the audience earnestly mystified each time the older man three rows up from me would clap, heavy, lumbering, echoing claps, and shout "Yes!" or "Bravo!" The nostalgic aspect of *Dolly,* in other words, flew high over my head, leaving me wondering what it was this man saw, what it was he remembered. Had he seen Channing's debut thirty years ago? Had he witnessed its original fluffy optimism during a time of civil unrest, and felt comforted by the return of a symbol of that star power? Had he known Channing to be on Nixon's hate list? Had he seen the revivals in the 1970s when Channing was playing merely her three thousandth show? Had he seen Ethel Merman or Pearl Baily or Mary Martin play Dolly on Broadway, women whose talent reportedly outshone the machinations of the star industry?[15]

Some reviewers suggested that the production might be most effective for those who saw the original show, but the audience that stood and cheered was clearly intergenerational. Additionally, the view that reading Dolly as a happy journey back to the days of authenticity is solely generationally based overlooks older audience members who might not assume theater to be an authenticating machine, or who might not subscribe to the "inspirational" model of Channing's attempts to erase age. What might the alternatives be? If the weight of authenticity and the burden of resurrecting an idealized individual and communal past are removed from stardom; if stage stardom is no longer predicated on the erasure and control of old age, what is left?

The Danger of Change

> World Beware: It's possible this woman is a substance that
> should be legally controlled.   —Vincent Canby, *New York Times*

Judith Butler's influential theories of performativity make a case for the coexistence of the momentum of history with disruptiveness of the present. In this light, then, a body carries both its history of social relations and a potential for change.[16] It is ensnared in history that seeks to isolate and freeze it, and yet with every performative entrance to culture, it is also unlocatable. In 1995 Channing parades across a set design from 1964 in a costume from 1964. What emerged for me in the performance was not just the elaborate attempts to create stasis by conjuring up an authentic, youthful, stage star. In fact, the time trickery in *Dolly* was fairly easily dissolved. If Penn and Teller had the chance, they might simply explain that Channing has excellent health care and a fabulous plastic surgeon. But Channing beat them to it, several times. While Channing's performance erases the physical evidence of aging in order to celebrate it, the performance also points to the differences of the present by marking her mask, and in turn, marking the performative aspect of *all phases* of the life course.[17]

Channing creates a *gestus*, a particularly loaded single image that accentuates the separation of the mask of stasis from her changing body and her craft as an actor. The scene is the Harmonia Gardens restaurant and dance hall. Dolly has finally cleared the field of suitors and sits to dine with Horace Vandergelder. Famished, she attacks her meal with ferocity. Clad in a long, red-sequined gown, Channing wears a choker with rhinestones around her neck, and white gloves that scale the length of her arms, nearly all the way up to the armpits. When she turns to eat, Channing takes off the gloves. The skin beneath her arms hangs loose, revealing her age in a way that up until this point had been nearly completely concealed. This moment of discovery is one Channing exploits. Cutting her food vigorously (Dolly has a voracious appetite), Channing wobbles the loose skin under her arms in a furious comic rhythm. The audience roared. Channing tells the joke and it is on her—and in turn on us. The punch line is the uncontrollability of aging, the control of which was the very thing the show set us up to desire. This moment of revealing comic excess, challenges and rewrites the star pact by making hypervisible the mortal, aging body. It may have been a slip, it may not. Regardless of whether the moment was planned, Channing presents of the contradictory images of fallen arms and lifted face and unsticks old age from being read solely as rigidity and stasis.

Channing's mask—her blond wig, her Cheshire Cat smile, and her enormous eyes—also acts as a *gestus*. Her features are wider now with plastic surgery. The blonde wig, somehow believable at forty-three, is anachronistic at seventy-four. Our knowledge of Channing's age and the differences in her body then and now that the mask does not hide, serves to make the mask appear more stylized than before. It has become a mask of a mask. Tellingly, reviewers likened the 1994–95 production to Japanese Kabuki and Greek comedy.[18] One reviewer likened her to Rushmore and to Galatea (Stern). In terms of acting techniques the younger Channing's mask could be naturalized and accepted as real. But at seventy-four, culturally defined as outside of femininity, her mask is "unnatural" and her clowning takes on a sense of danger. If one reads Channing's stardom as contingent on her remaining unchanged and her erasure of age, her clowning and mask of femininity prove her faded. If one reads her present and past in concert, *her mask of a mask* also becomes a mockery of the femininity that, being within it, was safer to parody in 1964.

Channing in 1964 (or 1974 or 1984) was no more Dolly Levi than she was in 1995 when I saw her perform. But naturalism in American acting onstage and screen is pervasive, and youthfulness is generally assumed to be *the* place to get off and linger as long as possible on the journey of life. Channing's early representations of Dolly are therefore assumed to equate Channing (Dolly) and youthfulness. Old age, the time when we suddenly *see* the writing of temporality on the body, is thought to be a mask of the former youthful self, automatically removing the possibility of naturalism in performance. "A garish exaggerated mask," writes Patricia Mellencamp, "hovers over as a reminder that we

want to be someone we no longer are" (1992, 293). Channing's clowning with/of her exaggerated mask mark both the earnestness and the
folly of such yearnings, making visible the mask of youthfulness and
the performative, temporal quality of the self *at every age.*

Performativity, the idea that one performs one's self across the
whole life course, can potentially open a space for the older performers
developing their crafts to hope for, even achieve the recognition they
deserve without adopting roles that lament the loss of stardom or erase
their age. Older adults can be and are both talented performers and
valuable social actors. Performance critic and theorist Janelle Reinelt,
however, astutely cautions against embracing performativity as an
inherently subversive social act, and I agree. It is, of course, not just *that*
we act, but *how* we act. *Hello, Dolly!* was and remains a celebration of
predominantly white, middle-class values. *Dolly* celebrates the love-
less, financially convenient marriage of a galvanizing, independent
widow to a grouchy, provincial, sexist (or, at best, simply misguided)
dry goods dealer.[19] The dangerous newness in Channing's performance that Canby ironically suggests might need to be legally controlled, also speaks a certain flexibility that her whiteness and economic
status allow. Still, in matters of age, recognizing the performances of
older adults as more than mere shadows of former selves, and as destabilizing youth as a privileged seat of subjecthood, no matter how fragmented, is a crucial first step.

Dolly Descending a Staircase

The tension is building. I've never seen *Hello, Dolly!* before, but even I
know what's coming: the triumphant descent. Back where she belongs.
The inverse of the decline narrative of aging. Like Duchamp's scan-
dalous 1911 painting *Nude Descending a Staircase,* Channing is both static and in motion. The young, handsome, all-male wait staff of the Harmonia Gardens restaurant has just completed its dance. The staircase
stands center stage. Long, narrow, empty—waiting.

It is nearly time. Dolly appears through the curtains at the top of
the stair. The red-sequined gown. The rhinestone and black velvet
choker. The long white gloves. Exactly the same as the photographs of
the 1964 opening I poured over at the New York Public Library of the
Performing Arts. Exactly the same as the publicity shots from 1978
when none of the review highlights used the word "still." She seems

Channing on the steep and narrow staircase. (*Photo by Joan Marcus.*)

exactly the same. The orchestra begins the first few bars and I'm surprised that I know the song. Despite my ignorance of musicals, this song has seeped into my memory, my history, my very being.

Well, hello, Dolly.

She places a foot on the first step. The 1964 photos. Statuesque height, blonde curls, wide smile, runway model thin. Exactly the same. She takes another step.

Yes, hello, Dolly.

Her foot wobbles just a bit. I suddenly become aware of how steep the stairs are and imagine the worst. I play the disastrous tumble over and over like a film loop in my mind. Her smile and outreached hands are like hardened concrete as she steadies herself. She takes yet another step.

It's so nice to have you back where you belong.

Led by the older man three rows ahead of me, spectators of all ages begin to rise to their feet, clapping. He shouts "Bravo! Bravo!" so force-fully that I laugh out loud as I stand and clap along, caught up in the swell of giddy enthusiasm. As I clap, I notice the backs of my hands, blue veins beginning to rise from smooth skin. I see her difference. I see my changing body and apparitions of changes yet to come. She steps again. Her gown is heavy, and extra material drapes around her feet. I'm worried, and watch them intensely. Her shoulders are bent slightly forward now, arms still reaching out; she seems to be embracing the crowd, who cheer and encourage her progress.

You're looking swell Dolly.

She's nearing the bottom of the stairs now and the tension releases. The waiters gaze up at her adoringly. Her confidence and charisma are comforting. The audience still stands, expressing what feels a complex gratitude. For the mask *and* for the reveal. The still-ness *and* the new-ness. Set against the trompe l'oeil painted flats, Channing's Dolly steps down a precariously narrow staircase, entering a moment of radically contradictory and shifting images and meanings of old age—of inter-nalized hatred of one's mirror image, and of embracing the freedoms that falling out of social roles can bring.

The lights come up. "I am sorry, she has had at least seventeen facelifts," said a middle-aged woman scornfully. "She is not a day under eighty-five" said another. "I think she's doing okay for an old girl," said a man who appeared to be in his sixties. This age-talk shows both the instability of these categories (old age, middle age, youth, etc.) and the lingering biases against the visibility of time on the body, par-ticularly for older women.

As I walked out, and back into the advertiser's battlefield of Times Square, I looked up at Kate Moss in her Calvins. With eyes freshly trained to see the performance of and passage of time, I try to imagine her at seventy-four. I feel a strange relief. Moss, who is the other extreme of Channing's mask, is aging too. The intergenerational audi-ence and the performance's hyperbolic attempts at stasis have given me as assurance of the certainty of change. Channing's mask, her wobble, her sexuality, are also glimmers that she has changed and that staying the same is really quite frightening. We shouldn't want it. Will the ground broken by the slight wobbles and the courage of Channing and Lee Roy Reams be enough? Coupled with the huge demographic changes to come, it is my hope that this and subsequent appearances of older women performers will lessen the pressure of stardom—the pressure not to visibly age. Ideally, they will make it okay for Moss to appear on this same billboard forty years from now with breasts and cheeks no longer taut—but beautiful. Hopefully, this will become the standard of beauty, and, rather than the 1996 Times Square billboard of a perfectly healthy, young model with her shirt open advertising for breast cancer research, there might be an image of a sixty-year-old model with one breast.[20]

9

Conclusion

The end surprised me. I imagine it always does. After all, until you get to the end itself, all thinking about the end, all its imaginings, are just that—imaginings. Several things surprised me. The memory sections I had carefully separated from the text in italics, setting them apart to underscore both my location as a relatively young woman and the important connections between memory and aging, rejoined the body of the last chapter. The point had been made with segregation. Integration now felt key.

The necessity for integration was driven home by my growing realization that the oldest and frailest old are too often forgotten in the efforts to redefine aging. Senior theater groups largely represent the "healthy" aged. They commonly avoid nursing home audiences as being "too depressing" for the performers. This is understandable for professionally oriented groups whose success turns on an audience's display of enthusiasm. But it also means that the transformative powers of performance are rarely tested on or by the frail old. Additionally, in the growing field of research in age studies in the humanities, the focus is primarily on the young and middle-aged. On the larger cultural scene the United States is experiencing shifts in social roles among the aged, from growing numbers of grandparents raising grandchildren to continued employment or the return to educational institutions. Yet these exciting shifts, largely due to improvements in health and extensions of life expectancy, seem to stop at the doors of the frail elderly, the oldest old. Those not lucky enough to be counted among the young-old, or the healthy aged, remain segregated from the rest of society. Except when they are paraded as the variously inspirational and/or tragic results of medical prolongevity efforts, the oldest old are tucked away into the corners of cultural consciousness. They are the embarrassing evidence of the shallowness of this country's romance with youthfulness and the conflation of youth with productivity and progress. They muddle gerontologists' efforts to separate aging from illness. In an effort to break down this spatial separation in my own life, I renewed my volunteer work at a long-term care facility. Throughout the year of writing this book, I tried to put some of my thoughts about performance into action with a population that seemed most in need of the possibilities of *becoming* that theater has to offer.

Others have gone this way before me and provided valuable models. Helen Kivnick assembled hours of interviews with older men and women considered role models by friends and relatives—role models for aging who happen to be living in nursing homes. Arthur Strimling of Roots & Branches Theater set up an arts program for Alzheimer's patients when the disease was first coming into common medical parlance in the late 1970s and early 1980s. Experiments by drama therapy and creative drama pioneers—including Thurman and Piggins (1982), McDonough (1981, 1994), Clark (1985), Weisberg and Wilder (1986), and Cattanach (1992)—have yielded a wealth of exercises designed specifically for or adaptable to the frail elderly. I arrived at the Marian Franciscan Care Center in Milwaukee well intentioned and armed with lists of dramatic exercises.

My initial visit stunned me back into reality. Overmedication, near complete physical dependency, the stinging smells of urine and illness; this was the stuff that fueled the nightmarish images of old age. This was the stuff that made sense of both Kevorkian and of radical medical measures to alleviate suffering in/of deep old age. My emotional reflexes kicked high and hard. *Preserve health. End suffering and loneliness. Avoid this prolonged suffering at all costs—personal and societal.* Gut reactions come fast. Answers, if there are any at all, are much, much slower.

I don't know exactly why I stayed. It was fear of letting down my second cousin, who worked as a music therapist in the same complex. It was fascination with and respect for how these many orderlies, these many residents, these many nurses and therapists, absorbed and made sense of this daily (sur)reality. It was hope that I could find even a small percentage of their strength. It was hope that the theories I'd been developing from the models of performance by older actors might have a positive impact on those at the farthest edges of aging and health.

The storytelling exercises that came of out my weekly sessions at the Marian Franciscan Center satisfied many of my hopes and have subsequently put these collected chapters into perspective. Again, like the Frolics, the majority of senior theater groups I have studied deal largely with the healthy aged, both in their casts and audiences. A small number of groups and individual artists, including Kazuo Ohno and Suzanne Lacy, challenge the transformative power of theater by featuring the frail elderly, those over the age of eighty-five. These performers actually transform *theater* by establishing their own standards of movement. Could these Alzheimer's patients, a group of people who have enormous difficulty discerning reality, understand and participate in the transformative power of performance? How would they (if they could at all) transform performance?

After a few attempts at role-playing misfired, we settled into a single exercise that seemed to work. I asked my regular group of four women, in various stages of Alzheimer's, to help tell a story from a picture I would bring in each week. Their answers were an indistinguishable blend of illness, creativity, and individual memories. A magazine ad of the Marlboro man became Fred Astaire, the "swanky" cowboy who lived on the plains of Oklahoma with his several Angora cats and three dogs, Bozo, Sandy, and Spotty. These cats and dogs, the women's own pets (I assume), emerged in nearly every story we told. The cows that Fred tended were black and white and said, "Moo" and "Hi Pat!" The latter clearly came out of one woman's cheerful confusion. When we reviewed the stories together, "Hi Pat!" was not a source of embarrassment or fear but laughter. This laughter was no miracle. Certainly, no one was cured by the stories. No one's cognitive ability radically improved. But the women's laughter drew surprised attention from staff and other residents. The transformation was not the performers' alone; it drew in the visitors, staff, and volunteers. It especially included me. Although it was no romantic picture of transformation, the residents' playfulness and their radical lack of understanding of linear time began to erode my own fears of Alzheimer's and late life. They helped me to see more clearly how life outside the institution is ruled by rigid constructs of ever-depleting, faster and faster flowing hiccups of time. Like sociologist Herman Coenen, I clearly saw the benefits that the world inside the institution could bring to those supposedly safely outside it.[1]

Exorcising the demons of the far ends of the life course and of physiological health enables us to let go of the manic clinging to youthfulness so prevalent in this country. Each of the performances I discuss in this book exorcises the *old* in old age in its own way. Each has its attributes and limitations. The Geritol Frolics makes inner youthfulness visible in and on older performers through the troupe's awe-inspiring, fast-paced, professional musical reviews. The Frolics uses music to create an atmosphere in which older audience members feel free to remember a shared past, while younger audience members learn of this past and see older community members as vibrant citizens. The Grandparents Living Theatre distinguishes old age from youth by accentuating the physical and psychological changes across the performers personal journeys through the life course. Based on both current political issues and the performers' experiences, GLT's performances connect local, individual visions of old age to both the present and the past. By having young and old performers sing, dance, and fight for common causes on the same stage, both Roots & Branches and Elders Share the Arts forge links between generations. The incredible diversity among the four hundred older women in Suzanne Lacy's *Crystal Quilt* as well the show's range of performance styles create the elderly performers as symbols of the living past and represent them as rich repositories of experience and as active, valuable citizens. Kazuo Ohno's *Water Lilies* imagines old age as inseparable from other life stages and one generation as inseparable from another. *Vidpires!* reminds us that, in spite of the persuasiveness of technological fantasies, the mortal body is inescapable. In a similar hyperbole of attempted stasis Channing's *Hello, Dolly!* reveals that "stardom" beyond the local level currently demands costly sacrifices in the value of old age. Although each of these performances constructs its own unique vision of old age, composed of local vocabularies of difference, they share a common attempt to ease the fears of old age by demonstrating the ability of older adults to represent and perform themselves even at the farthest reaches of the life course.[2]

The importance of reading localized constructions of old age cannot be overemphasized. Asserting local readings of age interrupts large-scale constructions of the meaning of old age that inevitably generalize differences such as race, class, and gender.[3] The creation of a local community in which one can age with respect, support, and challenge is the most common reason older actors cite when asked why they were drawn to and continue to perform. The importance of rallying community support in attempts to shift the roles and meanings of old age are particularly evident in the Frolics, GLT, R&B, ESTA, and *The Crystal Quilt*. *Water Lilies* as a touring show, *Vidpires!* as a newly relocated troupe, and *Hello, Dolly!* as a production of national scale provide helpful models for revisioning aging. But they also demonstrate the intimate connections between building community and shifting meanings of age by the relative absence or abstraction of these connections in the performances.

Emphasizing the ability of the oldest old to represent and perform themselves is of equal importance. Old age is commonly described as a mask, as a physical costume that shrouds, disguises, and burdens one's ageless sense of self (Kaufman 1986; Featherstone and Hepworth 1991). Encouraged to dye, exfoliate, moisturize, even surgically remove visual signs of aging, the mirror stage of old age, as Kathleen Woodward develops it through Freud and Lacan (1991), most commonly entails a fear-filled rejection of this mask. Considering aging as performative, however, suggests that the mask of old age is not so different from masks we carry across the life course. We just don't see them in youth. Cultural codes laminate them to our bodies. Youth is considered an object, a state of being more stable perhaps than the rigidity of personality we assign to older people, who supposedly become more and more themselves as they age. Theories of performativity and social acts, such as those of Judith Butler, Pierre Bourdieu, and Michel de Certeau, imagine that the body—its very materiality, its every entrance into the social field—is an iteration. Our bodies are the shifting, temporal products created by/in our social acts. What I have suggested throughout this book is that the space between being and becoming that performance reveals also makes visible the localized, individual performances and masks of youth. It is my hope that intergenerational relationships and an awareness of the life course in depth will be more possible through this common ground of masking. This is meant to be more than a sentimental call of "can't we all just get along." Besides easing fears and isolation, intergenerational relationships present largely untapped opportunities to question current cultural practices by creating a dialogue across historical locations, between the present and the past. Reforming Social Security, securing government loans for education, containing costs of health care—all these issues stand considerably more chance of effective change through intergenerational political alliances. Waiting for the Baby Boom to change the face of age ensures that intergenerational tensions will remain. Shifting the meanings and political implications of the shape of old age must be a collaborative, intergenerational effort, or the battle will need to be fought in perpetuity, as each generation enters old age.

I am optimistic about the possibilities for intergenerational relationships and the potential for changing the oppositional constructions of youth and old age. Here at the turn of the century, in a country reaching its own adulthood, there is a growing awareness of aging and old age. As more people live into deep old age, as marketers identify a consumer market of older adults, representations of old age in theater, film, television, and advertising are becoming increasingly common. I have witnessed these shifts on an individual level as well. In 1995 I participated in a lecture series on the representation of age at a Madison, Wisconsin, senior center, where an audience of thirty seniors absorbed, challenged, and assessed my recounting of aging in performance. In the spring of 1996 the Center for Twentieth Century Studies at the University of Wisconsin–Milwaukee hosted "Women and Aging," the first international conference within the humanities to focus on aging from the perspective of the arts and cultural studies. In January 1997 I returned to Las Vegas for the third and largest Senior Theatre USA festival.

This growing awareness is, much like the early phases of the second wave of feminism, largely focused on rooting out negative imagery and replacing it with positive models of activity, empowerment, and self-esteem. So much work remains to be done in shifting the attitudes toward aging and the aged, particularly for the oldest old, that this reactionary approach may be most effective in jump-starting cultural consciousness of aging as consisting of *more* than "The Today Show" segments on "how to care for an aging parent" or "how to stay young and fit." But the benefits of exuberantly positive images of old age are limited and ultimately do nothing to reshape the systems by which aging is valued.

Presenting, reading, contextualizing, and questioning performative models of aging from an intergenerational perspective, from across the full spectrum of the life course and in concert with unique generational and historical locations, can help shift how we think about aging

without slipping into simplistic and destructive positive/negative
poles. The groups and performances I selected to include in this study
represent a fraction of the important and inspirational work being done
in the field today. Liz Lerman's Washington, DC–based Dance
Exchange has encouraged movement and performance among the
elderly for two decades. Philadelphia's fourteen-year-old Full Circle
Theater does improvisational, issue-based, intergenerational performances that encourage audience interaction. Oakland, California's
StAGEbridge has been doing intergenerational performances and storytelling workshops for eighteen years. The senior theater program at
University of Nevada–Las Vegas continues its pioneering efforts to
establish a training program for older adults who aim for professional
acting as a second (perhaps even third) career. New and diverse
troupes are growing in number and range from choral singing groups
and kitchen bands to readers' theaters and senior orchestras. Broadway
and off-Broadway venues are also turning toward the topic of old age
and yielding more roles for older actors, such as the 1996 productions
of *Grace & Glorie* and *Curtains.* As the Baby Boom generation of avant-
garde artists continues its very public journey into old age, there will no
doubt be a tremendous increase in the representations of aging in their
work as well.[4]

The activity among older performers is certainly robust. There
remains, however, a clear need for scholars to shed apprehensions
about writing about and acknowledging age as a category of difference—one that permeates scholarly work. Invariably, when I share my
work with older colleagues, I hear the same uncomfortable laughter—
"Oh, you're writing about me!" No, I assure them, I'm writing about
me. Here I add that I'm writing about why these colleagues, often
barely denting middle age, *think* I'm writing about them. Addicted as I
am to the lighter side of life, I would never advocate the end of joking.
But it's long past time to ask what *compels* the uncomfortable laughter.

Notes

Chapter 1

1. I first saw this ad aired on 8 March 1995.

2. The possibility and purity of "live" performance is a matter of contention within the field of performance and media studies. I take up this topic in chapter 7.

3. See Gullette 1997, for a thorough description and deconstruction of the decline narrative of aging.

4. See Mary Harris's 1994 essay "Growing Old Gracefully: Age Concealment and Gender." Harris's study of 269 adults revealed that "most of the signs of aging were considered unattractive for both males and females" and that "aging women were seen as particularly unappealing" (149).

5. Borrowing a term from Richard Bolles, Thomas Cole refers to these stages as "three boxes." See, for example, Bolles's study *The Three Boxes of Life* (1979). Also see Cole for additional references (1992, 240). I prefer to emphasize the performative aspects of these "boxes" by calling them stages.

6. Infant mortality rates decreased from almost 100 out of 1,000 births in 1915 to 30 in 1930 and 9.9 in 1987 (Aiken 1989). Due to decreases in infant mortality rates and increasing longevity, life expectancy at birth has increased from 47 in 1900 to 75 in 1988. It is expected to reach 80 by the year 2000. It is important to note that these numbers represent a mix of race, class, and gender. Life expectancy for women is generally higher than men; life expectancy for African Americans, Native Americans, and Latinos is less than that of Caucasian and Asian Americans; and middle- and upper-class men and women have longer life expectancies than those in poverty. White women have consistently had the longest life expectancies since the turn of the century.

7. The term *geriatric* was not actually in common use until 1914, when I. L. Nascher published a text by that name. I use it here to differentiate it from *gerontology*, a term in common use after 1904. *Geriatrics* refers to medical research and care for the elderly; *gerontology* refers to a more general study of aging.

8. *Osteoperosis* refers to the loss of bone density especially common among older women. Geriatric doctors cite osteoperosis for the high number of and slow healing process of broken bones among older women, especially as they approach eighty and ninety years of age. According to Cole (1992), Nascher's findings were both important and influential and should be used to reconsider today's common practice of defining aging as a disease. Yet Cole is also careful to point out that Nascher did not account for differences in the aging process across lines of race, gender, or class.

9. Achenbaum (1978) refers to this change as the "obsolescence of old age."

10. Surprisingly, the scientific management of old age as a chronic disease and the growing sense that the aged were a problem for society was not reflected in any significant demographic changes in either the number of elderly or growing poverty levels. Brian Gratton and Carole Haber (1993) suggest that economic growth in the early decades of the twentieth century actually *improved* the status of the elderly and expanded their choices of living arrangements. The discursive history of old age as a category and the dramatic changes of modernization seem to have worked independently of actual changes in the living conditions and the number of the elderly. As Achenbaum writes, "the unprecedented denigration of older Americans arose independently of the most important observable changes in their actual status" (1978, 86).

11. The American Geriatric Society formed in 1942, the Gerontological Society in 1945. The first National Conference on Aging was held in 1950; the National Institute on Aging formed in 1974. For more on the establishment of journals and service organizations, see Achenbaum's study *Crossing Frontiers: Gerontology Emerges as Science* (1995).

12. Achenbaum writes: "The enactment of Medicare and Medicaid in the 1960s gave further impetus to the growth of commercial nursing homes. The promise of good return on investments, rather than altruism, created a nursing home boom" (1978, 151). He cites a 23 July *Business Week* article in 1966 that forecasted the growth of this industry: "The real action, say analysts will come in real estate deals or nursing homes—a complex and little-understood field that in the past has been characterized by converted ramshackle dwellings and old movie theatres, fast-dealing entrepreneurs and occasional scandals" (113).

13. The term *ageism* came into common use in 1968, when psychiatrist Robert Butler, who would become head of the National Institute on Aging from 1974 to 1982, used the term in a presentation, which was later published. "Ageism: Another Form of Bigotry" was published in the *Gerontologist* in 1969.

14. Erikson also identified basic characteristics of each life stage and a unique challenge the stage presented. The first stage of Infancy he characterized as a conflict between basic trust and basic mistrust that should ideally yield hope. In the second phase, Toddlerhood, one worked out issues of autonomy, shame, and doubt in order to develop one's "will." The third stage, Play Age, saw a conflict between initiative and guilt on the path toward building one's purpose. The other ages and their characteristic conflicts and rewards

include: School Age (industry and inferiority, yielding competence); Adolescence (identity and confusion, yielding fidelity); Young Adulthood (intimacy and isolation, yielding love); Middle Adulthood (generativity and self-absorption, yielding caring); and, finally, Older Adulthood (integrity and despair, yielding wisdom).

15. For more details on Erikson's formulations of the life course, see *The Life-Cycle Completed: A Review* (1982); *Adulthood* (1978); *Childhood and Society* (rev. ed., 1963); and the more recent *Vital Involvement in Old Age,* cowritten with Joan Erikson and Helen Kivnick (1986).

16. For more on Kuhn's ties to Erikson and Butler, see Hessel 1977.

17. Stephen Kern (1984) gives a similar analysis of the modern period. For more on Virilio's views of contemporary culture, see "The Third Interval" (1994). His 1995 book *The Art of the Motor* develops the ideas in "The Third Interval" and, more specifically, addresses their impact on the body.

18. Raymond Williams and Dana Polan use the nonstop "flow" of culture, as in, for example, the continuous flow of television programming, as one of the key characteristics of postmodern culture. See Polan's article "Brief Encounters: Mass Culture and the Evacuation of Sense," in Modeleski 1986. See Williams 1975.

19. The title and condition of the "Aging Society" is explored in Pifer and Brontë 1986.

20. Beth Soldo (1980) lists the ratio of dependents to workers as increasing from 18 to 100 in 1980, 26 to 100 in 2000, to as high as 32 to 100 in 2030.

21. Philip Longman, in *Born to Pay* (1987), synopsizes the issues for a general audience. Also see Bengtson and Achenbaum 1993.

22. See Vern Bengtson's essay "Is the Contract across Generations Changing?" (1993) for more on issues of generational equity. I address the emergence and variety of "Generation X" literature at more length in chapter 4.

23. Three recent books, for example—*The Handbook for the Humanities and Aging,* ed. Cole, Van Tassel, and Kastenbaum (1992); *Voices and Visions of Aging: Toward a Critical Gerontology,* ed. Cole, Achenbaum, Jakobi, and Kastenbaum (1993); and *Images of Aging,* ed. Mike Featherstone and Andrew Wernick (1995)—reflect a growing interest in discursive studies of the social construction of age. The recently developed *Journal of Aging Studies* offers a similar focus.

24. Chapters 2 and 3 of Friedan's book *The Fountain of Age* (1993), "The Two Faces of Age" and "The Youth Short Circuit," focus specifically on the limited samples and youthful standards of studies of aging. Friedan does not specifically use the work of postmodern theorists by name, but the aims of these two chapters reveal a basic tenet of postmodern philosophy: that research findings are dependent on research methods.

25. Exceptions include Woodward 1991; and Marc Kaminsky's extensive introduction to Myerhoff 1992.

26. Susan Bordo (1993) also identifies this strain of postmodern theory: "And contemporary culture, technologically armed, seems bent on defying aging, our various biological 'clocks,' and even death itself. . . . That which is

not-body is the highest, the best, the noblest, the closest to God; that which is body is the albatross, the heavy drag on self-realization" (4–5). I address this point in more detail in chapter 7, based on the work of performance artist Stelarc, who declares the obsolescence of the mortal body.

27. This nominal criticism of Foucault's work is echoed in Butler 1993; and Martin 1994.

Chapter 2

1. The college, which just recently changed its name, had been known, from the founding of the Frolics up until 1996, as the Brainerd Community College.

2. Drama therapy also emerged out of the creative drama movement. Drama therapy entails a special licensing process that ensures practitioners have training in psychology as well as theater. See Landy 1986, for more on the founding principles of the discipline.

3. I refer here to personal conversations with directors of these groups as well as panel discussions featuring the directors at both the 1993 and 1995 festivals.

4. London's Age Exchange Theater, directed by Pam Schweitzer, also has a multitiered structure. Age Exchange hires professional young actors to play out the stories of older men and women. Schweitzer has also formed a troupe of older, amateur performers who act out their own stories.

5. At the 1997 Senior Theatre USA Festival Jewell Fitzgerald, of Edgewood College in Madison, Wisconsin, presented vocal training techniques for those who have trouble memorizing. Marilyn Richardson of Ivins, Utah, presented a series of short one-woman movement pieces. Workshop sessions also featured readings of new, full-length plays by Kent R. Brown, Max Golightly, and Paullette MacDougal, winner of Dramatic Publishing and University of Nevada–Las Vegas' first National Senior Adult Theatre Playwriting Contest. Dorothy Perron of Santa Fe, New Mexico's Seniors Reaching Out, presented her oral history techniques, and Dr. Stuart Kandell and his Oakland-based troupe StAGEbridge shared their intergenerational storytelling and staging techniques.

6. Dryden reports that tickets for the first dozen performances sold out weeks before the show: "Publicity was strong, word of mouth was great, goodwill was everywhere. The only complaint heard was that the run of the show was not long enough" (4).

7. The Dallas troupe performed *A Musical Revue!* at the 1995 festival. The Fresno New Wrinkles troupe performed *A Ticket to Paradise* at the 1997 festival.

8. Shifting the gender distribution in the comic scenes, the Frolics' 1994 *Memories of the Thirties* featured two main comic performers, one man and one woman.

9. According to the American Association for Retired Persons, at age

sixty-five the ratio of men to women in the United States (without race or class differentials) is 82:100. At age eighty-five the ratio drops to 40:100.

10. Research and information on older gays and lesbians is scarce and is often blatantly overlooked in research on sex and gender in old age. For information on homosexuality in old age, see Quam 1992 and 1993.

11. In the January performace at the 1993 Senior Theatre USA Festival one man did appear in a wheelchair.

12. See Woodward 1991, for more a detailed reading of how psychoanalytic thought privileges an identity formed in youth and carried through life in a changing body.

13. Michel Foucault's often-quoted description of the construction of an inner reality—or soul—is applicable here. In *Discipline and Punish* Foucault writes:

> [The soul] has a reality, it is produced permanently around, on, within the body by the functioning of a power that is exercised on those punished— and, in a more general way, on those one supervises, trains and corrects. . . . This is the historical reality of this soul, which, unlike the soul represented by Christian theology, is not born in sin and subject to punishment, but is born rather out of methods of punishment, supervision and constraint. (1979, 29)

14. I am thinking specifically of Deepak Chopra's *Ageless Body, Timeless Mind* (1993), but there are a number of such self-help-oriented books in which physical changes of the aging body are underplayed while the spirit or soul is regaled.

15. Woodward parallels the mirror phase of old age with psychoanalyst Jacques Lacan's theory of the mirror phase of infancy (1977). In Lacan's model an infant between the six and eighteen months will recognize his or her reflection in a mirror. The moment is one of division, as the infant believes the reflection to be whole and cohesive, while experiencing him- or herself as fragmented and disjointed. Lacan believes the infant yearns for the cohesiveness of the reflection, taking it to be an image of immortality. In the mirror phase of old age, however, Woodward suggests that older people are encultured to reject their mirror images for the internalized memory of youth. When confronted with their reflection, the older person rejects the image, preferring instead the comfort of what is remembered to be a cohesive, internal, and youthful self. The memory of one's reflection as younger, a soothing image of immortality, now stands in contrast to the reflection as an old person, a haunting reminder of the imminence of death.

16. In lieu of the 1994 controversy in England over the postmenopausal woman who was "artificially" implanted with a younger woman's egg and her husband's sperm, the once-clear line between reproductive capabilities for both men and women is now suspect and riddled with questions of "natural" and "unnatural." For my purposes I refer to menopause (male and female) as a biological and social shift, after which gender roles can no longer be solely attributed to unassisted reproductive capacity.

17. Rossi's article presents interesting possibilities for reading old age as an illustration of the construction of youthful gender roles. The article, however, is problematic in her oversight of the impact of an androgynous culture on same-sex relationships.

18. I refer here to the phenomenon of the disappearance of childhood, which began to occur as those of the Baby Boom generation carried their youthful identity into middle age (see Postman 1994). This phenomenon is paralleled by the rise of the "young-old" as identified by Bernice Neugarten (1974).

19. Butler elaborates this point in *Bodies That Matter* (1993): "At best, it seems drag is a site of a certain ambivalence, one which reflects the more general situation of being implicated in the regimes of power by which one is constituted and, hence, of being implicated in the very regimes of power that one opposes" (125).

20. In his essay "Imperialist Nostalgia" (1989) Rosaldo outlines the paradox of this type of nostalgia:

> [A] person kills somebody and then mourns his or her victim. In more attenuated form, someone deliberately alters a form of life and then regrets that things have not remained as they were prior to his or her intervention. At one more remove, people destroy their environment and then worship nature. In any of its versions, imperialist nostalgia uses a pose of "innocent yearning" both to capture people's imaginations and to conceal its complicity with often brutal domination. (108)

21. These and subsequent comments from Frolics members are taken from personal interviews in Brainerd on 18 May 1994.

Chapter 3

1. I participated in two of Reilly's oral history workshops, one at the American Theatre in Higher Education Conference in Philadelphia in August 1993 and the second at the National Council on Aging in Washington, DC, in April 1994.

2. The international appeal of GLT's *I Was Young* drew the interest of a Broadway producer in 1993, but the production never materialized.

3. See part 1, "The Age Mystique," in Friedan 1993, for an introduction to this argument within the fields of popular culture, geriatrics, and gerontology.

4. Robert Butler writes:

> I conceive of the life review as a naturally occuring, universal mental process characterized by the progressive return to consciousness of past experiences, and, particularly, the resurgence of unresolved conflicts; simultaneously, and normally, these revived experiences and conflicts can be surveyed and reintegrated. (Qtd. in Neugarten 1974, 487)

5. Butler suggests that "probably at no other time in life is there as potent

a force toward self-awareness operating as in old age" (495), an observation that would seem to overlook the tumultuous adolescent years.

6. *Re-membering* is Myerhoff's term (based on Victor Turner's reasearch) for the reconstitution of self through memory.

7. Myerhoff, who approaches reminiscence from the discipline of anthropology, advocates life history for its communal (intergenerational and intragenerational) benefits.

8. As Middleton and Buchanan point out, the difficulty of translating the potential benefits of reminiscence into psychological statistics can leave the practice in an awkward limbo state—associated with psychological therapy yet also rejected by the discipline. Middleton and Buchanan point to Thornton and Brotchie's 1987 study as an example of the grounds on which reminiscence is excused: "the role of reminiscence as a therapeutic tool is doubtful, and it seems that at least as far as the normal and confused elderly are concerned, it is best regarded as a diversionary activity" (Middleton and Buchanan1987, 326).

9. Woodward writes:

> Theory like literature, is produced at a certain time and in a certain place in response to both external conditions as well as internal desires. . . . Erikson points to the development of his theory of the identity crisis from the perspective of his historical moment, a period in American society characterized by aggravated identity confusion. (1986, 143)

10. Reilly uses both these examples in her oral history workshops in hopes of encouraging similar responses.

11. GLT's repertoire includes a range of styles and structures, including *Woman: A Joyous Journey*, a ritually based show, again suggesting that the narrative form of I *Was Young* was a choice rather than illustrative of a normative pattern.

12. For more on alienation in Brecht's writings, see the essay "A Short Organum for the Theatre," in Willett 1982. This essay, a series of separate thoughts on theater, includes a description of the alienation effect.

13. These conclusions are also supported by a series of interviews with artistic directors, directors, and older actors in the Minneapolis / St. Paul and Chicago areas in 1993–95. Interviewees included Bill Partlan, artistic director of the Cricket Theater; Lou Bellamy, artistic director of the Penumbra Theater; Bonnie Morris, artistic director of the Illusion Theater; and Alberto Justiano, artistic director of Teatro del Peublo. Cross-cultural studies in the theatrical representation of age, particularly Japanese theatrical traditions, set in relief the Western, particularly American, practices of such "one-way" age representation, in which older people rarely play younger characters.

14. Of the artistic directors interviewed all named memory and physical movement problems as significant stumbling blocks to using older actors. A third major reason (the most important factor for Teatro del Pueblo) was the lack, or perceived lack, of older actors themselves.

15. Aging might also be considered an "event" in the terms of French

philosopher Gilles Deleuze. For Deleuze an event is a process of eternal becoming and demands a redefinition of time:

> Time must be grasped twice, in two complementary though mutually exclusive fashions. First, it must be grasped entirely as the living present in bodies which act and are acted upon. Second, it must be grasped entirely as an entity infinitely divisible into past and future, and into the incorporeal effects which result from bodies, their actions and their passions. (1993, 43)

16. Judith Litterman's *Trauma and Recovery* (1992) is illustrative of recent theories in psychology that addresses the imprinting of memory on/in the body. While this work can easily fall into an essentialism with which I am uneasy, it also speaks to the lingering traces of past experiences on/in the body.

17. I thank Jaqueline Zita for suggesting the connection between aging and disability in the construction of productivity. For more on the relationship between feminism and disability, see Thomson 1997.

18. For two examples of efforts to paint the aged as productive, see Butler and Gleason 1985; and Butler, Oberlink, and Schecter 1990. In Bond, Cutler, and Grams 1995, Eleanor M. Simonsick begins to question the accepted definitions of productivity in gerontological study and expands them to include the care of the self as a means of lessening the dependency ratio and its tax on the economy. This redefinition is the first step toward what Harry R. Moody (1986) describes as the revaluing of the contemplative in postmodern culture.

19. Baudrillard's essay "The Mirror of Production" suggests that Marx's idea of productivity relies on a "subject," an individual whose value is determined in his or her quantity and quality of output. Baudrillard reads this human subject as the creation of Marx's framework of the political economy. The passage to which I refer of Baudrillard's is worthy of quoting at length, as it speaks across disciplines:

> The double potentiality of man as needs and labor power, this double "generic" face of universal man is only man as produced by the system of political economy. And productivity is not primarily a generic dimension, a human and social kernel of all wealth to be extracted from the husk of capitalist relations of production (the eternal empiricist illusion). Instead, all this must be overturned to see that the abstract and generalized development of productivity (the developed form of a political economy) is what makes the *concept of production* itself appear as man's movement and generic end (or better, as the concept of man as producer). (1988, 104)

20. See, for example, Oakley 1974; Rubin 1975; Nicholson 1987; and articles collected in Kuhn and Wolpe 1978.

21. This questioning of how and why aging is produced in GLT's performance might be considered, in Fred Davis's terms, an example of "interpretted nostalgia" (1979). See chapter 2, for more on Davis' definitions of nostalgia.

Chapter 4

1. Other groups whose predominant focus is intergenerational performance include Liz Lerman's Dance Exchange, based in Washington, DC; StAGEbridge, in Oakland, California; and Full Circle Theatre, in Philadelphia.

2. Rushkoff 1994; and Howe and Strauss 1993, are also indicative of early Gen X literature.

3. The distinction of vertical and horizontal generations can be found in Evangelista et al. 1995.

4. Basing his study on both historical events and shifts in demographic patterns, Fernando Torres-Gil (1992) arrived at slightly different categoriza tions. Torres-Gil lays out the following generational lines: Swing (1900–26); Silent (1927–45); Baby Boomers (1946–64); Baby Bust or Boomerang (1965–79); Baby Boomlet or Echo (1980–current).

5. JASA, the Jewish Association for Services for the Aged, provides space and administrative support for the troupe.

6. *Shtarke* is Yiddish for "strong female."

7. Strimling suggested that the ensemble has come to measure the response of audiences composed largely of the frail elderly by their attentiveness rather than their laughter at jokes. According to Strimling, response time to jokes, unless they are really physical, are generally slower in these audiences (personal interview, November 1996).

8. Susan MacManus's (1996) extensive research into the voting practices and political interests of both old and young adults supports the generally assumed notion that, in spite of MTV's Rock the Vote, younger voting-age Americans largely do not exercise this civic right.

9. ESTA's observations bear particular weight in light of the fact that existing statistical studies on generational relationships are tricky to assess. For example, based on data from the International Social Survey Program, Janice Farkas and Dennis Hogan (1995) suggest that Americans have a relatively high proportion of contact between the old and young. But their study did not address the youngest age cohorts, nor did it attempt to assess the quality of the intergenerational kin contact.

10. Members of the Community Round Table for Senior Citizens include: Geraldine Moore, Carrie Raeford, Margaree Hall, Isabel Austin, Randolph Cherry, Sadell Coleman, Mary Dixon, Millie Hawkins, and Hattie Williams. Leonardo Macias, a young intern at the Round Table, also contributed to the creation of *Why Vote?*

11. This session at Bushwick Senior Center took place 4 April 1996.

12. In a personal interview (November 1996) Vladimir Auguste said that a young man stood up at one of the Long Island University performances and objected to the play's message that older and younger voters have common interests.

13. These comments come from two separate interviews: Randolph Cherry (May 1996); and Vladimir Auguste (November 1996).

14. Pam Schweitzer described her latest intergenerational effort with her

London-based Age Exchange theater company as a "disaster": "The show was fantastic. But the process was a nightmare. All the young people fell in desparate love with one another. When we were on the road, all the older people were in bed by nine and all the young people were up until four." Schweitzer spoke about Age Exchange's intergenerational performance in her workshop at the Senior Theatre USA Festival in Las Vegas, Nevada (January 1997).

Chapter 5

1. The mission statement evolved throughout the Whisper Minnesota project. This statement was finalized in September 1985 and was used in the packet circulated to potential funders and participants.

2. The Older Women's Leadership Series was conceived by Sharon Roe Anderson.

3. Lacy's collaborators at the Split Rock Arts Program included Lief Brush, Gloria de Felips Brush, and Judy Dwyer.

4. Myerhoff writes: "It is impossible to release the elderly from all standards of reasonable behavior. That ultimately is the most degrading position of all, with the final effect of reducing old people to nonpeople. . . . We must not allow old people to fall into purposelessness" (1992, 224). I adjust her generalization of older people here to older women for purposes of my argument.

5. I thank Carrie Sandahl for helping clarify this point. Sandahl's writing on "modern primitives" suggests that the collapse of performance and performativity is a tool to create the authenticity of the primitive other. Also see Dyer 1991b.

6. For more on Lacy's past performances and an extensive bibliography of writing on Lacy before 1988, see the trilogy of articles by Moira Roth, Diane Rothenberg, and Lucy R. Lippard in *TDR* (1988).

7. According to Roth, in Lacy's *Ablutions* (1972): "Lacy nailed raw beef kidneys to the wall as the tape-recorded voices of rape victims recited the details of their experiences" (1988, 50). Both *There Are Voices in the Desert* (1978), *Edna, May Victor, Mary and Me: An All Night Benediction* (1977), and *The Lady and the Lamb or The Goat and the Hag* (1978) use full, raw lamb carcasses. In the latter the carcass is bound in white bandages. See Roth 1988, for Lacy's full production history.

8. A potluck dinner was held as part of the overall *Whisper the Waves, the Wind* project, but neither that performance nor *The Crystal Quilt* involved food. I make the connection to food by the image of women seated at tables together and by Lacy's previous work, in which food has a significant presence. See Lippard 1988, for details on the potluck.

9. See, for example, Nicholson 1994.

10. For Bourdieu a social agent negotiates his or her way through a structured and structuring system divided into "fields" and "habitus." The field is a dynamic social space in which social agents act *in relationship* to one another.

Habitus is a structured "system of durable transposable dispositions" that sub-consciously guides the practices of a social agent. "Capital" are tools used in the struggles within ones' field. Capital can refer to, but is not limited to, econom-ics; Bourdieu divides capital into *symbolic capital*, markers of one's prestige or success in a field, and *cultural capital*, an "internalized code or a cognitive acqui-sition which equips the social agent with empathy towards, appreciation for or competence in deciphering cultural relations and cultural artefacts" (1984, 7).

11. See the section on nostalgia in chapter 2. In *Yearning for Yesterday: A Sociology of Nostalgia* Fred Davis posits that one can predict trends of nostalgia by subtracting twenty years from the current date.

12. Bowling Green University, for example, held a conference in March 1996 predicated on exploring generational relationships within feminisms.

13. This is, of course, a common criticism of applications of psychoana-lytic theory to literary and cultural studies. Although I point to this danger in psychoanalytic theory, I also acknowledge the connections between familial roles and the formation of the self and the valuable contributions of psychoan-alytic theory to the field of age studies.

14. Jagger (1983) and Case (1988) prefer the term *radical*, while Dolan (1988) opts for *cultural*. I use the terms according to whose categorical division I am addressing.

15. WTP makes consistent and concerted efforts to support the develop-ment of its graduate students by including them in the conference as presenters and planners and by ensuring their representation in the group's governing structure. The uneasiness with aging and generational relationships was coded in terms of methodolgy and revolved around the changes in academic roles and physical age among middle-aged scholars. On the opening evening of the 1994 conference, for example, long-time members of WTP shared their memo-ries of the organization. Some made apologies for subjecting others to their nos-talgia and seemed embarrassed at being identified as "old-timers" in the group. At a compelling panel session two days later a younger scholar playfully labeled her elders as "old broads." Her presentation bordered on parody, but the comment clearly struck a chord.

16. I thank Jerry Bloedow, head of the Minnesota Board on Aging during Whisper Minnesota, who graciously lent me the files he had collected during the planning, staging, and analysis phases of the project.

17. A similar movement in gerontology asserts that the contemporary cul-tural moment is "post-age," a period in which life stages lose their distinct char-acteristics and in which studies of aging serve mainly to construct and reify dif-ference across time (Neugarten and Neugarten 1986; Featherstone and Hepworth 1991).

18. Sue-Ellen Case uses a similar metaphor in "Theory/History/Revolu-tion." She writes: "In sum, the new historian/theorists today no longer sound the old, wheezing one note of the seamless narrative style" (1993, 427).

19. Lippard makes a similar observation but projects the image of multi-plicity onto Lacy. "Lacy abandoned neither the 'witch' who presided over those first years, nor her efforts to charm and control. She turned, however, to

a beneficent and outreaching aspect of her collective persona" (1988, 71). She later concludes that Lacy "takes her chosen diversity and forms a new hybrid: a multiple self. Thus she gets to be one woman and all-women: the maid, the bride, and the hag; the light and the dark madonna" (75). Lippard's notion of multiple selves was one of the founding ideas for this chapter, yet I redirect her approach from Lacy to the larger field of feminist performance and criticism.

Chapter 6

1. Throughout this chapter I refer to Kazuo Ohno as Ohno and his son as Yoshito.

2. See Featherstone 1995, for further exploration of the potential benefits and problems of virtual reality for older people.

3. For more on the cultural construction of aging in the United States, see Cole 1992; and Featherstone and Wernick 1995.

4. See Woodward 1991, for more on the mirror stage of old age.

5. My aim here is not to compare Western constructs of age to a reified vision of Japanese models of age that commonly suffer well-intentioned romanticizations. Aging in Japan has its own distinct and shifting constructions, eloquently described, for example, in Lock 1993.

6. For more on the history of butoh, see Viala 1988; Holborn 1987; Munroe 1994; and Stein 1986.

7. Ohno practices Christianity. He both writes about his beliefs and includes references to his faith in his dances.

8. This "timelessness" is more closely akin to Heidegger's and Merleau Ponty's than to Virilio's description of technoculture (1993, 1995). Merleau Ponty cites Heidegger in *The Phenomenology of Perception:*

> Time maintains what it has caused to be, at the very time it expels it from being, because the new being was announced by its predecessor as destined to be, and because, for the latter, to become present was the same thing as being destined to pass away. "Temporalization is not a succession (*Nacheinander*) of ecstases. The future is not posterior to the past, or the past anterior to the present. Temporality temporalizes itself as future-which-laspes-into-the-present." (1962, 420)

9. My ideas on the depth model of aging were sparked in part by dance theorist Mark Franko (1992). Franko concludes his essay on gender representation in *Water Lilies:* "[The performance] suggests a nonontological model of gender performance not bereft of depth, not reliant on death and resuscitation" (1992, 604).

10. Franko, more specifically focused on sex and gender roles in the performance, describes Ohno's *Water Lilies* in a similar way:

> Instead of producing that simulacrum of blending that we see as sexual ambiguity, Ohno simply opens the binaries to the possibility of mutual

self-inclusion, infolding their outer limits toward a center that is not conceptualized but purely performed. The performance suggests neither sexual blending nor a clinical doubling of the two sexes in one body but, rather, *a range of differences that bodies lay claim to*. (1992, 603; my emph.)

11. Anca Cristofovici finds that the essentially static medium of photography displays a similar play with layers of age: "If as pscyhic images, ages, like time, do not exist in isolation but rather simultaneously, so that we can read the younger woman through the older woman, the mother through the daughter, is it at all possible to isolate aging as a sign?" (forthcoming).

12. I refer here to some performance styles popular among senior theater troupes outlined in chapter 1. Liz Lerman's Dance Exchange is a twenty-year-old, Washington, DC–based intergenerational dance troupe. I am thinking specifically of "Flying into Middle Age" which I saw performed in December 1996.

13. Donna Haraway's writing on cyborgs is an excellent example. Although Haraway claims that immortality and omnipotence are not her goal in theorizing the cyborg as a merger of human and technology (1991, 188), the myth of the cyborg does not provide the tools to address aging and death, which cyborgs seem programmed to avoid. There have been several challenges to the cyborg's seeming immortality, including Katherine Hayles's "The Life Cycle of the Cyborg: Writing the Posthuman" (1995) and Margaret Morse's "What Do Cyborgs Eat?" (1994). Kathleen Woodward (1994) also addresses the value of aging (or the lack thereof) in technoculture.

14. For example, Foucault's vision of the body as determined by discourse appears to underscore the idea that aging is solely a process of decay:

The body is the inscribed surface of events (traced by language and dissolved by ideas), the locus of a dissociated Self (adopting the illusion of substantial unity), and a volume in *disintegration*. Genealogy, as an analysis of *descent*, is thus situated within the articulation of the body and history. Its task is to expose a body totally imprinted by history and the process of history's *destruction* of the body. (1977a, 148)

15. Foucault's spatial analysis is vital to an understanding of how discourse constructs the social field. But the sense that "history destroys the body" fuels the tendency to separate the soul and body that Foucault himself refutes and denies the body's hand in the production of time through its social practices. My awareness of this absence in Foucault's analysis was heightened by a footnote in Butler 1993, in which she writes:

The Foucaultian emphasis on *convergent* relations of power . . . implies a mapping of power relations that in the course of a genealogical process form a constructed effect. The notion of convergence presupposes both motion and space; as a result, it appears to elude the paradox . . . in which the very account of temporality requires the spatialization of the "moment." On the other hand, Foucault's account of convergence does not fully theorize what is at work in the "movement" by which power and discourse are said to converge. In a sense, the "mapping" of power does not fully theorize temporality. (245)

I do not want to polarize time and space here. Rather, I suggest that, in the effort to eliminate linear, chronological, and progress narratives, spatial analysis has flattened, frozen, and/or forgotten time. Thanks to Alice Rayner for suggesting this point.

16. Bourdieu and Wacquant cite Maurice Merleau-Ponty (*Phenomenology of Perception* [1962]) in a footnote to the passage I selected: "In every focusing moment my body unites present, past and future, it secretes time. . . . My body takes possession of time; it brings into existence a past and a future for a present, it is not a thing, but creates time instead of submitting to it" (1992, 138).

17. Biddy Martin (1994) forges similar ground. Her perceptive analysis is worth quoting at length here. Emphasizing the need to add temporal analysis to Foucault's spatial discourse analysis, Martin writes:

> When it comes to questions of gender, sexuality, and identity . . . temporality reminds us that inside/outside encounters have the effect again and again of making bodies and psyches with histories *that then exert their own pressures back on the boundaries between out and in, back on what we take to be the social world around a self or a person.* Though that body and psyche can be said to be effects of power, they are irreducible to it. Though never constituted outside of given social/discursive relations, power also moves from bodies/psyches/minds outward, not by virtue of will, but by virtue of the pressure exerted by what's given in the form of body and subjectivity. (119; my emph.)

Chapter 7

1. Margolis Brown Company's productions, which have met considerable acclaim, include *Bed Experiment One* and *Koppelvision*. Centered on the actor's body, each of the company's shows merges the body with media in order to create what they call "a modern theater of spectacle and celebration that is rich in metaphor" (production notes, 1995).

2. Alice Rayner makes a similar point in her discussion of the "borg" as alien/replicant (1994). She writes:

> The borg is alien because it is fully self-identical. It signals the imagined horror of total self-absorption and self-sameness that cannot stand outside itself and therefore cannot resist its own power. Heidegger imagined such self-absorption as the danger in technology. (138)

3. In *Being and Time* (1962) Heidegger describes the manipulatable object as displaying *Zuhandenheit*, or readiness-to-hand. The broken or useless object, on the other hand, is simply *Vorhanden*, or present-at-hand, becoming "conspicuously unusable" (103–4).

4. Sue-Ellen Case has also pondered the line between screened and material body from within the field of performance studies (1995a, 1995b). For Case the screened world is one that is spatially, rather than temporally, constructed:

> What is prompted by this technology is a change in the terms of political analysis from those of time, which determine the historical critique, to those of space—what is called the new geography or the topological critique. . . . Certainly, as some later French Marxists argued, including Henri Lefebvre and Michel Foucault, the correction of the critique from time to space suits the new politics of urban planning, space exploration, and finally, I would add the coming of virtual reality. (1995a, 18)

Spatial construction of identity and culture offer Case, a lesbian theorist, a way out of heterosexually based models of generational models of history. Case also takes up the vampire as a metaphor for homosexuality and for desire that produces no offspring (1991). According to Case, both the vampire and the homosexual are equated with the dead. Like my reading of Kazuo Ohno, Case reads homosexual desire, as embodied by the vampire, as puncturing "the life/death and generative/destructive bipolarities that enclose the heterosexist notion of being" (4).

5. For more on the cultural value of "flexibility," see E. Martin 1994.

6. Object status for a body can also be achieved through violence, illness, or pain. I certainly don't ignore this aspect of objectification but focus instead on self-objectification through technological means.

7. Writing of the visibility of age among older women on television, Mellencamp writes: "Given the uninsured cost of plastic surgery, 'looking old' might become just another disadvantage of being poor, as being fat is seen today as a sign of weakness and failure, the lack of control also attributed to alcoholism" (1992, 288).

8. Margaret Morse, specifically addressing the visual environment of virtual reality, writes: "It is as if the apparatus of virtual reality could solve the problem of the organic body, at least temporarily, by hiding it. Yet, the organic body as a problem has not been eluded: it has only been made momentarily invisible to the user" (1994, 105).

9. Baudrillard writes:

> But we want this immortality here and now, this real-time afterlife, without having resolved the problem of the end. For there is no real-time end, no real-time of death. This is an absurdity. The end is always experienced after it has actually happened, in its symbolic elaboration. It follows from this that real-time immortality is itself an absurdity (whereas imagined immortality was not: it was an illusion). (1992, 90)

10. I explore this point at greater depth in chapter 8 in my discussion of Carol Channing.

11. Jeffrey Ressner's essay "Dr. Tim's Last Trip" (1995) details Leary's illness and his plans for creating an Internet spectacle of his death.

Chapter 8

1. This question is especially fitting as a theater producer showed interested in taking *I Was Young* to play New York in the early 1990s.

2. At this writing Disney has also moved into Times Square, transforming the once seedy district as a place for wholesome family fun. The musical *Big* opened in April 1996. Along with *Beauty and the Beast, Big* marks Broadway's shift from older audiences toward more intergenerational audiences. I owe thanks to Mark Sussman (1996) for sharing his work on Times Square with me.

3. Kroll writes:

> Why this sudden divandalizing of Broadway? Wayne Koestenbaum, author of "The Queen's Throat," a study of opera and homosexuality, thinks the burgeoning gay culture has a lot to do with it. . . . "Stars who meant a lot me during my proto-gay youth are being brought back." Koestenbaum calls this "a beautiful moment. It's a sign of a certain artistic maturity and not a sign of senility that we're rummaging in theaters past like this." (1995a, 86)

Ironically, Kroll makes no mention of the potential interest in older characters or older actors.

4. I conflate middle age with youthfulness here with the understanding that the two very generalized time periods are generationally constructed and considerably different. I include them together in this point on stardom because middle age is a transitional time period when one can still pass as youthful with the right economic, aesthetic (physical appearance), and social power. In "old age," however, one is beyond the point of passing.

5. Because she has played the same role so many times, Channing is in a way the ultimate test of performativity theories. Although Andrews recreated her film role in the 1995–96 *Victor/Victoria*, her stardom is predicated on a greater variety of roles.

6. Richard Dyer also writes extensively about authenticity, stardom, and the use of the stage or unmediated venue as what he calls authenticating authenticity. In his essay *"A Star Is Born* and the Construction of Authenticity" Dyer writes:

> We must know that her star quality has nothing to do with recording techniques, with mechanical reproduction (even though what we are watching is perforce a recording), but is grounded in her own immediate (= not controlled), spontaneous (= unpremediatated) and essential (= private) self. that guarantees that her stardom is not a con, because an authenticated individual is acting as the guarantor of the truth of the discourse of her stardom. (1991b, 139)

7. Both Andrews and Burnett started their careers on Broadway but made the transition to film and television, respectively. Like Channing, but to a lesser degree, Burnett is also "confined" by the vivid cultural memories of roles she created in her long-running television comedy series. Burnett's fellow actors express her confinement more than Burnett is willing to. Philip Bosco,

her costar in *Moon over Buffalo*, suggests that audiences "don't see her as an actress; they see her as this great comedienne, and that poses a different set of circumstances over which no one has any control. . . . The audience sometimes reacts to her as Carol Burnett, this larger-than-life figure, rather than as an actress doing what she does" (Purdum 1995).

8. Mr. Reams, who met Jerry Herman through Channing, has performed with Herman throughout the years in a variety of venues from concerts to television specials.

9. New York–based public relations firm Boneau, Bryan-Brown sent me a press kit in November 1995. All references to promotional materials are taken from their press release copy.

10. Emily Mann's adaptation of *Having Our Say* (1995), based on the autobiography of the centenarian, African-American Delany sisters, did not rely on stars to sell the show. Instead, the show, and the book upon which it was based, created "real-life" stars of the sisters themselves.

11. In an interview with Lee Roy Reams (November 1996) the director said that Channing was hesitant to diverge from the successful portrayal of Dolly in past revivals and brought detailed notes of the original production to the first several rehearsals. After a while, however, Reams said that he and Channing agreed on the importance of playing the role and directing the production for what it is today, rather than what it was.

12. In another particularly brutal description, Kroll writes: "If Hello, Dolly! were a title fight, the septuagenarian Channing wouldn't be sanctioned by any athletic commission" (1995a).

13. "Before the Parade Passes By" is one of the songs in *Hello, Dolly!*—one that reviewers who had seen the show in various revivals suggest becomes more poignant as Channing ages.

14. I thank Margaret Morganroth Gullette for pointing out this reading of Channing's 1964 Dolly.

15. Tom Shales addresses this star power of days gone by most directly in his article "Curtains Rise, and Curtains Fall: *Dolly!* and Channing, Last of a Breed" (1995). Referring to the "communal orgasm" of *Hello, Dolly!* Tom Shales writes:

> Such moments are rare, but in the musical theater, they were once more common. The great big stars who could fill the great big stages, as Channing does the Opera House's, had a magic beyond talent, and an audience got rewards beyond mere entertainment. It was a lot more than a good time. (G1)

16. Kathleen Woodward puts it another way: "We both are and are not identical to ourselves throughout our lives. It is as important to stress continuity as it is difference" (1991, 159).

17. Although they emerge from radically different contexts, Channing's approach here is similar to the Grandparents Living Theatre's casting older actors as toddlers and adolescents and Kazuo Ohno's performance of the full life course.

18. Robert Sandia writes: "Always highly mannered (that's one of the

things people like about her) she [Channing] is as stylized in the current Dolly as a Kabuki actor" (1996, 98). Similarly, Ken Mandelbaum writes:

> What Channing does here can't precisely be described as acting, even if her work contains a number of beautifully judged moments of real emotion. This is, quite simply, star performing, the kind of thing we may have forgotten ever existed. Ritualized as Kabuki it may be. (1995)

19. In act 1 Horace Vandergelder leads the male ensemble in a chorus of "It Takes a Woman," a song that, with tongue in cheek, asserts the value of having a woman around the house.

20. I refer to a billboard by Kenar that appeared in Times Square in the summer of 1996 featuring model Linda Evangelista. The photograph subsequently appeared on the cover of the *New York Times Magazine,* 22 December 1996. This essay was originally delivered as a paper at the 1996 Women and Aging Conference at University of Wisconsin–Milwaukee's Center for Twentieth Century Studies. Thanks are due to Elinor Fuchs, Kathleen Woodward, and Amelie Hastie for their feedback on various versions of this chapter. I also thank Stacy Wolf for sharing with me her perceptive work on the intersections of queer theory and stardom in her essay on Mary Martin (1996).

Chapter 9

1. Thanks to Dale Jaffe for bringing Coenen's essay "Wandering through the Caves: Phenomenoloical Field Research in a Social World of Dementia"(1991) to my attention. Coenen observed that behavior inside the nursing home he studied was not so different from that of his own daily life: "So that which is so easily taken as a sharp and unbroken borderline between two non-interchangeable worlds is regularly crossed from both sides" (328).

2. *Vidpires!* is an exception here to a certain degree. The lead performers are in their forties, and the ensemble includes a man in his late fifties. While the performance clearly does not represent the "old," their mockery of dreams of suspending youth in perpetuity asserts the value of old age.

3. Rob Houtepen makes a similar point in his criticisms of recent work by David Callahan, Thomas Cole, and Harry Moody: "Meaning should be localized less at the level of global ideas and images and more at the level of local and heterogeneous practices" (1995). Although I agree with the need for localized meanings of old age, I also find that Moody's work is turning in this direction (1995).

4. A 1995 edition of *Performing Arts Journal* featured interviews with the "aging avant-garde," including Meredith Monk and Robert Wilson, among numerous others. The 31 December *New York Times* Arts and Leisure section ("For Boomers, the Cultural Clock Is Ticking Too") featured interviews with artists turning fifty in 1996 and played rather bitingly with the possible shifts that the aging Baby Boomers might bring to the arts in general.

References

Performances

1993 Geritol Frolics. Geritol Frolics. Dir. Bob Dryden. Brainerd Community College, Brainerd, MN. 16 May 1993.

Acting Up. Artreach Players. Dir. Kirsten Bonner. Milwaukee Public Library, Milwaukee, WI. 18 May 1996.

The Bag Lady and *The Nursing Home.* Marilyn Richardson. Aladin Hotel. Las Vegas, NV. 5 January 1997.

Bushwick, Why Vote? Elders Share the Arts. Dir. Peggy Pettitt. St. Ann's Church, Brooklyn, NY. 9 May 1996.

The Crystal Quilt. Dir. Suzanne Lacy. Crystal Court of the IDS Tower, Minneapolis, MN. 12 May 1987.

Encounters of the Third Age. Senior Players of the American River Community. Dir. Rita Ward Watson. Judy Bayley Theatre, University of Nevada, Las Vegas. 7 January 1997.

Hello, Dolly! Book by Michael Stewart. Music and lyrics by Jerry Herman. Dir. Lee Roy Reams. Lunt-Fontanne Theater, NY. 12 November 1995. Based on Thorton Wilder's play *The Matchmaker.*

I Was Young, Now I'm Wonderful. Grandparents Living Theatre. Dir. Joy Reilly. Hilton Hotel Ballroom, Washington, DC. 29 April 1994.

It's about Time! Roots & Branches Theater. Dir. Arthur Strimling. Jewish Association for Services for the Aged Housing, Far Rockaway, NY. 2 May 1996.

It's about Time! Roots & Branches Theater. Dir. Arthur Strimling. Kane St. Synagogue. Brooklyn, NY. 11 May 1996.

Liz Lerman Dance Exchange. Chor. Liz Lerman. Queens Theatre in the Park, Queens, NY. 7 December 1996.

Memories of the Thirties. Geritol Frolics. Dir. Dennis Lamberson. Brainerd Community College, Brainerd, MN. 18 May 1994.

New Wrinkles Plays Las Vegas. New Wrinkles. Dir. Tom Wright. Judy Bayley Theatre, University of Nevada, Las Vegas. 6 January 1997.

Old Is Not a Four-Letter Word. Third Age Theatre Company. Dir. Dr. Franklin L.
    Gray. Judy Bayley Theatre, University of Nevada, Las Vegas. 5 January
    1997.
Stelarc. Performance/lecture, University of Wisconsin–Milwaukee. 29 Septem-
    ber 1995.
———. Performance. University of Wisconsin–Milwaukee, remote site. 10
    November 1995.
Ticket to Paradise. Essex Community College, Senior Star Showcase. Dir. Arne
    Lindquist. Judy Bayley Theatre, University of Nevada, Las Vegas. 5 Janu-
    ary 1997.
Vidpires! Margolis Brown Company, Southern Theater, Minneapolis, MN. 4
    March 1994.
Water Lilies. Created and performed by Kazuo and Yoshito Ohno. Walker Art
    Museum, Minneapolis, MN. 30 October 1993.
We, the Memories: The Women of Spoon River. Senior Players of the American
    River Community. Dir. Melanie Smith. Paul Harris Theatre, University of
    Nevada, Las Vegas. 9 January 1995.

Interviews

Geritol Frolics Performers. 1994. Interview by author. Brainerd, MN, 18 May.
    Interview with C. Elmer Anderson, Leonard Bagne, Eleanor Bagne,
    Donna Deipolder, Don Forsberg, Phyl Glaser, Bob Holland, Vivian Hol-
    land, Pat Martinson, Ruth Meyers, Helen Molin, Bill Smithburg, Vivian
    Smithburg, and Joan Witham.
Roots & Branches performers. 1996. Interview by author. New York, 2 May.
    Interview with Yvette de Botton, Millie Gold, and Ida Harnden.
Roots & Branches performers. 1996. Interview by author. New York, 10 June.
    Interview with Etta Denbin, Ida Harnden, Jen Johnson, Michaela Lobel,
    Muriel Mervis, Yvette Pollack, and Molly Seif.
Allen, Claudia. 1994. Interview by author. Chicago, 27 July.
Auguste, Vladimir. 1996. Interview by author. Brooklyn, 8 November.
Bellamy, Lou. 1994. Telephone interview by author. 27 October.
Dryden, Bob. 1993. Interview by author. Brainerd, MN, 16 May.
Friars, Shewandasue. 1996. Interview by author. Brooklyn, 4 November.
Gibbons, June. 1994. Interview by author. Minneapolis, 19 October.
Justiano, Alberto. 1994. Interview by author. Minneapolis, 15 November.
Katz, Stephen. 1995. Conversation with author. 13 March.
Hill, Sue. 1996. Interview by author. Milwaukee, 2 March.
Hines, Kim. 1994. Telephone interview. 1 September.
Lacy, Suzanne. 1994. Telephone conversation with author. 23 September.
Morris, Bonnie. 1994. Telephone conversation with author. 18 August.
Partlan, Bill. 1994. Telephone conversation with author. 1 December.
Patterson, Barbara June. 1994. Interview by author. Minneapolis, 1 September.
Perlstein, Susan. 1995. Interview by author. Brooklyn, 16 November.

Pettitt, Peggy. 1996. Interview by author. Brooklyn, 14 March.

Quam, Jean. 1994. Interview by author. Minneapolis, 30 September.

Reams, Lee Roy. 1996. Telephone conversation with author. 11 November.

Reilly, Joy. 1995. Telephone conversation with author. 11 January.

———. 1994. Telephone conversation with author. 29 April.

———. 1993. Telephone conversation with author. 7 April.

Strimling, Arthur. 1995. Interview by author. New York, 24 November.

———. 1996. Interview by author. New York, 2 May.

———. 1996. Interview by author. New York, 22 November.

Williams, Diane. 1994. Telephone conversation with author. 22 September.

Books and Articles

Achenbaum, W. Andrew. 1978. *Old Age in the New Land.* Baltimore: Johns Hopkins University Press.

———. 1983. *Shades of Gray: Old Age, American Values, and Federal Policies since 1920.* Boston: Little, Brown.

———. 1986. *Social Security: Visions and Revisions.* New York: Cambridge University Press.

———. 1995. *Crossing Frontiers: Gerontology Emerges as a Science.* New York: Cambridge University Press.

Aiken, Lewis. 1989. *Later Life.* Hillsdale, NJ: Laurence Erlbaum Associates.

Allen, Jessie, and Alan Pifer, eds. 1993. *Women on the Front Lines: Meeting the Challenge of an Aging America.* Washington, DC: Urban Institute.

Aronowitz, Stanley. 1994. "Technology and the Future of Work." In Bender 15–30.

Auerbach, Nina. 1995. *Our Vampires, Ourselves.* Chicago: University of Chicago Press.

Auslander, Philip. 1992. "Live Performance in a Mediatized Culture." *Essays in Theatre* 11, no. 1 (November): 33–39.

———. 1994. "Live Performance in a Mediatized Culture, Part Deux." *Theatre Annual* 47:1–10.

Austin, Gayle. 1990. *Feminist Theories for Dramatic Criticism.* Ann Arbor: University of Michigan Press.

Balsamo, Anne. 1992. "On the Cutting Edge: Cosmetic Surgery and the Technological Production of the Gendered Body." *Camera Obscura* 28:207–37.

Baudrillard, Jean. 1988. *Selected Writings.* Ed. Mark Poster. Stanford: Stanford University Press.

———. 1992. *The Illusion of the End.* Trans. Chris Smith. Stanford: Stanford University Press.

Bauman, Zygmunt. 1992a. *Intimations of Postmodernity.* New York: Routledge.

———. 1992b. *Mortality, Immortality and Other Life Strategies.* Stanford: Stanford University Press.

Becker, Ernest. 1973. *The Denial of Death.* New York: Free Press.

Bender, Gretchen, and Timothy Druckrey, eds. 1994. *Culture on the Brink: Ideologies of Technology.* Seattle: Bay Press.

Bengtson, Vern L., and W. Andrew Achenbaum, eds. 1993. *The Changing Contract across Generations.* New York: Aldine de Gruyter.

Bengtson, Vern L., K. Warner Schaie, and Linda M. Burton, eds. 1995. *Adult Intergenerational Relations: Effects of Societal Change.* New York: Springer.

Bennet, Ruth, and Barry Gurland. 1981. *The Acting Out Elderly.* New York: Haworth Press.

Blau, Herbert. 1982. *Take Up the Bodies: Theatre at the Vanishing Point.* Urbana: University of Illinois Press.

———. 1990. *The Audience.* Baltimore: Johns Hopkins University Press.

Bolles, Richard. 1979. *Three Boxes of Life: And How to Get Out of Them.* Berkeley: Ten Speed Press.

Bordo, Susan. 1993. *Unbearable Weight: Feminism, Western Culture, and the Body.* Berkeley: University of California Press.

Bornat, Joanna, ed. 1994. *Reminiscence Reviewed: Perspectivies, Evaluations, Achievements.* Buckingham, Eng.: Open University Press.

Bourdieu, Pierre. 1984. *Distinction.* Trans. Richard Nice. Cambridge: Harvard University Press.

———. 1993. *The Field of Cultural Production.* New York: Columbia University Press.

Bourdieu, Pierre, and Löic J. D. Wacquant. 1992. *An Invitation to Reflexive Sociology.* Chicago: University of Chicago Press.

Boydston, Jeanne. 1990. *Home and Work: Housework, Wages, and the Ideology of Labor in the Early Republic.* New York: Oxford University Press.

Brecht, Bertolt. 1982. *Brecht on Theatre.* Trans. John Willett. London: Methuen.

Burger, Isabel. 1980. *Creative Drama for Senior Adults.* Wilton, CT: Morehouse-Barlow.

Butler, Judith. 1988. "Performative Acts and Gender Constitution: An Essay in Phenonmenology and Feminist Theory." *Theatre Journal* 40, no. 4: 519–31.

———. 1990. *Gender Trouble.* New York: Routledge.

———. 1993. *Bodies That Matter.* New York: Routledge.

Butler, Robert N. 1963. "The Life Review: An Interpretation of Reminiscence in the Aged." *Psychiatry* 26:65–76.

———. 1969. "Age-ism: Another Form of Bigotry." *Gerontologist.* 9:243–46.

———. 1975. *Why Survive?* New York: Harper and Row.

Butler, Robert N., and Herbert P. Gleason, eds. 1985. *Productive Aging: Enhancing Vitality in Later Life.* New York: Springer.

Butler, Robert N., Mia R. Oberlink, and Mal Schechter, eds. 1990. *The Promise of Productive Aging: From Biology to Social Policy.* New York: Springer.

Carlson, Marvin. 1996. *Performance: A Critical Introduction.* New York: Routledge.

Case, Sue-Ellen. 1988. *Feminism and Theatre.* New York: Methuen, 1988.

———. 1991. "Tracking the Vampire." *differences* 3, no. 2 (summer): 1–20.

———. 1993. "Theory/History/Revolution." In *Critical Theory and Performance,* ed. Janelle Reinelt and Joseph Roach, 418–29. Ann Arbor: University of Michigan Press.

———. 1995a. "Performing Lesbian in the Space of Technology: Part I." *Theatre Journal* 47, no. 1: 1–18.

———. 1995b. "Performing Lesbian in the Space of Technology: Part II." *Theatre Journal* 47, no. 3: 329–43.

Cattanach, Ann. 1992. *Drama for People with Special Needs.* New York: Drama Book Publishers.

Certeau, Michel de. 1984. *The Practice of Everyday Life.* Trans. Steven Rendall. Berkeley: University of California Press.

———. 1988. *The Writing of History.* Trans. Tom Conley. New York: Columbia University Press.

Charcot, J. M. 1881. *Clinical Lectures on the Diseases of Old Age.* Trans. Leigh H. Hunt. New York: William Wood and Co.

Chopra, Deepak. 1993. *Ageless Body, Timeless Mind: The Quantum Alternative to Growing Old.* New York: Harmony Books.

Chudacoff, Howard P. 1989. *How Old Are You? Age Consciousness in American Culture.* Princeton, NJ: Princeton University Press.

Clark, Patch. 1978. "Theatre Arts and the Aging." Master's thesis, Theatre Department of Virginia Commonwealth University, Richmond.

———. 1985. *Seniors on Stage: The Impact of Applied Theatre Techniques on the Elderly.* New York: Praeger Publishers.

Cleveland, William. 1992. *Art in Other Places: Artists at Work in America's Community and Social Institutions.* Westport, CT: Praeger Publishers.

Coenen, Herman. 1991. "Wandering through the Caves: Phenomenological Field Research in a Social World of Dementia." In *Social Organization and Process: Papers in Honor of Anselm L. Strauss,* ed. David Maines, 315–32. Hawthorne, NY: Aldine Publishing Corp.

Cohler, Bertram J. 1993. "Aging, Morale, and Meaning: The Nexus of Narrative." In *Voices and Visions of Aging,* ed. Thomas R. Cole, W. Andrew Achenbaum, and Patricia l. Jakobi, 107–33. New York: Springer.

Cole, Thomas R. 1992. *The Journey of Life.* New York: Cambridge University Press.

Cole, Thomas R., W. Andrew Achenbaum, and Patricia L. Jakobi, eds. 1993. *Voices and Visions of Aging: Toward a Critical Gerontology.* New York: Springer.

Cole, Thomas R., and Sally Gadow, eds. 1986.*What Does It Mean to Grow Old? Reflections from the Humanities.* Durham: Duke University Press.

Cole, Thomas R., David Van Tassel, and Robert Kastenbaum, eds. 1992. *Handbook for the Humanities and Aging.* New York: Springer.

Conley, Verena Andermatt, ed. 1993. *Rethinking Technologies.* Minneapolis: University of Minnesota Press.

Cornish, Roger. 1978. "Senior Adult Theatre—The State of the Art and a Call for Research." *Theatre News* (May): 1–2, 11.

Cornish, Roger, and John Orlock. 1976. *Short Plays for the Long Living.* Boston: Baker's Plays.

Cornish, Roger, and C. Robert Kase. 1981. *Senior Adult Theatre.* University Park: Pennsylvania State University Press.

Coupland, Douglas. 1991. *Generation X: Tales for an Accelerated Culture.* New York: St. Martin's.

Cristofovici, Anca. Forthcoming. "Touching Surfaces: Photography, Aging, and an Aesthetics of Change." In *Figuring Age: Women, Bodies, and Generations,* ed. Kathleen Woodward. Bloomington: Indiana University Press.

Davis, Fred. 1979. *Yearning for Yesterday: A Sociology of Nostalgia.* New York: Free Press.

Davy, Kate. 1993. "Fe/male Impersonation: the Discourse of Camp." In Reinelt and Roach 231–47.

deCordova, Richard. 1990. *Picture Personalities.* Urbana: University of Illinois Press.

Deleuze, Gilles. 1993. *The Deleuze Reader.* Ed. Constantin V. Boundas. New York: Columbia University Press.

Diamond, Elin. 1988. "Brechtian Theory / Feminist Theory: Toward a Gestic Feminist Criticism." *TDR* 32 (spring): 82–94.

Diamond, Irene, and Lee Quinby, eds. 1988. *Feminism and Foucault: Reflections on Resistance.* Boston: Northeastern University Press.

Dolan, Jill. 1988. *The Feminist Spectator as Critic.* Ann Arbor: University of Michigan Press.

———. 1993a. *Presence and Desire.* Ann Arbor: University of Michigan Press.

———. 1993b. "Geographies of Learning: Theatre Studies, Performance, and the 'Performative.'" *Theatre Journal* 45, no. 4 (December): 417–41.

Dollimore, John. 1991. *Sexual Dissidence: Augustine to Wilde, Freud to Foucault.* New York: Oxford University Press.

Dreyfus, Robert. 1996. "The End of Social Security as We Know It?" *Mother Jones* (November–December): 51–58.

Dryden, Bob. 1989. *Staging a Snazzy Senior Showcase.* Brainerd, MN: Brainerd Community College.

Durham, Scott. 1993. "The Technology of Death and Its Limits: The Problem of the Simulation Model." In *Rethinking Technologies,* ed. Verena Andermatt Conley, 156–72. Minneapolis: University of Minnesota Press.

Dychtwald, Ken. 1989. *The Age Wave: The Challenges and Opportunities of an Aging America.* Los Angeles: J. P. Tarcher.

Dyer, Richard. 1991a. "Charisma." In Gledhill 57–60.

———. 1991b. "*A Star Is Born* and the Construction of Authenticity." In Gledhill 132–40.

Erikson, Erik H. 1963. *Childhood and Society.* New York: Norton.

———. 1978. *Adulthood.* New York: Norton.

———. 1982. *The Life-Cycle Completed: A Review.* New York: Norton.

Erikson, Erik, Joan Erikson, and Helen Kivnick. 1986. *Vital Involvement in Old Age.* New York: Norton.

Estes, Carroll. 1980. *The Aging Enterprise.* San Francisco: Jossey-Bass.

Evangelista, Sylvia, et al. 1995. "Generations: Women's Tradition and the Handing Down of History." *Symposium* (summer): 130–35.

Fahey, Charles J., and Martha Holstein. 1993. "Toward a Philosophy of the Third Age." In Cole, Achenbaum, and Jakobi 241–56.

Farkas, Janice, and Dennis Hogan. 1995. "The Demography of Changing Intergenerational Relationships." In Bengtson, Schaie, and Burton 1–18.

Featherstone, Mike, and Mike Hepworth. 1991. "The Mask of Ageing and the Postmodern Life Course." In *The Body: Social Process and Cultural Theory*, ed. Mike Featherstone, Mike Hepworth, and Bryan S. Turner, 371–89. London: Sage.

Featherstone, Mike, and Andrew Wernick, eds. 1995. *Images of Aging: Cultural Representations of Later Life*. London: Routledge.

Foucault, Michel. 1965. *Madness and Civilization: A History of Insanity in the Age of Reason*. Trans. Richard Howard. New York: Pantheon.

———. 1973. *The Birth of the Clinic: An Archaeology of Medical Perception*. New York: Pantheon.

———. 1977a. "Nietzsche, Genealogy, History." In *Language, Counter-Memory, Practice: Selected Essays and Interviews*, ed. Donald Bouchard. Trans. Donald Bouchard and Sherry Simon. Ithaca: Cornell University Press.

———. 1977b. *Discipline and Punish*. Trans. Alan Sheridan. New York: Pantheon.

———. 1978. *History of Sexuality*, vol. 1. Trans. Robert Hurley. New York: Random House.

Franko, Mark. 1992. "Where He Danced: Cocteau's Barbette and Ohno's Water Lilies." *PMLA* 107, no. 3: 594–607.

———. 1995. *Dancing Modernism / Performing Politics*. Bloomington: Indiana University Press.

Friedan, Betty. 1993. *The Fountain of Age*. New York: Simon and Schuster.

Frueh, Joanna. 1994. "The Erotic as Social Security." *Art Journal* (spring): 66–72.

Garner, Stanton B., Jr. 1994. *Bodied Spaces: Phenomenology and Performance in Contemporary Drama*. Ithaca: Cornell University Press.

Geertz, Clifford. 1983. *Local Knowledge: Further Essays in Interpretive Anthropology*. New York: Basic Books.

Gledhill, Christine. 1991. *Stardom: Industry of Desire*. London: Routledge.

Goffman, Erving. 1959. *The Presentation of Self in Everyday Life*. Garden City, NJ: Doubleday.

Graebner, William. 1980. *A History of Retirement*. New Haven: Yale University Press.

Gratton, Brian, and Carole Haber. 1993. "Rethinking Industrialization: Old Age and the Family Economy." In Cole 134–59.

Gray, P. 1974. *Dramatics for the Elderly: A Guide for Residential Care Settings and Senior Centers*. New York: Teachers College, Columbia University Press.

Grossberg, Lawrence. 1992. *We Gotta Get Out of This Place: Popular Conservatism and Postmodern Culture*. New York: Routledge.

———. 1994. "Is Anybody Listening? Does Anybody Care?: On Talking about 'The State of Rock.'" In Ross 41–58.

Gullette, Margaret Morganroth. 1997. *Declining to Decline: Cultural Combat and the Politics of the Midlife*. Charlottesville: University Press of Virginia.

Habermas, Jürgen. 1979. *Communication and the Evolution of Society*. Trans. Thomas McCarthy. Boston: Beacon.

———. 1987. *The Theory of Communicative Action*. 2 vols. Trans. Thomas McCarthy. Boston: Beacon.

Hables Gray, Chris, ed. 1995. *The Cyborg Handbook*. New York: Routledge.

Hall, Elizabeth. 1980. "Acting One's Age: New Rules for Old." *Psychology Today* 13 (April): 66.

Haraway, Donna J. 1990."A Manifesto for Cyborgs: Science, Technology, and Socialist Feminism in the 1980s." Rptd. in *Feminism/Postmodernism*, ed. Linda Nicholson, 190–233. New York: Routledge.

———. 1991. *Simians Cyborgs, and Women*. New York: Routledge.

Harris, Mary. 1994. "Growing Old Gracefully: Age Concealment and Gender." *Journal of Gerontology: Psychological Sciences* 49, no. 4: 149–58.

Hart, Linda, and Peggy Phelan, eds. 1993. *Acting Out: Feminist Performances*. Ann Arbor: University of Michigan Press.

Hayles, N. Katherine. 1993. "The Seductions of Cyberspace." In Conley 173–90.

———. 1995. "The Life Cycle of Cyborgs: Writing the Posthuman." In Hables Gray 321–35.

Heidegger, Martin. 1962. *Being and Time*. New York: Harper and Row.

Herman, Judith Lewis. 1992. *Trauma and Recovery*. New York: Basic Books.

Hessel, Dieter. 1977. *Maggie Kuhn on Aging: A Dialogue*. Philadelphia: Westminster.

Hoffman, Yoel. 1986. *Japanese Death Poems*. Tokyo: Charles E. Tuttle.

Holborn, Mark. 1987. *Butoh, Dance of the Dark Soul*. New York: Aperture Foundation.

Holtz, Geoffrey. 1995. *Welcome to the Jungle*. New York: St. Martin's.

Houtepen, Rob. 1995. "The Meaning of Old Age and the Distribution of Health-Care Resources." *Ageing and Society* 15, no. 2: 219–43.

Howe, Neil, and Bill Strauss. 1993. *13th Gen: Abort, Retry, Ignore, Fail?* New York: Vintage.

Jackson, James S., Linda M. Chatters, and Robert Joseph Taylor, eds. 1993. *Aging in Black America*. New York: Sage.

Jaggar, Alison M. 1983. *Feminist Politics and Human Nature*. Totowa, NJ: Rowman and Allanheld.

Jameson, Frederic. 1988. *Postmodernism and Its Discontents*. Ed. E. Ann Kaplan, 13–29. London: Verso. First printed in *The Anti-Aesthetic*, ed. Hal Foster, 111–25. Port Townsend, WA: Bay Press, 1983.

Kain, Philip J. 1993. "Marx, Housework, and Alienation." *Hypatia* 8, no. 1 (winter): 121–44.

Kaminsky, Marc. 1984. *The Uses of Reminiscence*. New York: Haworth.

———. 1993. "Definitional Ceremonies: Depoliticizing and Reenchanting the Culture of Age." In Cole 257–74.

Kastenbaum, Robert. 1994. *Defining Acts: Aging as Drama*. Amityville, NY: Baywood.

Kaufman, Sharon. 1986. *The Ageless Self*. Madison: University of Wisconsin Press.

Kern, Stephen. 1983. *The Culture of Time and Space: 1880–1918.* Cambridge: Harvard University Press.

King, Barry. 1991. "Articulating Stardom." In Gledhill 167–82.

Kivnick, Helen. 1993. "Everyday Mental Health: A Guide to Assessing Life Strengths." *Generations* 17, no. 1 (spring): 13–20.

Koestenbaum, Wayne. 1994. *The Queen's Throat: Opera, Homosexuality, and the Mystery of Desire.* New York: Vintage.

Kroker, Arthur. 1992. *The Possessed Individual: Technology and the French Postmodern.* New York: St. Martin's.

Kroker, Arthur, and David Cook, eds. 1986. *The Postmodern Scene: Excremental Culture and Hyper-Aesthetics.* New York: St. Martin's.

Kroker, Arthur, and Marilouis Kroker, eds. 1987. *Body Invaders: Panic Sex in America.* New York: St. Martin's.

Kroll, Jack. 1995a. "Hello, Dolly!" *Newsweek,* 30 October, 78.

———. 1995b. "Exaltation of Divas." *Newsweek,* 18 September, 86.

Kübler Ross, Elizabeth. 1969. *On Death and Dying.* New York: Macmillan.

Kuhn, Annette, and Ann Marie Wolpe. 1978. *Feminism and Materialism: Women and Modes of Production.* London: Routledge and Kegan Paul.

Kundera, Milan. 1984. *The Unbearable Lightness of Being.* Trans. Henry Heim. New York: Harper and Row.

Lacan, Jacques. 1977. *Ecrits: A Selection.* Trans. Alan Sheridan. New York: Norton.

Lacy, Suzanne. 1985. Project Description of Whisper Minnesota. MS, private files of Jerry Bloedow.

Lambert, Pam, Lois Armstrong, and Joyce Wagner. 1995. "The Vanishing." *People Weekly* 43, no. 8: 32–42.

Landy, Robert. 1986. *Drama Therapy.* Springfield, IL: Charles C. Thomas.

Laslett, Peter. 1991. *A Fresh Map of Life: The Emergence of the Third Age.* Cambridge: Harvard University Press.

Leary, Timothy. 1994. *Chaos and Cyber Culture.* Berkeley: Ronin Publishing.

Levin, Charles. 1987. "Carnal Knowledge of Aesthetic States." In Kroker and Kroker 99–111.

Lippard, Lucy. 1988. "Suzanne Lacy: Some of Her Own Medicine." *TDR* 32, no. 1: 71–81.

Lipsitz, George. 1990. *Time Passages.* Minneapolis: University of Minnesota Press.

———. 1994. "We Know What Time It Is: Race, Class and Youth Culture in the Nineties." In Ross and Rose 17–28.

Lock, Margaret. 1993. *Encounters with Aging: Mythologies of Menopause in Japan and North America.* Berkeley: University of California Press.

———. 1996. Lecture. 9 February. Center for Twentieth Century Studies, University of Wisconsin–Milwaukee.

Longman, Phillip. 1987. *Born to Pay: The New Politics of Aging in America.* Boston: Houghton Mifflin.

Lugones, Maria. 1994. "Purity, Impurity, and Separation." *Signs* 19, no. 2: 458–79.

Lyotard, Jean-François, and Jean-Loup Thébaud. 1984. *The Postmodern Condition: A Report on Knowledge*. Minneapolis: University of Minnesota Press.

———. 1985. *Just Gaming: Conversations*. Minneapolis: University of Minnesota Press.

———. 1993. *The Postmodern Explained: Correspondence, 1982–1985*. Ed. Julian Refanis and Morgan Thomas. Minneapolis: University of Minnesota Press.

Maclay, Elise. 1990. *Green Winter: Celebrations of Later Life*. New York: Henry Holt.

MacManus, Susan. 1996. *Young v. Old: Generational Combat in the 21st Century*. Boulder, CO: Westview.

Mandelbaum, Ken. 1995. "Musical Theater Review: 'Hello Dolly!'" *Theater Week* 6 (November): 45–46.

Marranca, Bonnie. 1994. "Ages of the Avant-Garde." *Performing Arts Journal* 46:9–57.

Martin, Biddy. 1994. "Sexualities without Genders and Other Queer Utopias." *Diacritics* 24, nos. 2–3: 104–21.

Martin, Emily. 1994. *Flexible Bodies: Tracking Immunity in American Culture from the Days of Polio to the Age of AIDS*. Boston: Beacon.

McCullough, Laurence B. 1993. "Arrested Aging: The Power of the Past to Make Us Aged and Old." In Cole 184–204.

McDonald, Barbara. 1990. "Politics of Aging: I'm Not Your Mother." *MS* (July–August): 56–58.

McDonough, Ann. 1994. *The Golden Stage: Dramatic Activities for Older Adults*. Dubuque, IA: Kendall/Hunt.

———. (Del Vecchio). 1981. "Modifying Creative Drama for Senior Adult Participants: The Theories and Methods of Selected Practitioners." Ph.D. diss., University of Minnesota, 1981.

Mellencamp, Patricia. 1992. *High Anxiety: Castastrophe, Scandal, Age, and Comedy*. Bloomington: Indiana University Press.

Merleau-Ponty, Maurice. 1962. *Phenomenology of Perception*. Trans. Colin Smith. London: Routledge and Kegan Paul. New York: Humanities.

Michaels, Claire. 1979. "Geridadrama, Drama Therapy with Senior Citizens." In *Drama in Therapy*, ed. Gertrude Schaffner and Richard Courtney, 175–92. New York: Drama Book Specialists.

Middleton, David, and Kevin Buchanan. 1993. "Is Reminiscence Working? Accounting for the Therapeutic Benefits of Reminiscence Work with Older People." *Journal of Aging Studies* 7, no. 3: 321–33.

Minkler, Meredith, and Carroll L. Estes. 1991. *Critical Perspectives on Aging*. Amityville, NY: Baywood.

Modleski, Tania. 1986. *Studies in Entertainment: Critical Approaches to Mass Culture*. Bloomington: Indiana University Press.

Mondale, Clarence. 1988. "Under Reduced Circumstances: Space and Place for the Aging." *Journal of American Studies* 22, no. 3: 347–70.

Moody, Harry. 1986. "The Meaning of Life and the Meaning of Old Age." In Cole and Gadow 9–40.

———. 1993. "Overview: What Is Critical Gerontology and Why Is It Important?" In Cole, Achenbaum, and Jakobi xv–xli.

————. 1995. "Aging, Meaning and the Allocation of Resources." *Ageing and Society* 15, no. 2: 163–85.

Morse, Margaret. 1994. "What Do Cyborgs Eat? Oral Logic in an Information Society." *Discourse* 16, no. 3: 86–123.

Munroe, Alexandra. 1994. *Japanese Art after 1945: Scream against the Sky.* New York: Abrams.

Myerhoff, Barbara. 1992. *Remembered Lives: The Work of Ritual, Storytelling and Growing Older.* Ed. Marc Kaminsky. Ann Arbor: University of Michigan Press.

Nascher, I. L. 1909. *Geriatrics.* Philadelphia: P. Blakiston's Son and Co.

Neugarten, Bernice. 1974. "Age Groups in American Society and the Rise of the Young Old." *Annals of the American Academy of Political and Social Science.*

Neugarten, Bernice L., and Dail A. Neugarten. 1986. "Changing Meanings of Age in the Aging Society." In Pifer and Bronte 33–51.

Newton, Judith, and Deborah Rosenfeld, eds. 1985. *Feminist Criticism and Social Change: Sex, Class, and Race in Literature and Culture.* New York: Methuen.

Nicholson, Linda. 1994. "Feminism and the Politics of Postmodernism." In *Feminism and Postmodernism,* ed. Margaret Ferguson and Jennifer Wicke. Durham: Duke University Press.

Nolter, M. 1973. "Drama for the Elderly: They Can Do It." *Gerontologist* 12:153–56.

"No Purpose in Dying." 1993. *U.S. News and World Report,* 8 March, 72.

Oakley, Ann. 1974. *The Sociology of Housework.* New York: Pantheon, 1974.

Ohno, Kazuo. 1986. "Performance Text: *The Dead Sea.*" *TDR* 30, no. 2: 170.

————. 1986. "Selections from the Prose of Kazuo Ohno." *TDR* 30, no. 2: 156–62.

Olshansky, S. Jay. 1993. "The Human Life Span: Are We Reaching the Outer Limits?" *Geriatrics* 48, no. 3 (March): 85–88.

Palmore, Erdman, and Daisaku Maeda. 1985. *The Honorable Elders Revisited = Otoshyori Saiko: A Revised Cross-Cultural Analysis of Aging in Japan.* Durham: Duke University Press.

Parker, Andrew, and Eve Kosofsky Sedgwick, eds. 1995. *Performativity and Performance.* New York: Routledge.

Pettitt, Peggy, and the Bushwick Round Table Intergenerational Collective. 1996. *Bushwick, Why Vote?* MS.

Pflanzer, Howard. 1992. "Older People Act Up: Making the Ordinary Extraordinary." *TDR* 36, no. 1 (spring): 115–23.

Phelan, Peggy. 1993. *Unmarked.* New York: Routledge.

Pifer, Alan, and Lydia Brontë, eds. 1986. *Our Aging Society: Paradox and Promise.* New York: Norton.

Polan, Dana. 1986. "Brief Encounters: Mass Culture and the Evacuation of Sense." In Modeleski 167–87.

Postman, Neil. 1994. *The Disappearance of Childhood.* New York: Vintage.

Quam, Jean. 1992. "Adaptation and Age-related Expectations of Older Gays and Lesbians." *Gerontologist* 32, no. 3 (June): 367–75.

————. 1993. "Gay and Lesbian Aging." *Siecus Report* 21, no. 5 (June–July): 10–13.

Rayner, Alice. 1994. "Cyborgs and Replicants: On the Boundaries." *Discourse* 16, no. 3: 124–43.

Reinelt, Janelle. 1986. "Beyond Brecht: Britain's New Feminist Drama." *Theatre Journal* 37:154–63.

———. 1994. "Staging the Invisible: The Crisis of Visibility in Theatrical Representations." *Text and Performance Quarterly* 14:97–101.

Reinelt, Janelle, and Joseph Roach. 1992. *Critical Theory and Performance.* Ann Arbor: University of Michigan Press.

Ressner, Jeffrey. 1996. "Dr. Tim's Last Trip." *Time,* 29 April.

Roiphe, Katie. 1993. *The Morning After: Sex, Fear, and Feminism on Campus.* Boston: Little, Brown.

Rosaldo, Renato. 1989. "Imperialist Nostalgia." *Representations* 26:107–22.

Rosen, Jonathan. 1995. "Rewriting the End: Elizabeth Kübler-Ross." *New York Times Magazine,* 22 January, 22–25.

Ross, Andrew. 1988. *Universal Abandon.* Minneapolis: University of Minnesota Press.

Ross, Andrew, and Tricia Rose, eds. 1994. *Microphone Fiends: Youth Music and Youth Culture.* New York: Routledge.

Rossi, Alice. 1986. "Sex and Gender in the Aging Society." In Pifer and Brontë 111–40.

Roth, Moira. 1988. "Suzanne Lacy: Social Reformer and Witch." *TDR* 32, no. 1: 42–60.

Rothenberg, Diane. 1988. "Social Art / Social Action." *TDR* 32, no. 1: 61–70.

Rowles, Graham D. 1993. "Evolving Images of Place in Aging and 'Aging in Place.'" *Generations* 17, no. 2 (spring–summer): 65–70.

Rushkoff, Douglas. 1994. *The Gen X Reader.* New York: Ballantine.

Russel, Cheryl, and Susan Mitchell. 1995. "Talking about Whose Generation?" *American Demographics* 17, no. 4 (April): 32–33.

Sandia, Robert. 1996. "Hello, Dolly!" *Dance Magazine* 70, no. 1 (January): 98.

Schaie, K. Warner, and W. Andrew Achenbaum, eds. 1993. *Societal Impact on Aging: Historical Perspectives.* New York: Springer.

Schatner, Gertrud, and Richard Courtney. 1981. *Drama in Therapy.* Vol. 2, *Adults.* New York: Drama Book Specialists.

Schechner, Richard. 1985. *Between Theatre and Anthropology.* Philadelphia: University of Pennsylvania Press.

———. 1986. "Kazuo Ohno Does Not Commute." *TDR* 30, no. 2: 163–69.

Schecter, David, and Arthur Strimling. 1996. *It's about Time!* MS.

Schor, Julet B. 1992. *The Overworked American: The Unexpected Decline of Leisure.* New York: Basic Books.

Schrof, Joannie. 1993. "Feminism's Daughters." *U.S. News and World Report,* 27 September, 68.

Simon, John. 1995. "Hello, Dolly!" *New York,* 6 November, 52.

Simonsick, Eleanor M. 1995. "Demography of Productive Aging." In *Promoting Successful and Productive Aging,* ed. Lynne A. Bond, Stephen J. Cutler, and Armin Grams, 69–90. Thousand Oaks, CA: Sage Publications.

Soldo, Beth J. 1980. "America's Elderly in the 1980s." *Population Bulletin* 35, no. 4: 3–47.

Sontag, Susan. 1972. "The Double Standard of Aging." *Saturday Review* 55:29–38.

Stein, Bonnie Sue. 1986. Butoh: "Twenty Years Ago We Were Crazy, Dirty, and Mad." *TDR* 30, no. 2: 107–26.

Stelarc. 1995. "From Psycho to Cyber Strategies: Prosthetics, Robotics and Remote Existence." MS.

Straka, Gerald A. 1986. "Television and the Elderly." In *Education and Aging,* ed. David A. Peterson, James E. Thornton, and James E. Birren, 93–117. Englewood Cliffs, NJ: Prentice-Hall.

Strauss, William, and Neil Howe. 1991. *Generations: The History of America's Future, 1584–2069.* New York: Quill, Willliam Morrow.

Sussman, Mark. 1996. "New York's Facelift." Paper presented at the Association for Theatre in Higher Education, 7–10 August, New York.

Telander, M., F. Quinlan, and K. Verson. 1982. *Acting Up! An Innovative Approach to Creative Drama for Older Adults.* Chicago: Coach House Press.

Terdiman, Richard. 1993. *Present Past: Modernity and the Memory Crisis.* Ithaca: Cornell University Press.

Thomson, Rosmarie. 1997. *Extraordinary Bodies: Figuring Physical Disability in American Culture and Literature.* New York. Columbia University Press.

Thornton, S., and J. Brotchie. 1987. "Reminiscence: A Critical Review of the Literature." *British Journal of Clinical Psychology* 26:93–111.

Thurman, Anne H., and Carol Ann Piggins. 1982. *Drama Activities with Older Adults: A Handbook for Leaders.* New York: Haworth Press.

Torres-Gil, Fernando. 1992. *The New Aging: Politics and Chante in America.* New York: Auburn House.

Turner, Victor. 1974. *Drama, Fields, and Metaphors: Symbolic Action in Human Society.* Ithaca: Cornell University Press.

———. 1976. "Social Dramas and Ritual Metaphors." *Ritual, Play and Performance: Readings in the Social Sciences / Theatre,* ed. Richard Schechner and Mady Schutzman, 97–120. New York: Seabury Press.

———. 1982. *From Ritual to Theatre: The Human Seriousness of Play.* New York: PAJ Publications.

Van Gennep, Arnold. 1960. *The Rites of Passage.* Trans. Monika B. Vizedom and Gabrielle L. Caffe. Chicago: University of Chicago Press.

Viala, Jean. 1988. *Butoh: Shades of Darkness.* Tokyo: Shufunotomo.

Virilio, Paul. 1989. *War and Cinema: The Logistics of Perception.* London: Verso.

———. 1993. "The Third Interval: A Critical Transition." In Conley 3–10.

———. 1994. *The Vision Machine.* Bloomington: Indiana University Press.

———. 1995. *The Art of the Motor.* Minneapolis: University of Minnesota Press.

Vorenberg, Bonnie. 1985. *A Guide to 49 New Plays for Senior Adult Theatre.* Portland, OR: Arts for Elders.

———. 1987. *New Plays for Mature Actors.* Chicago: Coach House Press.

Walker, Barbara. 1985. *Crone: Woman of Age, Wisdom, and Power.* New York: Harper and Row.

Weisberg, Naida, and Rosilyn Wilder. 1986. *Drama Therapy with Older Adults.* New Haven, CT: National Association for Drama Therapy.

Wexler, Michael, and John Hulme. 1994. *Voices of the Xiled: A Generation Speaks for Itself.* New York: Mainstreet Books.

Williams, Raymond. 1975. *Television: Technology and Cutural Form.* New York: Schocken.

Wolf, Naomi. 1990. *The Beauty Myth.* London: Chatto and Windus.

Wolf, Stacy. 1996. "The Queer Pleasures of Mary Martin and Broadway: 'The Sound of Music' as a Lesbian Musical." *Modern Drama* 39, no. 1 (spring): 51–64.

"The Wonderful Leveling Off." 1950. *Time Magazine,* 9 January, 50–55.

Woodward, Kathleen. 1986. "Reminiscence and the Life Review: Prospects and Retrospects." In Cole and Gadow 135–61.

———. 1991. *Aging and Its Discontents.* Bloomington: Indiana University Press.

———. 1994. "From Virtual Cyborgs to Biological Time Bombs: Technocriticism and the Material Body." In Bender 47–64.

———. 1995. "Tribute to the Older Woman: Psychoanalytic Geometry, Gender and the Emotions." In *Psychoanalysis, Feminism and the Future of Gender,* ed. Joseph H. Smith, 91–108. Baltimore: Johns Hopkins University Press.

Wyatt-Brown, Anne. 1992. "Literary Gerontology Comes of Age." In Cole, Van Tassel, and Kastenbaum 331–51.

Yates, Francis. 1966. *The Art of Memory.* Chicago: University of Chicago Press.

Newspapers

Canby, Vincent. 1995. "Hello, Dolly!" *New York Times,* 20 October.

Jefferson, Margo. 1995. "Goddesses of the Theater, Hear Our Prayer." *New York Times,* 5 November, national ed.

Klein, Julia M. 1995. "The Dolly Is Back Again." *Philadelphia Inquirer,* 26 February.

Lacey, Carol. 1987. "Women Raise Their Voices." *St. Paul Pioneer Press Dispatch,* 10 May.

Mordden, Ethan. 1995. "Quick: Name a Hot, New Musical Star." *New York Times,* 28 January.

Norman, Michael. 1996. "Living Too Long: The Human Species Is Experiencing Profound Change in the Stages of Life, and There's a Catch." *New York Times Magazine,* 14 January.

Purdum, Todd S. 1995. "Carol Burnett Comes Round to Where She Started From." *New York Times,* 24 September.

Roca, Octavio. 1994. "Dolly's Back Where She Belongs." *San Francisco Chronicle,* 5 May, C1+.

Shales, Tom. 1995. "Curtains Rise, and Curtains Fall: 'Dolly!' and Channing, Last of a Breed." *Washington Post,* 1 October.

Sommers, Pamela. 1994. "You're Looking Swell, Dolly!" *Washington Post,* 1 September, D1, D5.

Stern, Alan. 1994. "Look at the Old Girl Now! 'Dolly' as Classy as Ever." *Denver Post,* 16 July.

Index

Achenbaum, W. Andrew, 10
Acting Up! 60
advertising, 5–6
Age Exchange Theater, 190n. 4, 195n. 14
age makeup, 77
aging
  association between old age and out-of-date, 128, 130, 131
  binary categories, 135, 136, 141, 143–45, 148
  as category of difference, 186
  in depth, 22 (*see also* depth model of aging)
  as feminist issue, 125–28
  as mark of poverty, 154, 201n. 7
  as narrative of decline, 2, 5, 9, 23, 27, 166, 167, 173, 176
  as natural, 10, 19
  as normal, 12, 19
  as obsolete, 13
  as pathology, 12, 17, 19
  as process, 135, 136, 193n. 15
  as social construction, 10
aging society, 6, 16, 146, 167
Alzheimer's Disease, 1, 29, 162, 181, 182
Andrews, Julie, 164, 165, 181, 182
Aronowitz, Stanley, 155

Artreach Players, 31–33
Association for Theatre in Higher Education (ATHE), 113
ATHE. *See* Association for Theatre in Higher Education
At the Foot of the Mountain Theater, 116, 117
Auerbach, Nina, 148
Auguste, Vladimir, 103, 105–6
Auslander, Philip, 153–56
Austin, Gayle, 129
authenticity, 169, 172–74, 202n. 6

Baby Boom(ers), 1, 5, 14, 16, 20, 84, 87
Bagne, Eleanor, 39
Baudrillard, Jean, 150–51, 156, 158, 160, 194n. 19, 210n. 9
Bayme, Gabrielle, 103, 104–6
Bengtson, Vern, 86
bifocal theater groups, 31–34, 90–91
binary categories. *See* aging, binary categories
Black Theatre Network (BTN), 21, 114, 133
Blau, Herbert, 148, 167
Boal, Augusto, 102
Boline, Matt, 89
Bordo, Susan, 135
Bosco, Philip, 202n. 7

Bourdieu, Pierre, 79, 124, 125, 196n. 10
Brecht, Bertolt, 76
Brown, Tony, 148, 159, 160
BTN. *See* Black Theatre Network
Buchanan, Kevin, 69, 193n. 8
Buckley, Betty, 164, 170
Burnett, Carol, 164, 169–70
Butler, Judith, 2, 7–9, 45, 48, 141, 143, 154, 168, 174, 199n. 15
Butler, Robert, 15, 19, 26, 66–68, 70–72, 79, 102, 188n. 13, 192n. 4, 192n. 5
butoh, 136–37, 140, 141

Caldwell, Zoe, 164, 170
Canby, Vincent, 171, 172, 174
Cantwell, Alice Davis, 3
Case, Sue-Ellen, 128–29, 197n. 14, 197n. 18, 201n. 4
Center for Twentieth Century Studies (University of Wisconsin–Milwaukee), 185, 204n. 20
Champion, Gower, 170
Channing, Carol, 5, 22, 134, 163–78, 183
Charcot, Jean Martin, 12
Cherry, Randall, 106
Chopra, Deepak, 72, 191n. 14
Chudacoff, Howard, 11
Coenen, Herman, 182, 204n. 1
Cohen-Cruz, Jan, 89
Cohler, Bertram, 70
Cole, Thomas, 12
Coleman, Sadell, 104
Cornish, Roger, 27
counter-memory, 52–53
Coupland, Douglas, 85, 88
Creative Drama, 26–28, 181
Cristofovici, Anca, 141, 199n. 11
critical gerontology, 19
Crystal Quilt, The, 20–21, 112–14, 115–23, 130–33, 183, 184
cultural capital, 125, 132, 197n. 10
cyborgs, 150, 199n. 13

Dance Exchange. *See* Liz Lerman's Dance Exchange
Davis, Fred, 50, 51
Davy, Kate, 45–46, 49
DeBotton, Yvette, 92, 93, 96, 99
de Certeau, Michel, 2, 123–26, 132, 168
decline narrative of age. *See* aging, as narrative of decline
definitional ceremony, 119
Deleuze, Gilles, 194n. 15
Denbin, Etta, 90, 99
Dennis, Nancy, 116
dependency ratio, 16, 189n. 20
depth model of aging, 136, 140–43, 148, 149, 156, 161, 184
Dickerson, Glenda, 114, 133
Diepolder, Donna, 38, 54
disability, 39, 79–81, 135, 191n. 11, 194n. 17
diversity
    in *The Crystal Quilt,* 119–20, 123
    in ESTA, 100
    feminist scholarship 126
    in the Geritol Frolics, 38
    in GLT, 31, 60–61
    lack of, 31
    in R&B, 31
    in StAGEbridge, 31
Dolan, Jill, 128–29
Dollimore, John, 141
drag, 44–49, 192n. 19
Drama Therapy, 27–28, 181, 190n. 2
Dryden, Bob, 28, 34–36, 39, 42, 56
Dyer, Richard, 202n. 6

Elders Share the Arts (ESTA), 21, 27, 31, 83–84, 100–110, 183, 184
Encounters at the Border, 30–31
Erikson, Erik, 14–15, 17, 19, 27, 66–68, 70, 72, 102, 188n. 14
ESTA. *See* Elders Share the Arts

Featherstone, Mike, 17, 18
feminism

cultural/radical, 128–30
    liberal, 128–29
    materialist, 128–29, 132, 133
    post-, 131
Forsberg, Don, 40, 54
Foucault, Michel, 17, 19, 43, 191n. 13, 199n. 15, 200n. 17
Franko, Mark, 22, 143, 198n. 9, 198n. 10
Free Street, 26
Free Street Too, 26–27
Frias, Sue, 103, 108
Friedan, Betty, 17, 126
Full Circle Theater Company, 186
Furlow, Etta, 119

generations
    defined, 86–88, 132, 195n. 4
    horizontal and vertical, 126–28
Generation X, 5, 16, 85–86
Gentlemen Prefer Blondes, 168–69
Geras, Stephan, 148
geriatrics, 12, 187n. 7
Geritol Follies, 34
Geritol Frolics, The, 7, 8,10, 24–55 *passim*, 56, 60, 75, 78, 81, 90, 98, 102, 104, 172, 182, 183, 184
gerontology, 12, 187n. 7
gestus, 174, 175
GLT. *See* Grandparents Living Theatre, The
Gold, Millie, 93, 95–96
Grandparents Living Theatre, The (GLT), 8, 20, 21, 30, 73–82, 90 92, 102, 104, 118, 119, 164, 183, 184
    diversity and, 30–31
    multitier structure of, 33
Gullette, Margaret Morganroth, 166, 187n. 3

Hagen, Uta, 164
Haraway, Donna, 150, 199n. 13
Harndon, Ida, 92–93, 98–99
Having Our Say, 164

Heidegger, Martin, 153, 198n. 8, 200n. 3
Hello, Dolly! 5, 22, 134, 163, 166–78, 183
Henry, Patrick, 26
Hepworth, Mike, 17, 18
Herman, Jerry, 170
Hijikata, Tatsumi, 137
Holland, Bob, 40
Holland, Vivian, 41
Houtepen, Rob, 204n. 3
Howe, Neil, 87, 90, 109
Husserl, Edmund, 152

immortality, 22, 23, 144, 148–51, 153–62 *passim*, 199n. 13, 201n. 9
infant mortality, 187n. 6
integration, 14, 27, 66, 67, 70, 103
intergenerational alliances, 5, 21, 23, 184, 185, 195n. 9
intergenerational tensions, 83
intergenerational troupes, 83–111, 195n. 1
I Was Young, Now I'm Wonderful, 62 66, 72 82, 164

Jameson, Frederic, 45, 50, 53
JASA. *See* Jewish Association for Services for the Aged
Jewish Association for Services for the Aged (JASA), 97
Johnson, Jennifer, 92, 96, 99
Jorasalow, Risa, 30

Kaminsky, Marc, 68–69, 71
Kandell, Stuart, 27
Kase, C. Robert, 27
Kaufman, Sharon, 44, 91
Kern, Stephen, 11
King, Barry, 169
Kivnick, Helen, 17–18, 181
Koestenbaum, Wayne, 165
Koppelvision, 155
Kroll, Jack, 165, 167, 169, 171
Kuhn, Maggie, 15, 189n. 16
Kundera, Milan, 131

Lacan, Jacques, 191n. 15
Lacy, Suzanne, 20, 21, 112–13, 115–17,
    119–24, 130–33, 182, 183
    production history, 196n. 7
Ladies Who Lunch, 117
Lamberson, Dennis, 34, 35, 37, 41
Laslett, Peter, 17
Leary, Timothy, 162, 201n. 11
Lenton, Thelma, 103
life course
    vs. life cycle, 17
    modern, 10, 13, 14, 17
    postmodern,10, 15
life review, 62, 66–73, 102
    defined, 192n. 4
Lindquist, Arne, 30
Lipsitz, George, 52–53, 88
Living History Festival, 31, 101, 102,
    105
Liz Lerman's Dance Exchange, 26, 27,
    143, 186, 199n. 12
Lobel, Michaela, 91
Lock, Margaret, 125, 198n. 5
Lugones, Maria, 21, 131
Lyotard, Jean-François, 18

MacDonald, Barbara, 125
MacManus, Susan, 87, 90, 195n. 8
Mandelbaum, Ken, 173
Mann, Emily, 164
Margolis Brown, 20, 22, 147–49, 155,
    159, 160, 164
    production history, 200n. 1
Margolis, Kari, 148, 159, 160
Marian Franciscan Center (Milwau-
    kee), 181, 182
Martin, Biddy, 200n. 17
mask of age, 175, 176, 178, 184
Master Class, 164, 170, 181
McDonough, Ann, 26
media culture, 147, 148, 156, 161
Medicare, 13
Mellencamp, Patricia, 154, 175, 201n.
    7
Mercedes, Jorge, 102

Merleau-Ponty, Maurice, 198n. 8,
    200n. 16
Mervis, Muriel, 92, 93
Metchnikoff, Elie, 12
Meyer, Ruth, 38
middle age, 18, 202n. 4
Middleton, David, 69, 193n. 8
Miller, Susan 89
Minnick, Michele, 95, 96
mirror phase of old age, 44, 136, 184,
    191n. 15
Molin, Helen, 37
Monroe, Marilyn, 169
Moody, Harry, 18, 19, 80, 144, 204n. 3
Moon over Buffalo, 164, 170, 202n. 7
Mordden, Ethan, 169
Morse, Margaret, 201n. 8
mortality, 155, 159, 161
Myerhoff, Barbara, 40, 52, 68, 71, 102,
    118, 196n. 4

Nascher, I. L., 12
National Council on Aging (NCOA),
    35, 57, 58, 62, 63, 76
NCOA. *See* National Council on Aging
Neugarten, Bernice, 18
New Fogey Follies, 33
New Wrinkles Review, 33, 35, 190n. 7
nostalgia, 21, 50–53, 124, 149, 151,
    153, 154, 192n. 20, 197n. 11

Ohno, Kazuo, 10, 20, 21, 132, 136–46,
    148, 182
Ohno, Yoshito, 134, 137–40, 143,
    144
old
    frail, 180, 181
    healthy, 180, 182
    oldest, 184, 185
    young-, 180, 192n. 18
Older Americans Act, 13
onnagata, 137, 139
oral history, 56, 57, 59–61, 66, 71, 73,
    81, 113
osteoporosis, 12, 188n. 8

parody, 45, 74–78, 81, 92, 97, 143
Pearls of Wisdom, 102, 104
performance and performativity
    blurring distinctions, 119, 120, 142,
        145, 196n. 5
    defined, 6–10
performativity, 167, 168, 176, 184
Perlstein, Susan, 27, 100–103
personal mythology, 68–69
Pettitt, Peggy, 102, 104–5
Pflanzer, Howard, 89
Piggins, Carol, 28, 181
Platinum Follies, 35
Pomeroy, Pat, 42, 43
post-age, 197n. 17
postfeminism. See feminism, post-
postmodern theory, 16–19, 22, 70–71,
        136, 144, 146
    perpetual present, 15, 189n. 18
Primus Players, 30
productivity, 11, 13, 79–80, 118, 124,
        135, 136, 146, 181, 194n. 18
professional standards, 25, 28, 104–5,
        180, 183

Quam, Jean, 112

R&B. See Roots & Branches
Raeford, Carrie, 104, 106
Rayner, Alice, 200n. 2
re-membering, 52, 193n. 6
Reams, Lee Roy, 170, 178, 203n. 11
Reik, Agnes, 119
Reilly, Joy, 56, 60–62, 66–71, 102
reminiscence, 21, 27, 62, 66–71, 102,
        193n. 8
restored behavior, 6–7
retirement, 13
Robert Morris College, 60
Roberts, Vera Mowry, 27, 123
Roca, Octavio, 169
Roiphe, Kate, 126
Roots & Branches (R&B), 21, 30, 31,
        83–84, 89–100, 102, 104, 109–10,
        183, 184

Rosaldo, Renato, 50, 192n. 20
Rose, Phyllis Jane, 116
Rossi, Alice, 48, 192n. 17
Roth, Moira, 120, 130

Sandahl, Carrie, 196n. 5
Sandia, Robert, 203n. 18
Schapiro, Miriam, 122
Schacter, Zal, 72
Schechner, Richard, 6–8, 142
Schechter, David, 90
Schein, David, 27
Schrof, Joannie, 127–28
Schweitzer, Pam, 190n. 4, 195n. 14
Seif, Molly, 89, 90, 96, 97
Senior Players of the American River
    Community (SPARC), 30, 33
Senior Star Showcase, 29, 33, 35, 60
Senior Theatre in Renaissance (STIR),
        60
Senior Theatre USA festival, 4, 25, 28,
        31, 33, 35, 36, 58, 60, 65, 185,
        190n. 5
Shales, Tom, 171, 172
Silver Foxes, 29
Simon, John, 165
Smith, Iris, 133
Smithburg, Bill, 41
Smithburg, Vivian, 41
Social Security, 13, 16, 85, 87, 88,
        96
Sommers, Pamela, 171, 172
SPARC. See Senior Players of the
    American River Community
spirituality, 21, 114, 130, 131, 133
StAGEbridge, 27, 61, 186, 190n. 5,
        195n. 1
stardom, 22, 164, 166, 167, 170, 171,
        175, 179, 183, 202n. 6, 204n. 18
Stelarc, 22, 151–54, 156
STIR. See Senior Theatre in Renais-
    sance
Stone, Susan, 122
Strauss, William, 86–87, 90, 109
Streisand, Barbra, 169

Strimling, Arthur, 89, 95, 97, 99, 181, 195n. 7
Sunset Boulevard, 164, 170
Swanson, Bea, 119

Teer, Barbara Ann, 114, 133
temporality, 200n. 15, 200n. 17
Terdiman, Richard, 124
therapeutic models, 28, 29, 186
Third Age Theatre Company, 33
Thurman, Anne, 28, 181
time, 11, 198n. 8, 200n. 16, 201n. 4
Torres-Gil, Fernando, 195n. 4

University of Nevada-Las Vegas, 4, 29, 186

Vaughn, Muriel, 119
Victor/Victoria, 164
Vidpires! 20, 22, 147–50, 155–61, 164, 183
Virilio, Paul, 15, 18, 124, 126, 152, 189n. 17
Vorenberg, Bonnie, 57

Walker, Barbara, 121

Water Lilies, 134–46
Wells, Ella Richey, 72
Whisper Minnesota, 115–20
Whisper, the Waves, the Wind, 115, 131
Wilder, Thornton, 168
wisdom, 67, 70
Witham, Joan, 54
Women and Aging Conference, 1996, 204n. 20
Women and Theatre Program (WTP), 21, 113–14, 118, 129, 130, 132, 185, 197n. 15
Woodward, Kathleen, 18, 44, 70, 144, 184, 191n. 15, 193n. 9, 203n. 16
World Wide Web, 152
WTP. *See* Women and Theatre Program
Wyatt-Brown, Anne, 70–71

youth
  as idealized, 172
  as peak of life course, 135, 136, 142, 164, 175, 176
  as the real, 167
  as soul, 43, 54